MAX WEBER:

The Interpretation of Social Reality

MAX WEBER:
THE INTERPRETATION
OF SOCIAL REALITY

Edited and with an introductory essay by
J. E. T. ELDRIDGE
UNIVERSITY OF BRADFORD

NELSON

THOMAS NELSON AND SONS LTD
36 Park Street London W1Y 4DE
PO Box 18123 Nairobi Kenya

Thomas Nelson (Australia) Ltd
597 Little Collins Street Melbourne 3000

Thomas Nelson and Sons (Canada) Ltd
81 Curlew Drive Don Mills Ontario

Thomas Nelson (Nigeria) Ltd
PO Box 336 Apapa Lagos

Thomas Nelson and Sons (South Africa) (Proprietary) Ltd
51 Commissioner Street Johannesburg

Copyright © J. E. T. Eldridge 1971
First published in Great Britain 1971 by Michael Joseph Ltd
Published in Nelson's University Paperbacks 1972

ISBN 0 17 712080 0
Printed in Great Britain by A.Wheaton and Co., Exeter

ACKNOWLEDGEMENTS

My thanks are due to the following for permission to quote from works by Max Weber in which they hold the copyright: George Allen & Unwin Limited, *The Protestant Ethic And The Spirit Of Capitalism*; Free Press Inc., New York, *The Methodology Of The Social Sciences*; Harvard University Press, *Law In Economy And Society*; William Hodge & Co. Ltd., *The Theory Of Social And Economic Organisation*; The Journal of General Education, Pennsylvania, *The Social Causes of the Decay of Ancient Civilisation*; Southern Illinois University Press, *The Rational And Social Foundations Of Music*.

Finally I should like to thank the editor of this series, Ronald Fletcher, for his advice and encouragement in the writing of this book.

CONTENTS

Introduction by Ronald Fletcher

The work of Max Weber was unquestionably one of the most outstanding contributions to the making of sociology. Rich, complex, many-sided—like the work of all the great theorists—it cannot possibly be satisfactorily characterised in any simple, summary statement. Even so, his achievement can be said to be distinctive in this chiefly: that it clarified, beyond any doubt, those features and problems which *crucially distinguished* the subject-matter of the new science of society from the subject-matter of all the other sciences, and successfully constructed a clear method-ology whereby it could be studied rigorously and reliably in accordance with the testable procedures of science.

In this achievement, Weber successfully dealt with what is still taken, by some, to be an insuperable obstacle in the way of applying the methods of science to the study of man and society: namely, that men are not just 'phenomenal objects'—like rocks, trees, and even animals—about which 'laws of regularity' can be established, but are thinking, feeling, calculating, purposive beings. Weber agreed with this 'objection'. He agreed that no *causal* explanation of human social configurations could possibly be sufficient unless—in addition to the study of all their relevant 'phenomenal' and 'quantitative' attributes—there was an accurate *understanding* of the social *actions* of men in terms of *meaning*. But—far from regarding this as an insuperable obstacle—Weber made it the firm and indispensable basis upon which he then built a satisfactory method for social science.

He was not the first man either to raise this issue or to deal with it. All theorists from Comte onwards had insisted that the *action* of men in society was a qualitatively different *level* of subject-matter from that of the phenomenal *events* studied by the natural sciences. The early Americans—Giddings especially—had already clarified 'types of social action' very similar to those proposed by Weber. Tonnies had provided a most thorough 'typological' explanation of that pattern of social change which he took to be of central cultural significance in modern times. Weber's contribution was therefore couched within the context of others. Even so— at his hands, these specific dimensions of sociological analysis, these particular tools of sociological study, came to be most definitively clarified and used.

To understand Weber is therefore to understand one of the most central components of sociological analysis: a component essential to the satisfactory stating and testing of theories of society.

In this new presentation of Weber's work, Professor Eldridge has provided an introduction and a selection of writings which successfully represents the wide range of Weber's studies, but which also reflects—in a very useful way—his own interests and approaches. Professor Eldridge is himself research-oriented. His teaching interests have chiefly been in methods of investigation and sociological theory, but he has been more or less continuously engaged in empirical investigations in the field of his chief interest: Industrial Relations. Besides giving a satisfactory coverage of those areas of Weber's work which are generally known, he has therefore also introduced new material—related to his own interest —with which not many can be familiar: the most interesting being Weber's discussion of methodological issues in his approach to the study of industrial workers, and also his lecture on 'Socialism'. These have been specially translated for this volume. In addition, there is other material which has not so far been easily available to students—such as, for example, Weber's important and interesting article on the social causes of the decay of ancient civilization.

This book therefore provides a reliable foundation for the study of Weber's distinctive contribution to the subject, making available to students representative selections of established and essential work, and also new material which is of the greatest interest, and of direct relevance to our own immediate problems.

Abbreviations of Weber's works referred to in the text:

AJ Ancient Judaism.

EN The Meaning Of Ethical Neutrality In Sociology And Economics (in Methodology).

GEH General Economic History.

Law On Law In Economy And Society.

Logic Critical Studies In the Logic Of The Cultural Sciences (in Methodology).

Methodology The Methodology Of The Social Sciences.

Objectivity Objectivity In Social Science And Social Policy (in Methodology).

PE The Protestant Ethic And The Spirit Of Capitalism.

Science Science As A Vocation (in From Max Weber).

SR The Sociology Of Religion.

Theory The Theory Of Social And Economic Organisation.

Preface

A brief introductory word about the plan of this book—the nature of the introductory essay, and the arrangement of the selection of writings—might be helpful.

Max Weber is a complex author. His work is detailed; his range of interests wide; and not all scholars have been agreed in their interpretation of him. It has therefore been thought fitting that the introductory essay should not be an 'introduction' in the sense of a simple 'guide', but—from the beginning—a critical discussion of a number of central methodological and theoretical questions which any careful reading of Weber's sociology is bound to provoke. The issues raised are often of a controversial nature; and nothing can be served by avoiding this. It is as well to recognise at the outset the simple point that controversy operates at different levels. There are disagreements, sometimes, over where Weber really stands on this or that question; and there are disagreements which may be expressed about Weber's position on particular matters—on the *assumption* that one *knows* where he stands. Even in his own lifetime, Weber was a controversial figure, engaged in many intellectual battles, and the passage of time has not dimmed the conflicts which surround his work. It is in an appreciation of the controversies themselves that we can best come to an understanding of the distinctive nature of his contribution.

The selections from Weber's work have been grouped into three chapters—preceded, in each case, by brief introductory remarks, so that no further comment is necessary here. The choice has been centrally guided by a desire to represent as wide a range as possible of Weber's interests. However, studies which are relatively unfamiliar have been introduced in conjunction with the work more generally known. These include, for example, his methodological approach to the study of industrial workers and his lecture on socialism (both of which have been specially translated for this volume by D. Hÿtch), and also his lecture on the social causes of the decay of ancient civilization. The organization of the selections within each chapter needs no special justification, but it will be noted that it deliberately cuts across traditional ways of dividing his work—into the sociology of economic life, law, religion, and so on. By drawing these several spheres of interest together within the same chapter it is probable that the mode of Weber's sociological analysis may be more sharply revealed; when, that is, it can be seen similarly applied to different matters.

J. E. T. Eldridge
University of Bradford,
November, 1970

Introductory Essay:

Max Weber: some comments, problems and continuities

(A) Sociological Explanation and the Problem of Knowledge

THE SOCIOLOGIST AS SCIENTIST

For Max Weber sociology was a science. What sociologists shared with other scientists in Weber's view was a 'rational method': the acceptance that in whatever sphere of inquiry one was engaged, the only explanations which could be treated as 'valid' were those which were embedded in a structure of logical thinking. The approach to the study of causality in scientific inquiry necessarily demanded the precise formulation of concepts, a preoccupation with the rules of evidence and logical basis of inference. 'All scientific work presupposes that the rules of logic and method are valid.'[1] The scientific activity may be viewed as a tool 'in the service of self-clarification and knowledge of interrelated facts'.[2] This 'rational method' Weber saw as making the highest demands on those who practised it. His own view upon this is superbly expressed in the following passage:

> . . . whoever lacks the capacity to put on blinkers, so to speak, and to come up to the idea that the fate of his soul depends upon whether or not he makes the correct conjecture at this passage of this manuscript may as well stay away from science. He will never have what one may call the 'personal experience' of science. Without this strange intoxication ridiculed by every outsider: without this passion, this 'thousands of years must pass before you enter into life and thousands more wait in silence'—according to whether or not you succeed in making this conjecture: without this you have *no* calling for science and

[1] *Science as a Vocation* in *From Max Weber*, p. 143.
[2] *Science*, p. 152.

9

you should do something else. For nothing is worthy of a man unless he can pursue it with passionate devotion.[1]

There is then, one may note in passing, a form of irrationality which provides the motive force for those who utilise 'the rational method'. That is to say, one cannot justify this 'strange intoxication' with scientific activity in scientific terms. It is indeed in this sense of the term 'irrationality' that we can see why Weber quotes Tolstoi with approval: 'Science is meaningless because it gives no answer to our question, the only question important for us: "What shall we do and how shall we live".'[2] Indeed, far from suggesting, as some of his contemporaries do, that science was the way to 'art', 'nature', 'happiness', 'God' or some other ultimate value, Weber sees scientific activity as a major agent in the demystification of the world. It is the very use of 'the rational method' which makes it so.

The fact that in Weber's sociology attention is paid to the way in which the sociologist can interpret the meaning men attach to their behaviour is not to suggest that sociological knowledge may be obtained simply by inspired intuition. We shall spell out some of the assumptions and implications of Weber's interpretative sociology below, but we may say at the outset that the interpretative approach is to be seen as an integral part of the rational method in sociology and not as opposed to it. Schutz, in his study,[3] has expressed the point very clearly:

Sociology can claim no monopoly on the rational method. The methodologies of all true sciences are rational, involving, as they do, the use of formal logic and interpretative schemes. All true sciences demand the maximum of clarity and distinctiveness for all their propositions. There is no such thing as an irrational science. We must never cease reiterating that the method of Weber's sociology is a rational one and that the position of interpretative sociology should in no way be confused with that of Dilthey, who opposes to rational science another so-called 'interpretative' science based on metaphysical presuppositions and incorrigible 'intuition'.

[1] *Science*, p. 135.   [2] *ibid.*, p. 143.
[3] A. Schutz, *The Phenomenology of the Social World* (Northwestern University Press, 1967), p. 240.

THE PROBLEM OF KNOWLEDGE

If sociology is to be characterised as an empirical science, as Weber suggests, it must be recognised that the 'explanations' it propounds about social phenomena and their interrelations are necessarily limited in scope and incomplete in execution. Weber is most specific on this when he considers the problem of knowledge. In 'Objectivity in Social Science and Social Policy' he points out, for example, that:

> . . . as soon as we attempt to reflect about the way in which life confronts us in immediate concrete situations, it presents an infinite multiplicity of successively and coexistently emerging and disappearing events both 'within' and 'outside' ourselves. The absolute infinitude of this multiplicity is seen to remain undiminished even when our attention is focused upon a single 'object' for instance, a concrete act of exchange, as soon as we seriously attempt an exhaustive description of all the individual components of this 'individual phenomena' to say nothing of explaining it causally . . .[1]

One cannot in the nature of the case, Weber argues, give a causal explanation of even an individual fact in any final sense, nor even exhaustively describe 'the smallest slice of reality'.

> The number and types of causes which have influenced any given event are always infinite and there is nothing in the things themselves to set them apart as alone meriting attention. A chaos of individual judgements about countless individual events would be the only result of a serious attempt to analyse reality 'without pre-suppositions'. And even this result is only seemingly possible, since every single perception discloses on closer examination an infinite number of constituted perceptions which can never be exhaustively expressed in a judgement.[2]

It is precisely upon the basis of statements such as these that Salomon has correctly observed:

[1] In *Methodology of the Social Sciences*, p. 72.
[2] *ibid.*, p. 78.

Weber assumed at the outset that no individual science is capable of furnishing an authentic 'copy' of reality. The utmost that can be accomplished by such sciences, either in the historical or the social disciplines, is, through reasoned thought, to bring order into the world of reality, which is in a state of ceaseless flux. The principles of classification by which this order is to be achieved, cannot, however, draw upon reality, but must be imposed by the scientist himself.[1]

The question which arises, then, is what kind of pre-supposition do we make tacitly or explicitly when as social scientists we seek to make statements about social phenomena? What we do in practice is to select certain aspects of the world around us as both problematic and worthy of study. The direction of a social scientist's interest introduces an element of subjectivity at the outset of the scientific enterprise. It is in this sense that Weber propounds the view that: 'There is no absolutely "objective" scientific analysis of culture—or put perhaps more narrowly but certainly not essentially differently for our purposes—of "social phenomena" independent of special and one-sided viewpoints according to which —expressly or tacitly, consciously or unconsciously—they are selected, analysed and organised for expository purposes'.[2]

Each of these 'one-sided viewpoints' could, so to speak, throw shafts of light on to social phenomena. Weber sought to maintain the position that one viewpoint had as much justification as another in principle, and conversely to deny the monopolistic claims of any one viewpoint. So, although in much of his work he sympathised with economic interpretations of history as an approach to the understanding of empirical reality, he took the view that other evaluative presuppositions could equally well be made by a social scientist. One's subjective viewpoint, then, will be reflected in the problem one selects for study and also in the concepts one employs as tools for study. We may add, however, that the problem does not determine the concepts. This is illustrated in Gouldner's essay, 'Anti-Minotaur: the Myth of a Value-Free Sociology',[3] where he describes in passing the differing stances of the Chicago

---

[1] A. Salomon, 'Max Weber's Methodology', in *Social Research*, Vol. 1 (1934), p. 157.
[2] *Objectivity*, p. 72.
[3] Horowitz, I. L. (ed.), *The New Sociology* (O.U.P., 1965).

sociologists as against the Columbia and Harvard sociologists in their studies of medical practioners.

The Chicago group evinced uneasiness with the concept of profession as a guideline for study, preferring the more open-ended concept of occupation. The approach to empirical reality for them was to see the sociological similarities of a doctor's job with a whole range of other jobs, whereas the Harvard and Columbia studies were more prone to view the practice of medicine as a noble profession. If they more readily regard the profession in terms of its own claims, the Chicago group were more inclined to investigate 'the seamier side of medical practice'.[1]

The relativistic position of Weber is reinforced by his view of the cultural sciences as those to which 'eternal youth is granted' because the 'eternally onward flowing stream of culture perpetually brings new problems'.[2]

It is directly from this assumption that Weber draws an important inference:

The history of the social sciences is and remains a continuous process passing from the attempt to order reality analytically through the construction of concepts—the dissolution of the analytical constructs so constructed through the expansion and shift of the scientific horizon—and the reformulation anew of concepts of the foundations thus transformed. It is not the error of the attempt to construct conceptual systems *in general* which is shown by this process—every science, every single descriptive history, operates with the conceptual stock-in-trade of its time. Rather, this process shows that in the cultural sciences concept-construction depends on the setting of the problem, and the latter varies with the content of culture itself. The relationship between concept and reality in the cultural sciences involves the transitoriness of all such syntheses. The great attempts at theory-construction in one science were always useful for recording the limits of the significance of those points of view which provided their foundations. The greatest advances in the sphere of the social sciences are substantively tied up with the shift in practical cultural problems and take the guise of a critique of concept-construction.[3]

[1] Horowitz, I. L. (ed.), *The New Sociology*, p. 208.
[2] *Objectivity*, p. 104.   [3] *ibid.*, pp. 105–6.

It is precisely because of the position here elaborated by Weber that we support Albert Salomon's contention when he observes: 'Every attack on Weber's lack of system . . . is meaningless, since Weber by his fundamental theory of knowledge, rejected such a desire and he repeatedly gave utterance to this view *expressis verbis*. In order to undermine this absence of system, therefore, it would be necessary to attack the logical foundations of his sociology and not his sociology as such.'[1]

This assessment is, of course, at variance with Parsons' view that Weber failed to see that he could have developed a general systems theory via a functional mode of analysis.[2] The point is rather that, for reasons which he states clearly enough, he chooses not to proceed in that direction. Given his orientation to the nature of sociological theory, as indicated in the preceding quotation, it is difficult to imagine him writing a book entitled *The Social System*. In other words, what Parsons tends to view as a scientifically more primitive position from which Weber could by taking thought have escaped, is rather, we suggest, a position to which, for better or for worse, Weber is necessarily wedded precisely because of his view of the eternal youth of the discipline.

And certainly he chose to grapple with the problem of causal analysis in sociology rather than functional analysis. He takes the position that as a provisional mode of orientation a functionalist analysis in which the 'whole' is taken as the point of departure and the 'parts' or 'individual acts' assessed in relation to it, is

> . . . not only useful but indispensable. But at the same time if its cognitive value is overestimated and its concept illegitimately 'reified' it can be highly dangerous. . . . In the case of social collectivities precisely as distinguished from organisms, we are in a position to go beyond merely demonstrating functional relationships and uniformities. We can accomplish something which is never attainable in the natural sciences, namely the subjective understanding of the action of component individuals. . . . We do not 'understand' the behaviour of cells, but can only observe the relevant functional relationships and generalise on the basis of these observations. This additional

[1] Salomon, 'Max Weber's Sociology' in *Social Research*, Vol. 2 (1935), p. 68.
[2] See for example Parsons' introduction to *Theory of Social and Economic Organization* pp. 18 ff.

achievement of explanation by interpretative understanding, as distinguished from external observation, is of course obtained only at a price—the more hypothetical and fragmentary character of its results. Nevertheless, subjective understanding is the specific characterisation of sociological knowledge.[1]

There is in Parsons' critique of Weber an underlying contention that Weber is not enough of a positivist in his approach to sociology. Parsons maintains that Weber draws too sharp a distinction between the natural sciences and the cultural sciences. In so far as Parsons shows that the natural sciences are also relativisitic in that the selection of natural science problems is determined by the scientist's 'direction of interest', and that in terms of motivation these are more variable than Weber seemed to imagine, we see this as a helpful corrective statement; not least because in this sense all scientific activity has subjectivist foundations, not only the social sciences. But Parsons implies more than this: 'Weber should have gone all the way to the view that in a purely *logical* aspect there is no difference whatsoever [i.e. between natural and social sciences]. The differences all lie on a substantive level.'[2]

For Parsons this means the possibility of analytical science (natural or social) being able to make law-like statements of the kind that Weber had associated only with natural sciences. The point of difference is well brought out in Parsons' comments on *The Theory of Social and Economic Organisation* when he properly notes that Weber's sociological generalisations are 'ideal typical' in form and not therefore 'methodologically equivalent to most of the laws of physics, especially of analytical mechanics. The latter do not generally formulate a concrete course of events, but rather a uniform relationship between the values of two or more variables. Weber does not even consider the possibility of formulating laws of the latter type, essentially because he does not develop social theory explicitly in the direction of setting up a system of interdependent variables, but confines it to the ideal type level'.[3]

For Weber, by contrast, there was a deep dissatisfaction with those social scientists who claimed that their task was to discover

[1] *Theory*, pp. 103-4.
[2] T. Parsons, *The Structure of Social Action*, p. 595.
[3] *Theory*, p. 108.

laws in the social world which had the same logical status as those in the physical universe:

> It has often been thought that the decisive criterion in the cultural sciences, too, was in the last analysis, the regular recurrence of certain causal relationships. The 'laws' which we are able to perceive in the infinitely manifold stream of events must—according to this conception—contain the scientifically 'essential' aspect of reality. . . . Accordingly, even among the followers of the Historical School we continually find the attitude which declares that the ideal which all the sciences, including the cultural sciences, serve and towards which they should strive even in the remote future is a system of propositions from which reality can be 'deduced' . . .[1]

To accept this as a valid goal of cultural science was, Weber maintained, to attempt 'to construct a closed system of concepts in which reality is synthesised in some sort of *permanently* and *universally* valid classification and from which it can again be deduced.'[2]

This position identified by Weber as the naturalistic viewpoint (or prejudice!) is rejected by him fundamentally because he does not accept that cultural scientists can have a direct awareness of the structure of human actions in all their reality. One of his targets here was the kind of economic writing which in his day asserted that there were economic laws which could be so articulated: '. . . . the fantastic claim has occasionally been made for economic theories—e.g. abstract theories of price, interest, rent, etc.—that they can, by ostensibly following the analogy of physical science propositions, be validly applied to the derivation of quantitatively stated conclusions from given real premises, since given the ends, economic behaviour with respect to means is unambiguously "determined".'[3]

The given real premises turn out to be psychological axioms which allegedly crystallise a universal truth about human behaviour, such as the acquisitive impulse. Since Weber himself laid great emphasis on the understanding of the motivation of human action it is necessary to point out why he regarded this position as untenable. His comment is illuminating because it reveals that

[1] *Objectivity*, pp. 72–3.   [2] *ibid.*, p. 84.   [3] *ibid.*, p. 88.

although he might properly be termed a methodological individualist, he cannot reasonably be described as a psychological reductionist.

> . . . the partly brilliant attempts which have been made hitherto to interpret economic phenomena psychologically show . . . that the procedure does not begin with the analysis of psychological qualities, moving then to the analysis of social institutions, but that, on the contrary, insight into the psychological preconditions and consequences of institutions presupposes a precise knowledge of the latter and the scientific analysis of their structure. In concrete cases, psychological analysis can contribute then an extremely valuable deepening of the knowledge of the historical cultural *conditioning* and cultural *significance* of institutions. The interesting aspect of the psychic attitude of a person in a social situation is specifically particularised in each case, according to the special cultural significance of the situation in question. It is a question of an extremely heterogeneous and highly concrete structure of psychic motives and influences. Social psychological research involves the study of various very disparate *individual* types of cultural elements with reference to their interpretability by our empathic understanding. Through social psychological research with the knowledge of individual institutions as a point of departure, we will learn increasingly how to understand institutions in a psychological way. We will not however deduce the institution from psychological laws or explain them by elementary psychological phenomena.[1]

This position separates Weber from John Stuart Mill who argued that social institutions could ultimately be explained as derivatives of the laws of human nature. It is not entirely a dead controversy as is testified to, for example, by the more recent writings of George Homans who suggests that sociological statements rest necessarily upon the propositions of behavioural psychology. Even though the causal chains might be long and complicated, ultimately explanations even of social institutions rest upon propositions which describe the characteristics of man as man.[2]

---

[1] *Objectivity*, pp. 88–9.
[2] See, for example, *Sentiments and Activities* (Routledge, 1962), pp. 47–8.

It is interesting to recall that Durkheim shared Weber's distrust of the status of economic theories. They are more adequately thought of, argued Durkheim, as 'maxims for action or practical precepts in disguise':

> The famous law of supply and demand for example, has never been inductively established, as should be the case with a law referring to economic reality. No experiment or systematic comparison has ever been undertaken for the purpose of establishing that *in fact* economic relations do conform to this law. All that these economists do, and actually did do, was to demonstrate by dialectics that, in order properly to promote their interests, individuals ought to proceed according to this law, and that every other line of action would be harmful to those who engage in it and would imply a serious error of judgement. It is fair and logical that the most productive industries should be the most attractive and that the holders of the products most in demand and most secure should sell them at the highest prices. But this quite logical necessity resembles in no way the necessity that the true laws of nature present. The latter express the regulations according to which facts are really interconnected, not the way in which it is good that they should be inter-connected.[1]

Like Durkheim, Weber argued that economic theory had a tendency to treat presuppositions as self-evident when they were nothing of the kind. They were both also uneasy over the way in which economic statements were converted into ideological statements about ethically desirable ends. Durkheim suggested that the language of economics was impregnated with ideological concepts (*Rules*, p. 25), and Weber maintained that a statement based, for example, on the premise of free trade is sometimes 'transformed from a very useful heuristic instrument into a by no means self-evident evaluation as soon as one begins to derive value judgements from it.'[2]

However, the crucial difference between Durkheim and Weber in their respective commentaries is that for Durkheim, in principle,

---

[1] E. Durkheim, *The Rules of Sociological Method* (Free Press, 1938), p. 26.
[2] 'Ethical Neutrality in Sociology and Economics' in *Methodology*, op. cit., p. 36.

social laws are discoverable which describe reality. Social facts are facts of nature. They are different from the conceptions which men have of the world since they express things as they actually are. Consequently they have an 'objective' existence and the discovery of causal connections between social facts is to make manifest a social law: 'Far from being a product of the will [social facts] determine it from without; they are like moulds in which our actions are inevitably shaped. This necessity is often inescapable . . . Thus, in considering social phenomena as things, we merely adjust our conceptions in conformity to their nature.'[1]

This at least was Durkheim's formal methodological position, even though it is clear that in his substantive work he introduced concepts which were not consistent with his definition of what constituted social facts. But Weber moves in another direction. Certainly there were 'facts' which could be identified in the real world, and which the sociologist may have to take into account— death rates, migratory movements, the life cycle of human beings, wage rates and so on. And the seriousness with which Weber treated such facts is well illustrated in his Methodological Introduction for the survey of the Society for Social Policy concerning selection and adaptation (choice and course of occupation) for the workers of major autonomous industrial enterprises (see below pp. 103–155).

So, for example, Weber counselled the research team to get certain economic facts, such as the capital requirement for the firms studied and the breakdown into the component costs for buildings, machines, raw materials, wages and other essentials. But such facts, relevant though they might well be for sociological investigation, were to be distinguished from analytical concepts which as a genus may be labelled ideal-types.

The point we are making here is paralleled in Rex's observation that: '. . . research into what Weber called the "life chances" of human beings strictly speaking forms no part of sociology. True it poses a problem for the sociologist who asks whether the differential distribution of life-chances is indicative of a particular power system or whether it means the emergence of segregated ways of life. But by itself it is simply a part of the study of human biology in which exact descriptive and mathematical techniques have been developed to a high level.'[2]

[1] *Rules*, p. 29.   [2] J. Rex, *Key Problems of Sociological Theory*, p. 189.

WEBER'S APPROACH TO CAUSAL ANALYSIS

Weber makes an important distinction between two forms of causal analysis: *ratio essendi* and *ratio cognoscendi*, notably in his essay 'Critical Studies in the Logic of the Cultural Sciences'. In the first form the scientist seeks to establish real causal linkages in explaining historical events. Indeed for Weber, 'the meaning of history as a science of reality can only be that it treats particular elements of reality not merely as heuristic *instruments*, but as the subject of knowledge and particular causal connections not as premises of knowledge but as *real* causal factors.'[1]

How can one demonstrate the validity of such causal linkages?

> Obviously not by the simple 'observation' of the course of events . . . certainly not if one understands by that a 'presuppositionless' mental 'photograph' of all the physical and psychic events occurring in the space-time region in question— even if such were possible. Rather does the attribution of effects to causes take place through a process of thought which includes a series of *abstractions*. The first decisive one occurs when we *conceive* of one or a few of the actual causal components as modified in a certain direction and then ask ourselves whether under the conditions which have been thus changed, the same effect (the same, i.e. in 'essential' points) or some other effect 'would be expected'.[2]

Weber is here introducing the notion of 'objective possibility' as a means of discriminating between factors which are relevant and those which are not in accounting for certain specified observed effects. In making such judgements, the historian does of course have the benefit of hindsight. Thus, in assessing the significance of the Greek victory over the Persians at the battle of Marathon, he is aware of the general effects of Greek culture on Western European thought forms. The result of the battle, therefore, may be said to be causally relevant in accounting for the significant influence of Greek culture on the Western world. Had the Persians won then, in the light of the historian's knowledge of other Persian conquests, he would judge that the cultural life of

[1] *Logic*, in *Methodology*, op. cit., p. 135.   [2] *Logic*, p. 171.

Greece would have been very different in character. The method Weber is recommending in this kind of causal analysis is that of imaginative reconstruction. But his process of attributing significance to causal factors has to take place within the context of the historian's grasp of certain empirical regularities of behaviour: 'The simplest historical judgement represents not only a categorically formed intellectual construct but it also does not acquire a valid content until we bring to the "given" reality the whole body of our "nomological" empirical knowledge.'[1]

If one asks in advance of an event how predictable it is, answers might vary depending upon the degree of one's knowledge of the relevant empirical regularities, from unpredictable (pure chance outcome), moving through various degrees of objective possibility towards objective probability:

> Despite the familiar and fully justified notice which warns against the transference of the calculus of probabilities into other domains, it is clear that the . . . case of favourable chance or 'objective probability' determined from general empirical propositions or from empirical frequencies, has its analogues in the sphere of of all concrete causality, including the historical.[2]

Clearly the degree of certainty attained, as far as empirical regularities are concerned, is very important in enabling one to judge the causal significance of particular factors. In discussing this Weber uses the concept of 'adequate causation'. The reasons for and significance of this position are well brought out by R. Aron:

> Let us suppose that the judgement of sufficient cause (development of the Greeks under Persian rule) is based on analogies, that is, the Persian policy in other countries. The analogy between the case under consideration and other cases is only partial. Moreover, the facts which are being compared are fragments of social statistics, separated perhaps arbitrarily, checked by decree at a certain date. Our judgements, then, when most favourably considered are adequate and not necessary, since abstract relations are not the whole of the concrete singularity, because historical comparisons involve something

[1] *Logic.*, p. 175. [2] *ibid.*, p. 183.

of the arbitrary, and isolated systems are always subject to outside influences.[1]

When Weber applies the notion of causal adequacy to sociological inquiry, he points out the sense in which causally adequate explanations must be linked with meaningfully adequate explanations of social actions to form a basis for sociological generalisations. We may, on the basis of generalisations from experience, indicate the likelihood of particular outcomes in particular situations:

> A correct causal interpretation of a concrete course of action is arrived at when the correct action and the motives have both been correctly apprehended and at the same time their relationship has become meaningfully comprehensible. A correct causal interpretation of typical action means that the process which is claimed to be typical is shown to be both adequately grasped on the level of meaning and at the same time the interpretation is to some degree causally adequate. If adequacy in respect to meaning is lacking, then no matter how high the degree of uniformity and how precisely its probability can be numerically determined, it is still an incomprehensible statistical probability, whether dealing with overt or subjective processes. On the other hand, even the most perfect adequacy on the level of meaning has causal significance from a sociological point of view only in so far as there is some kind of proof for the existence of a probability that action in fact normally takes the course which has been held to be meaningful. For this there must be some degree of determinable frequency of approximation to an average or pure type.
>
> Statistical uniformities constitute understandable types of action . . . and thus constitute 'sociological generalisations' only when they can be regarded as manifestations of the understandable subjective meaning of a course of social action.[2]

It is important here to distinguish between two kinds of probabilistic statement, both of which can properly be thought of as

[1] R. Aron, *Introduction to the Philosophy of History* (Weidenfeld and Nicolson, 1961), p. 164.
[2] *Theory*, pp. 99–100.

conditional generalizations. The one we might term an empirical tendency statement based upon statistical knowledge—for example the tendency of certain groups of people to be located in the commanding positions in a society. The other we might term ideal typical constructions with built-in statements about probability, which may be utilised as a bench mark against which to analyse the actual course of behaviour. It is this second kind of analysis which is distinctively sociological since it is used as an heuristic device to demonstrate causal adequacy and adequacy at the level of meaning. It is common for such 'typicalities' to be constructions based on ideas of rational action—for example, how two commanders locked in battle would have acted, each given adequate knowledge of his own situation and that of his opponent:

> Then it is possible to compare with this the actual course of action and to arrive at a causal explanation of the observed deviations, which will be attributed to such factors as misinformation, strategical errors, logical fallacies, personal temperament, or considerations outside the realm of strategy.[1]

Nevertheless, there is no reason in principle why the concepts of typical action should not be constructed as irrational or emotive abstractions against which to analyse the actual course of behaviour. In either case the use of these conceptual tools enables us to understand the actual course of events more proficiently than we otherwise would.

Causal analysis of the form *ratio cognoscendi* is treated by Weber as having a logically different structure from that of *ratio essendi*. It represents the attempt to construct type concepts—a type of man, a type of culture, a type of authority—which are elaborated as heuristic instruments.

Particular facts of history are related to these type concepts in two ways: they assist in the elaboration of type concepts which the sociologist constructs, and they serve as historical illustrations of the typical. The sociologist, in other words, has certain notions of what is 'characteristic' in the phenomenon he is studying (say captalism, bureaucracy, socialism, the state), and he crystallises them in ideal type concepts. Weber insists that whether they realise it or not historians and economists have had to orient their

---

[1] *Theory*, p. 111.

work by using such conceptualisations. This interpretative construction of 'historical individuals' represents an area of study which for us has relevance to our values. The distinction between *ratio essendi* and *ratio cognoscendi* is brought out in the following comment:

> . . . in constructing historical individuals I elaborate in an explicit form the focal points for *possible* 'evaluative' attitudes which the segment of reality in question discloses and in consequence of which it claims a more or less universal 'meaning', which is to be sharply distinguished from causal 'significance'.[1]

Discussions at the level of *ratio essendi* take consciously or not as their point of departure formulations at the level of *ratio cognoscendi*:

> The construction of abstract ideal types recommends itself not as an end but as a *means*. Every conscientious examination of the conceptual elements of historical exposition shows . . . that the historian, as soon as he attempts to go beyond the bare establishment of concrete relationships and to determine the *cultural* significance of even the simplest individual event in order to characterise it, *must* use concepts which are precisely and unambiguously definable only in the form of ideal types.[2]

Perhaps the important thing to bear in mind here is that while the type statements elaborated at the level of *ratio cognoscendi* are not concerned to establish causal linkages in actual courses of action, they do ultimately rest on concepts of types of action. This comes out very clearly in the following comment:

> In *all* cases, rational or irrational, sociological analysis both abstracts from reality and at the same time helps us to understand it, in that it shows with what degree of approximation a concrete historical phenomenon may be in one aspect 'feudal', in another 'patrimonial', in another 'bureaucratic', and in still another 'charismatic'. In order to give a precise meaning to these terms, it is necessary for the sociologist to formulate pure ideal types of the corresponding forms of action which in each case

[1] *Logic*, p. 149.   [2] *Objectivity*, p. 92.

involve the highest possible degree of logical integration by virtue of their complete adequacy on the level of meaning. But precisely because this is true, it is probably seldom if ever that a real phenomenon can be found which corresponds exactly to any one of these ideally constructed pure types.[1]

It is indeed this preoccupation with the forms of social action which makes it possible to describe Weber as a methodological individualist.

METHODOLOGICAL INDIVIDUALISM

In 1920, not long before he died, Max Weber wrote in a letter to Robert Liefmann: '. . . . if I have become a sociologist . . . it is mainly in order to exorcise the spectre of collective conceptions which still lingers among us. In other words, sociology itself can only proceed from the actions of one or more separate individuals and must therefore adopt strictly individualistic methods'.[2]

What was this spectre of collective conceptions which needed to be exorcised? The language of every society embodies collective conceptions of course: 'the family', 'the school', 'the state', and so on. One immediate problem is that if simply taken over and used in an undifferentiated way by a social scientist, such terms can impede rather than aid social explanation. In his essay 'Objectivity in Social Science and Social Policy' (in *Methodology of the Social Sciences*, op. cit.) Weber discusses this in some detail with reference to the collective concept 'the interests of agriculture'.[3] He has no difficulty in illustrating the fact that within the agricultural sphere a whole range of specific interests may be located, some of which are antagonistic to others. These interests may be tied to the specific produce of a farm, to whether one is buying or selling land, to whether one has a subordinate or dominant position in the system of social stratification which characterises the agricultural sphere. Further, Weber suggests that one can distinguish broadly between interests derived from 'material' values (for example, the desire to maximise profits), and interests derived from 'ideal'

[1] *Theory*, p. 110.
[2] Quoted by W. Mommsen in 'Max Weber's political sociology and his philosophy of world history', *Int. Soc. Sc. Jnl.*, Vol. 17 (1965), p. 25.
[3] *Objectivity*, pp. 108–10.

values (for example, beliefs that one way of rural life is intrinsically preferable to another even though the individual may be worse off in an economic sense in consequence). In real life the distinction may not be clear cut, but Weber's point is that unless this kind of analytical distinction were introduced, the explanation of partic-ular forms of social behaviour could not be adduced. Against all this, of course, may be set the material and ideal interests of those outside the agricultural sphere; from these they derive their own conceptions of 'the interests of agriculture' which may contain beliefs about what farmers should be producing, at what prices and with what resources.

Clearly, if one wishes to consider 'the interests of agriculture' in relation to 'the interests of the state', the underlying complexity of the first collective concept is surpassed only by the complexity of the second. The lesson for sociological analysis is, according to Weber, that 'the clear-cut sharply defined analysis of the various possible standpoints is the only path which will lead us out of verbal confusion'.[1] Hence vague classificatory concepts have to be supplanted by analytical concepts which can serve to get a research problem into focus.

THE ACTION FRAME OF REFERENCE

In confronting the problem of knowledge, as we have seen, Weber settled on the concept of action as a basic unit for sociological analysis. There is a similarity here to the young Marx, especially to his Theses on Feuerbach. Lefebvre, commenting on Marx's position in this respect, writes:

The 'problem of knowledge' as speculative philosophers treat it is a false problem. Abstract logical consistency theories divorced from social activity and practical verification, have no value whatever. The essence of man is social, and the essence of society is praxis—acts, courses of action, interaction. Separated from praxis, theory vainly comes to grips with falsely formu-lated or insoluble problems, bogs down in mysticism and mystification.[2]

---

[1] *Objectivity*, p. 110.
[2] Lefebvre, *The Sociology of Marx* (Allen Lane, 1968), p. 34.

The emphasis on acts, courses of action and interaction is reiterated in Weber, notably in *On Law in Economy and Society*. However, in Marx certain emanationist considerations come into the reckoning. So conservative praxis, which refers to patterns of action that have as their goal the preservation of the established order and its institutions, is to be opposed by revolutionary praxis which questions the legitimacy of the established social order. And it is revolutionary praxis which is superior. Why?

Thanks to it, thought and feeling are once again brought into accord with reality, institutions into accord with the productive forces (the base) social forms into accord with their contents. Here again we encounter the fundamental idea of going beyond a given historical stage, of progressing to a higher stage. It creates intelligibility as living reason in the heads of men and as rationality in social relations.[1]

Now there are occasional passages in Weber in which he exhibits a similar concern that living reason might reign in the heads of men. For example, in 'The Meaning of Ethical Neutrality in Sociology and Economics' he comments on the shallowness of the routinised existence of contemporary man. But deliverance is not necessarily to be obtained by revolutionary action (which, as he elsewhere pointed out, might have unexpected and unintended consequences); rather, he points to an existentialist 'solution':

The fruit of the tree of knowledge, which is distasteful to the complacent but which is, nonetheless, inescapable, consists in the insight that every single important activity and ultimately life as a whole, if it is not to be permitted to run on as an event in nature, but is instead to be consciously guided, is a series of ultimate decisions through which the world—as in Plato—chooses its own fate, i.e. the meaning of its activity and existence.[2]

But as a sociologist Weber set his face against recommending certain courses of action or political programmes as ethically desirable, meeting man's essential needs, or promoting progress. Rather he embarked upon the classification of types of action as tools for the explanation of actual courses of action. And in

[1] Lefebvre, *The Sociology of Marx*, p. 53.   [2] *Ethical Neutrality*, p. 18.

action is included 'all human behaviour when and in so far as
the acting individual attaches a subjective meaning to it'.[1]

THE CONCEPT OF 'UNDERSTANDING' IN WEBER'S SOCIOLOGY

A crucial feature of sociological explanation for Weber was the
establishment of propositions concerning human behaviour which
were 'adequate at the level of meaning'. To understand the
meaning which men give to their acts is, in a word, to understand
their intentions. In his essay, 'The Meaning of Ethical Neutrality
in Sociology and Economics', Weber observes: 'The means
employed by the method of understanding explanation are . . . on
the one hand the conventional habits of the investigator and
teacher in thinking in a particular way and, on the other, as the
situation requires, his capacity to "feel himself" empathically into
a mode of thought which deviates from his own and which is
normatively "false" according to his own habits of thought.'[2]

In *The Theory of Social and Economic Organisation* he makes
a distinction between direct observational understanding and
explanatory understanding. This hinges on the conviction that
some acts directly reflect the intention of the actor so that low
level inferences may be drawn concerning the connection between
act and intention by the observer; whereas other acts have to be
related to a context of meaning not immediately apparent to the
observer before he is in a position to comment on the intention of
the actor.

The observer may be interested in the intentions that produce
the actions of a particular individual. This Weber saw as a
characteristic of the historical approach. It may well be that the
observer can call upon the findings of social psychology to
sensitise himself to the complications of human motivation.

Weber himself writes of the complementary part which a
verstehen psychology may play in sociological and historical
research. One thinks, for example, of G. Faber's reinterpretation
of Newman and his associates in the Oxford Movement in the
light of Freudian psychology.[3] But it is not just a matter of

---

[1] *Theory*, p. 88.   [2] *EN*, p. 41.   [3] *Oxford Apostles* (Penguin, 1954).

arriving at ever better modes of depth psychology; there remains the historian's traditional concern for the rules of evidence in describing and accounting for the plans and projects of men. Collingwood has well described this as equivalent to effective detective work or, as in the quotation below, to a thorough cross-examination:

> . . . history finds its proper method when the historian puts his authorities in the witness box—by cross-questioning extorts from them information which in their original statements they have withheld either because they did not wish to give it or because they did not possess it. Thus a commentator's despatches may claim a victory: the historian reading them in a critical spirit will ask: 'If it was victory why was it not followed up in this or that way?' and may thus convict the writer of concealing the truth.[1]

Thus regarded, the historian's job, then, is to interpret the meaning of particular actions, improving wherever possible upon previous interpretations.

It is indeed instructive to recall that Collingwood in his historical methodology lays a stress similar to Weber's on the centrality of intention for historical investigation:

> There are certain kinds of act which cannot be done . . . except reflectively by a person who knows what he is trying to do and is therefore able when he has done it to judge his own action by reference to his intention. It is characteristic of these acts that they should be done as we say 'on purpose': that there should be a basis of purpose upon which the structure of the act should be erected and to which it must conform. Reflective acts may be roughly described as the acts which we do on purpose and these are the only acts which can become the subject-matter of history.[2]

It is recognised by Collingwood that purposes may change as the activity proceeds but 'the purpose is always in advance of the act'.[3] This position is broadly equivalent to Schutz's treatment of

---

[1] R. G. Collingwood, *The Idea of History* (O.U.P., 1946), p. 237.
[2] *ibid.*, p. 309.   [3] *ibid.*, p. 310.

projects and 'in-order-to' motivation.[1] Schutz speaks of action as being determined by the project of the actor. 'The project is the intended act imagined as already accomplished, the in-order-to motive is the future state of affairs to be realised by the projected action.'[2]

Accordingly for Schutz, the distinction between behaviour and action is that action is the execution of a projected act. If one asks the further question, why does a person choose one project rather than another, Schutz argues that a different kind of motivational explanation is called for; one which refers to the actors' past experiences to provide a 'reason' or 'cause' and designated by Schutz as a 'because-motive'.

Weber portrays two other levels at which the method of understanding may be applied: the average or approximation to the meaning actually intended, which may help to explain 'sociological mass phenomena', and intention constructed by the investigator for heuristic purposes—the scientifically formulated pure types. It is this last-named procedure which has led some writers to characterize Weber's sociology as formalistic and to liken it to that of Simmel or von Wiese; and Lazarsfeld and Oberschall have argued that Weber's objective was to develop an action schema through which sociological concepts could be organised: that he was not therefore concerned with the empirical study of social action, which was rather a task for psychologists.[3]

It is true, as we have seen, that Weber did see psychology as performing work complementary to sociology in the explanation of human action. This could broadly be identified with the 'because motivations' as subsequently designated by Schutz. And, as we have also seen, Weber never thought that an act could be wholly reproduced in an empirical description. However, Weber was concerned with real action as well as with the conscious construction of fictional actors with fixed goals and modes of orientation devised by the sociologist for heuristic reasons. This double interest is evident in Weber's discussion of concepts and their application in *The Theory of Social and Economic Organisa-*

---

[1] See particularly *The Phenomenology of the Social World.*
[2] 'The Social World and The Theory of Action' in D. Braybrooke, *Philosophical Problems of the Social Sciences* (Collier-Macmillan, 1965), p. 60.
[3] In 'Max Weber and Empirical Research', *A.S.R.*, Vol. 30, No. 2 (1965), pp. 197–8.

tion. The concept of legitimate order will serve us as a good example:

> Action, especially social action, which involves social relationships may be oriented by the actors to a *belief* (*Vorstellung*) in the existence of a 'legitimate order'. The probability that action will actually be empirically so oriented will be called the 'validity' (*Geltung*) of the order in question. . . . The subjective meaning of a social relationship will be called an 'order' only if action is approximately or on the average oriented to certain determinate 'maxims' or rules. Furthermore, such an order will only be called 'valid' if the orientation to such maxims includes, no matter to what actual extent, the recognition that they are binding on the actor, or the corresponding action constitutes a desirable model for him to imitate. Naturally, in concrete cases, the orientation of action to an order involves a wide variety of motives. But the circumstance that along with the other sources of conformity the order is also held by at least part of the actors to define a model or to be binding, naturally increases the probability that action will in fact conform to it, often to a very considerable degree.[1]

It is this very fact that there are regularities of action that makes an interpretative sociology possible. The method of understanding is certainly not to be confused with psychological reductionism. Raymond Aron in his *Introduction to the Philosophy of History* has put the matter very well:

> If we suppose the noble savage, dear to the eighteenth century, to be back among us, confronted with the Stock Exchange, or a train, it is not to the psychologist that he would apply for an understanding of what takes place. Physics would help him to interpret the behaviour of the engine driver, the rules of railroad management, the behaviour of the station master, the techniques of financial exchange, that of the brokers.[2]

If the sociologist is concerned with the understanding of the social action, he is concerned with the circumstances which hinder or fulfil the intentions being realised, whether they be non-

[1] *Theory*, p. 124.   [2] Pp. 65–6.

sociological factors or whether they can be traced to the behaviour of others. Here we may appropriately recollect Weber's pre-occupation with the problem of power in social life. 'Power (*Macht*)', he says, 'is the probability that one actor within a social relationship will be in a position to carry out his own will despite resistance, regardless of the basis on which this probability rests.'[1]

The intentions of one actor may then be carried out over and against the intentions of another. Thus, although Weber's sociology has often been described as voluntaristic (with its emphasis on actors pursuing goals), the social world he describes is not peopled by actors necessarily striving to please one another and provide one another with mutual benefits. It is a world in which one may be effectively constrained and coerced.

This is reflected in Weber's discussion of law, custom and convention and in his treatment of domination in social orders. Moreover, it is not simply that an actor may lose out in his personal struggles with contemporaries: his life may be effectively constrained by preceding generations. Thus:

> The Puritan wanted to work in a calling; we are forced to do so. For when asceticism was carried out of monastic cells into everyday life and began to dominate worldly morality, it did its part in building the tremendous cosmos of the modern economic order. This order is now bound to the technical and economic conditions of machine production which today determine the lives of all the individuals who are born into this mechanism, not only those directly concerned with economic acquisition, with irresistible force.[2]

It is possible in principle, then, for the interpretative sociologist to understand, better than the actor himself, the context in which action succeeds or fails in its intention.

[1] *Theory*, p. 152.
[2] Weber, *The Protestant Ethic and the Spirit of Capitalism*, p. 181.

(B) The Sociology of Capitalism

CAPITALISM IN THE WESTERN WORLD

A preoccupation with the phenomenon of modern capitalism which had emerged in Western societies pervades much of Weber's writing. The basic questions he asked were:

1. How may modern capitalism be described?
2. How can one account for its emergence?
3. Why did it emerge in the West and not elsewhere in the world?

An approach to answering the first question can be made by asking whether any generic definition of capitalism may be formulated over and against 'non-capitalism'. In *The Protestant Ethic and the Spirit of Capitalism* such a definition is offered: 'We will define a capitalistic economic action as one which rests on the expectation of profit by the utilisation of opportunities for exchange, that is on (formally) peaceful chances of profit.'[1] This is set against the notion of acquisition of profit by force. (In other words, it is not acquisitive activity as such which is identical with 'capitalism'). Certain differentiating characteristics within this generic definition may then be propounded which seem to delineate different types of capitalism.

One such procedure emphasises the difference between 'politically oriented capitalism' and 'industrial capitalism'. The former refers to situations where the opportunity exists, and is taken, to obtain profitable exchanges by, for example, providing loan support to politicians, financing their wars and so on. Or, as in the case of tax-farming schemes, plantation economies and suchlike, the capitalist may take advantage of the profit opportunities made available to him by the structure and sanctions of political authority. Industrial capitalism was exemplified in situations where continuous productive enterprises sought to exploit a market situation, making use of capital accounting techniques in the process.

[1] Weber, *The Protestant Ethic and the Spirit of Capitalism*, p. 17.

33

A second form of differentiation is between 'rational' and 'irrational' capitalism. The important consideration for Weber in delineating 'rational' capitalistic behaviour 'is always that a calculation of capital in terms of money is made, whether by modern book-keeping methods or in any other way, however primitive and crude. Everything is done in terms of balances: at the beginning of the enterprise an initial balance, before every individual decision a calculation to ascertain its probable profitableness, and at the end a final balance to ascertain how much profit has been made. . . . So far as the transactions are rational, calculation underlies every single action of the partners'.[1] Weber contrasts this with the activities of financial and trade speculators, tax farmers, money lenders and colonial entrepreneurs, which he regarded as essentially irrational, that is to say not based upon calculation.

Types of Capitalism		
Type of Economic Behaviour	Types of Capitalism	
	Political	Industrial
Irrational	1	2
Rational	3	4

In the chart above it is categories 1 and 4 that operate as points of contrast in Weber's analysis, namely, irrational political capitalism and rational industrial capitalism. It is important to recognise, however, that Weber did not claim that rational industrial capitalism was identified with modern capitalism: 'Capitalism and capitalistic enterprises, even with a considerable rationalisation of capitalistic calculation, have existed in all civilised countries of the earth, so far as economic documents permit us to judge. In China, India, Babylon, Egypt, Mediterranean antiquity and the Middle Ages, as well as in modern times.'[2]

It is necessary to introduce another differentiation into that segment of the classification. The distinctive characteristic of

[1] Weber, *The Protestant Ethic and the Spirit of Capitalism*, pp. 18-19.
[2] *ibid.*, p. 197.

modern industrial capitalism is, says Weber, the rational organisation of (formally) free labour. Such labour Weber sees as con-
trasting favourably with slave labour from the entrepreneur's
point of view.[1] It is a cheaper capital investment. The labourer, not
the entrepreneur has to support his own family; he can be
selected on the basis of his ability and willingness to work whilst,
at the same time, the risk of dismissal if he does not meet the
employer's requirements should keep him working hard.

To explain, therefore, the origins of modern capitalism, one has
to account both for the emergence of formally free labour in the
West and for the emergence of the entrepreneurs who were both
willing and able to utilise it. Weber explored these theories in
many discussions throughout his work. But in his *General Economic History* is located a good summary statement to the question:
Why is it that only in the Western world is the entrepreneurial
organisation of formally free labour to be found?

If this development took place only in the occident the reason
is to be found in the special features of its general cultural
evolution which are peculiar to it. Only the Occident knows the
state in its modern scale, with a professional administration,
specialised officialdom, and law based on the concept of citizenship. Beginnings of this institution in antiquity and in the
Orient were never able to develop. Only the Occident knows
rational law, made by jurists and rationally interpreted and
applied, and only in the occident is found the concept of
citizens (civis Romanus, citoyen, bourgeois) because only in the
Occident again are there cities in the specific sense. Furthermore, only the occident possesses science in the present-day
sense of the word. Theology, philosophy, reflection on the
ultimate problems of life, were known to the Chinese and the
Hindu, perhaps even of a depth unreached by the European:
but a rational science and in connection with it a rational
technology remained unknown to these civilisations. Finally,
western civilisation is further distinguished from every other
by the presence of men with a rational ethic for the conduct of
life. Magic and religion are found everywhere; but a religious
basis for the ordering of life which consistently followed out

See, for example, *Theory*, pp. 276–7.

must lead to explicit rationalism is again peculiar to western civilisation alone.[1]

It can readily be seen that such a statement could only meaningfully be made after a period of prolonged scholarship in which historical research into the culture of the Occident had been undertaken in the context of comparative studies of other civilisations. Each of these aspects of Western civilization has to be explained, so to speak, in its own right, and its absence in other cultures accounted for. It is Weber's concern both for historical detail (the prerequisite for adequate evidential statements) and for the panoramic comparative perspective which makes his sociological achievement so impressive.

If Weber saw free labour as a key factor differentiating modern capitalism from its earlier forms, it was because he believed that without it economic activity based on exact calculation was impossible.[2] On the other hand if one forms the question slightly differently and asks, as Weber also did, what was the prerequisite for exact calculation, free labour becomes only one factor among several, which necessarily buttress 'rational capital accounting' in industrial undertakings. Others include:

(a) The appropriation of all physical means of production as disposable property of autonomous private industrial enterprise and

(b) Freedom of the market from 'irrational' limitations of trading in the market (such as class factors affecting the purchase of commodities or labour);

(c) A rational technology, as for example, is implied in the mechanisation of production;

(d) A framework of calculable law such that an industrial organisation can depend upon calculable adjudication and administration;

(e) The commercialisation of economic life such that commercial instruments may be used to represent share rights in enterprises and property ownership.[3]

It is in Part 4 of the *General Economic History* that Weber indicates the ways in which these various strands emerged in Western Europe, weaving together to form a unique cultural configuration.

[1] *GEH*, pp. 232–3.   [2] See *PE*, p. 22.   [3] See *GEH*, pp. 238–9.

PROTESTANTISM AND CAPITALISM

Weber's monograph *The Protestant Ethic and the Spirit of Capitalism*[1] first appeared as two separate essays in the *Archiv für Sozialwissenschaft und Sozialpolitik* in 1904 and 1905. By the time they were reprinted in book form in 1920 the essays had already been the subject of much critical discussion. Weber took the opportunity of adding extensive footnotes to his work. In them he replied to his major critics, notably Brentano and Sombart; he sought to clarify his argument, provide further evidence on points which had been challenged, and deal with what he believed to be misunderstandings about the task he had set himself and the position he had adopted. It is important for us to recognise afresh the significance of these footnotes. They do not remove all the problems, but if we neglect them it is simply not possible to do justice to what has come to be known as 'the Weber thesis'.

In *The Protestant Ethic and the Spirit of Capitalism* Weber sets out to discuss the part which the religious ideas of ascetic Protestantism played in accounting for the emergence of an ethos which he believed characterised the economic life of Western capitalist societies. In doing this he explicitly adopted, as a conscious research strategy, a one-sided causal analysis. The virtue of this strategy had been argued at some length in his essay 'Objectivity in Social Science and Social Policy'.[2] He sees it as a technical expedient, since scholars could become skilled in handling particular kinds of conceptual schemes and in 'the observation of the effects of qualitatively similar categories of causes'.[3] To the charge that this was an arbitrary procedure Weber's reply was essentially two-fold: it was not arbitrary if in practice it produced insights into certain kinds of interconnections which made up the reality of a particular culture; it was not arbitrary if it was accepted that it was a contribution to a further explanation of cultural reality rather than an exhaustive statement. There is in principle a plurality of one-sided explanations which needs to be pursued if an adequate grasp of the social processes which contribute towards cultural reality is to be obtained. Thus, Weber refused to accept

[1] Allen & Unwin, 1948.
[2] In *Methodology of the Social Sciences*, op. cit.
[3] *Objectivity*, p. 71.

that an explanation of social life solely in terms of economic causes was satisfactory. Not even an explanation of economic life: 'In principle a banking history of a nation which adduces only economic motives for explanatory purposes is naturally just as unacceptable as an explanation of the Sistine Madonna as a consequence of the social-economic basis of the culture of the epoch in which it was created. It is in no way more complete than, for instance, the explanation of capitalism by reference to certain shifts in the context of the religious ideas which played a role in the genesis of the capitalistic attitude; nor is it more exhaustive than the explanation of a political structure from its geographical background.'[1] But the last thing that this methodological position should be taken to imply is that economic considerations should be neglected when moving towards a comprehensive analysis of a particular culture. Indeed, he argues explicitly that he considers 'the influence of economic development on the fate of religious ideas to be very important',[2] and points out that a further statement than the one he advanced in *The Protestant Ethic* would need to show 'how Protestant ascetism was in turn influenced in its development and character by the totality of social conditions, especially economic'.[3] After all, if, as has been noted above, economic life could not be wholly explained by reference to the economic sphere, neither could religious life be explained solely by referncee to the religious sphere.

What appears to have happened in much of the subsequent debate surrounding the Weber thesis is that a research strategy has been treated as though it was a complete explanation, despite Weber's own clear assertion that it was not his intention to substitute for a one-sided materialistic interpretation 'an equally one-sided spiritualistic causal interpretation'.[4] Tawney was right when he observed drily: 'If Weber did not in his articles refer to the economic consequences of the discovery of America, or of the great depreciation, or of the rise to financial pre-eminence of the Catholic city of Antwerp, it was not that these bashful events had at last hit on an historian whose notice they could elude'.[5] Such matters are of course treated in Weber's *General Economic History*. Yet in his Foreword to the English translation of *The Protestant Ethic* Tawney had himself fallen into this kind of misreading of

Weber. 'Why insist that causation can only work in one direction? Is it not a little artificial to suggest that capitalist enterprise had to wait, as Weber appears to imply, till religious changes had produced a capitalist spirit? Would it not be equally plausible, and equally one-sided, to argue that the religious changes were themselves merely the result of economic movements.'[1]

R. Bendix has suggested that much of the controversy surrounding the Weber thesis is beside the point since it concentrates on the problem of the causal significance of the Protestant ethic for the rise of capitalism, whereas Weber had insisted that he had not been trying to explain the origin or the expansion of capitalism.[2] What lies behind this suggestion is the fact that, for example, Weber cites the existence of capitalistic business organisation before the Reformation as sufficient refutation of any theory which wished to maintain that the economic system of capitalism was a creation of the Reformation. And the view that the 'spirit of capitalism' could only have arisen as a result of certain efforts of the Reformation Weber dismisses as a 'foolish and doctrinaire thesis'.[3] But Weber's strategy of a one-way causal analysis does imply that certain kinds of linkages between Protestant asceticism and particular features of modern capitalism can be articulated. He sets out his own position in the following way:

We only wish to ascertain whether and to what extent religious forces have taken part in the qualitative formation and quantitative expression of that [capitalist] spirit over the world. Furthermore, what concrete aspects of our capitalistic culture can be traced to them. In view of the tremendous confusion of interdependent influences between the material basis, the forms of social and political organisation, and the ideas current in the time of the Reformation, we can only proceed by investigating whether and at what points certain correlations between forms of religious belief and practical ethics can be worked out. At the same time we shall as far as possible clarify the manner and general *direction* in which, by virtue of those relationships, the religious movements have influenced the development of material culture.[4]

---

[1] *PE*, p. 8.
[2] R. Bendix, *Max Weber: An Intellectual Portrait* (Heinemann, 1960), p. 72.
[3] *PE*, p. 91.   [4] *ibid.*, pp. 91-2.

So these religious ideas may in certain circumstances exercise some leverage over economic life. But their influence has to be assessed in the context of a particular cultural configuration. Thus, for example, the fact that Calvinism in Scotland was not associated with marked capitalistic development of the economy is no refutation of Weber's position.[1] Let us try then to state the salient features of Weber's thesis. There is first of all a distinction made between the 'form' of modern capitalistic enterprise and the 'spirit' of modern capitalism. One may comment on this by reference to the following chart:

Type of Production System	Type of 'Spirit'	
	Modern Capitalist	Traditionalist
Non-capitalist	1	2
Capitalist	3	4

To those who accept as a guide to their own conduct the idea of increasing one's capital as an end in itself and out of a sense of duty (an ethical imperative) Weber attributes 'the spirit of modern capitalism'. It is a spirit which characterises labour when in an individualistic way the workman calculates how he can maximise his earnings and will respond to economic incentives (designed to improve his productivity) to the best of his ability; whilst at the same time he manifests a sense of responsibility towards his work and a specific willingness to work hard and systematically. It is also a spirit which characterises an entrepreneur who accepts the pursuit of money as virtuous in itself and systematically organises himself and his productive resources to that end. His business is the *raison d'être* of his whole existence. Weber quotes particularly from the writings of Benjamin Franklin to illustrate how honesty, thrift, frugality, punctuality and hard work, because they promoted economic gain, were extolled as moral virtues.

This 'spirit of modern capitalism' is contrasted with a 'traditional spirit'. It is reflected in both the worker and the employer who simply wish to earn sufficient money to enable them to carry

[1] Albert Hyma thinks otherwise, as shown in *Renaissance to Reformation* (Grand Rapids, 1955).

on living in a way which, for them, is already established and acceptable. Changes in ways of working or in the character of market relationships (with customers and fellow competitors) are seen as undesirable and, given this kind of orientation, are resented and resisted.

By separating the 'form' from the 'spirit' of modern capitalism Weber is able to suggest first that non-capitalist types of production systems, although they will most likely be dominated by a traditionalist spirit, may in fact be imbued with the spirit of modern capitalism. Thus he maintains, for example, that Franklin's printing business did not, in the first instance, differ in form from any handicraft enterprise, while Franklin himself was imbued with the spirit of capitalism. Conversely, a capitalistic form of enterprise (i.e. enterprises carried on by private entrepreneurs by utilising capital to make a profit, purchasing the means of production and selling the product)[1] could be characterised by a traditionalistic spirit: indeed, it was this spirit which could enable an entrepreneur to gear his activities to 'the traditional manner of life, the traditional rate of profit, the traditional amount of work, the traditional manner of regulating the relationships with labour and the essentially traditional circle of customers and the manner of attracting new ones'.[2] We may see, therefore, that all four of the situations which are designated if we cross-tabulate the type of production system with the type of 'spirit', as we have done in the chart above, have some anchorage in empirical reality.

One crucial question which then emerges is this: who are the people who bring into conjunction the form of capitalist enterprise with the spirit of capitalism? Weber's answer is clear: it is primarily the self-made parvenu, the rising strata of the lower middle classes,[3] rather than the capitalistic entrepreneurs of the commercial aristocracy whom he sees as operating more typically in a traditionalistic spirit. This brings out a point which, although plainly stated by Weber, is often blurred in discussion of the thesis: 'The assumption is . . . by no means justified *a priori*, . . . that on the one hand the techniques of the capitalistic enterprise and on the other the spirit of professional work which gives to capitalism its expansive energy must have had their original roots in the same social classes.'[4]

While, then, as we have seen, Weber was not attempting to

[1] *PE*, p. 64.   [2] *ibid.*, p. 67.   [3] *ibid.*, p. 65.   [4] *ibid.*, p. 200.

explain the origin of modern capitalism, he was interested in the origin of this 'expansive energy'. How does one account for the behaviour which enables a man to become a self-made parvenu? The motivation must be very strong for him to withstand the criticism and resentment of the traditionalists (capitalist and non-capitalist) and to feel himself justified. It is here that the linkage with Puritanism is suggested. Puritanism is used as a generic term to refer to 'the ascetically inclined religious movements in Holland and England without distinction of church organisation or dogma, thus including Independents, Congregationalists, Baptists, Mennonites and Quakers'.[1] Despite the diversity of dogma, however, Weber selected the Calvinist doctrine of predestination—as outlined, for example, in the Westminster Confession—in trying to draw out the significance of the linkage between Puritanism and the capitalist spirit. Thus: 'By the decree of God, for the manifestation of His glory, some men and angels are predestined unto everlasting life, and others foreordained to everlasting death'.[2] And again: 'All those whom God hath predestined unto life, and those only, He is pleased in His appointed and accepted time eventually to call by His word and spirit (out of that state of sin and death, in which they are by nature) . . . renewing their wills, and by His almighty power determining them to that which is good . . .'.[3].

The logical consequence of this doctrine was that no one who believed it could be certain of his salvation; no man in his sinful finiteness could assure you, and God resided in unapproachable transcendence and kept His own counsel on the matter. However, since within this framework one's eternal destiny was of immense significance, the psychological need to obtain some certainty of one's calling and election was very pressing. It was this need, Weber suggested, which was met by 'proving' one's (God-given) faith in worldly activity. A life of diligent, systematic hard work could become the religious equivalent of a monastic asceticism, though the economic consequences were very different. 'Christian ascetism strode into the market-place of life, slammed the door of the monastery behind it, and undertook to penetrate just that daily routine of life with its methodicalness, to fashion it into a life in the world, but neither of nor for this world.'[4] Weber held that it was of strategic importance to consider the doctrine of pre-

[1] *PE*, p. 217.   [2] Quoted *ibid.*, p. 100.   [3] *ibid.*,   [4] *ibid.*, p. 154.

destination, because the dilemma of 'proving' one's salvation was posed in its most extreme form and hence 'its psychological effect was extraordinarily powerful' on the character and conduct of the believer. He recognised, however, that not all Puritans adhered to this doctrine, but they did nevertheless have to cope with the question: How do I know I am saved? And what was widespread in Puritan thinking was the notion that while works performed for the glory of God were not the cause of one's state of grace, they were a sign of it: even eighteenth-century Methodism, which in its mainstream theology rejected the doctrine of predestination, shared this perspective with earlier English Puritanism. The doctrine of Christian perfection in the Methodist context could serve as a practical substitute for the doctrine of predestination, forming the religious basis of ascetic conduct. The incentive to enter into 'the eternal struggle for perfection'[1] is well brought out in the following hymn of Charles Wesley:

> A charge to keep I have,
> A God to glorify,
> A never-dying soul to save,
> And fit it for the sky.
>
> To serve the present age,
> My calling to fulfil;
> O may it all my powers engage
> To do my Master's will.
>
> Arm me with jealous care,
> As in Thy sight to live;
> And O Thy servant, Lord, prepare
> A strict account to give!
>
> Help me to watch and pray,
> And on Thyself rely,
> Assured if I my trust betray,
> I shall for ever die.

But one may perhaps still ask why was it that the idea of fulfilling one's calling was interpreted in practice as fulfilling one's occupational calling. Antoni has argued that although this is not clearly

[1] *PE*, p. 143.

explained in Weber's work, it is in fact directly derived from the Calvinist idea of God: 'God's glory consists in His will being done. But what is His will? He desires that men work, even the rich, without the riches produced being consumed in voluptuary self-indulgence or being squandered. . . . Here . . . is the discovery of the world as a rational, useful creation. . . . The idea that work represents the glory of God means, in fact, that economic activity is consecrated and seen as having an autonomous value'.[1] It is for this reason that Antoni suggests that the spirit of capitalism is both the logical and the psychological consequence of Calvinism. By the same token 'Weber's thesis loses that eloquent, paradoxical equality in which consequences are held to appear in opposition to the principles as unexpected and surprising results'.[2]

The concentration on one's occupational calling was therefore at the expense of other activities. Any impulsive enjoyment of life—sport, dancing, the theatre, the public house—was seen as the enemy of that rational asceticism with its central life-interest of work. And since one was expected to give account of one's work as a faithful steward, the use to which one's money was put was of great importance:

> The greater the possessions the heavier, if the ascetic attitude towards life stands the test, the feeling of responsibility for them, for holding them undiminished for the glory of God and increasing them by restless effort. The origin of this type of life also extends in certain roots, like so many aspects of the spirit of capitalism, back into the Middle Ages. But it was in the ethic of ascetic Protestantism that it first found a consistent ethical foundation.[3]

What remains paradoxical, or certainly unintended so far as the Puritan theologians were concerned, is the secularisation of the spirit of capitalism, such that the call to work hard, be thrifty and accumulate capital becomes justified for its own sake and enclosed in a utilitarian value system as exemplified in the writings of Benjamin Franklin, from which Weber quoted so liberally. One may note in passing that those who chide Weber for using

[1] C. Antoni, *From History to Sociology* (Wayne State University Press, 1959), pp. 156–7.
[2] *ibid.*, p. 159.   [3] *PE*, p. 170.

Franklin as an example of the spirit of capitalism, whilst not being a Calvinist, misunderstand the point at issue.[1] Franklin is used to illustrate the fully developed spirit of capitalism ('accumulation for its own sake') which was only attained in its secular phase. Franklin is, as Weber puts it, 'expressly denoted as a man who stood beyond the direct influence of the Puritan view of life'.[2] To say, as Bendix does, that this paradox is diminished when one recognises that the secular phase was made possible by the whole history of Western civilisation[3] is obviously true, but the realisation of that possibility still remains one of the ironies of history.

FURTHER COMMENTS AND CONTINUITIES ON THE WEBER THESIS

One recent stimulating reconsideration of the Weber thesis is that of Trevor-Roper. He argues that the thesis has 'a solid, if elusive, core of truth'.[4] One of his qualifications, however, takes the form of arguing that not only in Protestant but also in Catholic countries, it is the Calvinists who are the great entrepreneurs in the mid-seventeenth century. 'They are an international force, the economic *élite* of Europe. They alone, it seems, can mobilise commerce and industry and, by so doing, command great sums of money, either to finance armies or to reinvest in other great economic undertakings.'[5] But did these Calvinists bear the imprint of the character structure of Protestant asceticism? They did not. They lived magnificently, acquiring hereditary nobilities and buying large estates, and gambled in the grand manner. To this qualification, one might suppose that Weber could reply that most of the examples quoted were of bankers, financiers and state capitalists, most of whom could be subsumed under the heading of 'traditional capitalism'. It is consistent with Weber's thesis to recognise that 'there were at all times large bankers and merchants'[6] and that 'absolute and conscious ruthlessness in acquisition has often stood in the closest connections with the strictest conformity

[1] See, for example, K. Samuelsson, *Religion and Economic Action* (Harper, 1964), pp. 55 ff.
[2] *PE*, p. 198.   [3] R. Bendix, *Max Weber* op. cit. p. 286.
[4] Trevor-Roper, *Religion, the Reformation and Social Change* (Macmillan, 1967), p. 6.
[5] *ibid.*, p. 13.   [6] *PE*, p. 200.

to tradition'.[1] By the same token the fact that some of these great financiers were often aliens in the countries they served (such as the notable Hans de Witte who went from his home in Antwerp to Prague to serve the Catholic powers) is not necessarily important. On this very point, Weber had commented:

> The migration of exiles of all the religions of the earth, Indian, Arabian, Chinese, Syrian, Phoenician, Greek, Lombard, to other countries as bearers of the commercial lore of highly developed areas, has been of universal occurrence and has nothing to do with our problem. . . . Bankers of foreign extraction have existed at all times and in all countries as the representatives of commercial experience and connections. They are not peculiar to modern capitalism. . . .[2]

The point at issue also comes out with some clarity in Weber's short essay 'The Protestant Sects and the Spirit of Capitalism',[3] where Weber notes that a great number of the American 'captains of industry' often had some formal connection with a sect such as the Baptists. Their religiosity, like that of some of the Calvinists noted by Trevor-Roper, was often of dubious sincerity. But these he sees as having more in common with capitalist figures of all ages and he specifically distinguishes them from 'the strata ascending with and out of the middle classes' who were 'the bearers of the specifically Occidental bourgeois mentality'.[4] A point which Trevor-Roper does not develop but which is found in Weber's own analysis is the effect of change of residence in stimulating the labourer's willingness to work:

> The simple fact of working in quite different surroundings from those to which one is accustomed breaks through the tradition and is an educative force. It is hardly necessary to remark how much of American economic development is the result of such factors. In ancient times the similar significance of the Babylonian exile for the Jews is very striking, and the same is true of the Parsee. But for the Protestants, as is indicated by the undeniable difference in the economic characteristics of the

[1] *PE*, p. 58.   [2] *ibid.*, p. 190.
[3] In H. Gerth, and C. W. Mills, *From Max Weber* (Routledge, 1948).
[4] *PE*, p. 309.

Puritan New England colonies from Catholic Maryland, the Episcopal South and mixed Rhode Island, the influence of their religious belief quite evidently plays a part as an independent factor. Similarly in India, for instance, with the Jains.[1]

However, some forms of migration could be conducive to the development of modern capitalism, as Weber to some extent acknowledged, and one of the merits of Trevor-Roper's essay is the emphasis he gives to the importance of 'diaspora Calvinism'— albeit diminishing the importance of Calvinism as an explanatory factor in its own right so far as the capitalist spirit was concerned. He notes that none of 'the four obvious Calvinist societies', Holland, Scotland, Geneva and the Palatinate, produced their own entrepreneurs. Most successful entrepreneurs were immigrants, mainly from the Netherlands. They were predominantly Flemish, often though not always Calvinist. The historical question for Trevor-Roper is: What was it that drove both entrepreneurs and workmen to migrate in the first place? The answer we can here note only cryptically:

> In its year of panic (after the Reformation) the bloated rigid Church of the Inquisitors and the friars saw the Erasmianism of the entrepreneurs as a form of Lutheranism: *Erasmus posuit ova, Lutherus eduxit pullos*: and it saw the 'primitive Christianity' of weavers and miners as a form of German Anabaptism. So it drove both out of the fold.[2]

Trevor-Roper sees the Calvinist International as a movement which Erasmian merchants could espouse. It not only solved a crisis of conscience for them as individuals but enabled them to take a position which differentiated them from both the Catholic princes of the Mediterranean and Burgundy who wished to preserve their old supremacy, and from the Lutheran princes of Germany, who headed the nationalist revolt against Mediterranean domination and exploitation.

We may turn now to another recent consideration of the impact of religious life on economic life which in an important sense may be reckoned an extension of Weber's thesis. Weber's analysis centred upon the religious attitude which originally served as an

[1] *PE, p. 191.*   [2] Trevor-Roper, op. cit., p. 41.

underpinning for the bourgeois business man. He did little more than note that such a business man was enormously helped in his endeavour if religious asceticism had moulded the character of the work force. It could, indeed, provide him with 'sober, conscientious and unusually industrious workmen, who clung to their work as a life purpose willed by God'.[1] Weber certainly had England very much in mind and in fact suggests that Baxter's reflections on what constitutes a saintly workman appear to indicate that 'the interests of God and of the employers are curiously harmonious!'[2] Now it is in the English context that E. P. Thompson has suggested that 'Methodism obtained its greatest success in serving *simultaneously* as the religion of the industrial bourgeoisie (although here it shared the field with other Nonconformist sects) and of wide sections of the proletariat'.[3] Weber was conscious of the importance of work discipline among the labour force as a prerequisite of successful industrial capitalism. Thompson asks how it was achieved. He depicts Andrew Ure as the Richard Baxter of Cottonopolis with his advice to employers who wished to command superior workmanship 'to organise his moral machinery on equally sound principles with his mechanical'.[4] And this moral machinery could receive its momentum in Ure's view from the transforming power of the cross of Christ:

> It is the sacrifice which removes the guilt of sin: it is the motive which removes love of sin: it mortifies sin by showing its torpitude to be indelible except by such an awful expiation it atones for disobedience: it excites to obedience; it purchases strength for obedience; it makes obedience practicable; it makes it acceptable; it makes it in a manner unavoidable for it constrains to it; it is finally not only the motive to obedience, but the pattern of it.[5]

Thompson argues that Methodism, especially during the period 1790–1830, was able to inculcate this pattern of obedience among the proletariat for three main reasons: first because of the psychological impact of its indoctrination. Young children at Wesleyan

---

[1] *PE*, p. 177.   [2] *ibid.*, p. 281.
[3] E. P. Thompson *The Making of the English Working Class* (Gollancz, 1963), p. 255.
[4] *Ure's Philosophy of Manufactures*, quoted *ibid.*, 361.
[5] Quoted *ibid.*, p. 362.

Sunday Schools were taught the virtues of hard work, industry and submission to authority and to behave in the sure knowledge that they were being watched by an all-seeing eye. The adults were reached through the typical conversion process of the 'religion of the heart'. This Thompson describes as a 'psychic ordeal in which the character structure of the pre-industrial labourer or artisan was violently recast into that of the submissive industrial worker'.[1] The second reason relates to the Methodist community sense: one can see, for example, how the Methodist church membership ticket could act as a passport for the migrant industrial worker to gain entrance to a religious community which had 'its own drama, its own degrees of status and importance, its own gossip and a good deal of mutual aid'.[2] In this respect the fellowship of Methodist people could serve as a substitute for the older social patterns of living which were being undermined by the process of industrialisation. The third and more tentative reason put forward is that Methodist revivalism with its appeal to the compensation of the after life was a 'chiliasm of the defeated and the hopeless'.[3]

The stifling of revolution in late eighteenth-century England could lead to a religion which based its message on the virtue of resignation and obedience. It is possible that religious revivalism took over just at the point where 'political' or temporal aspirations met with defeat.[4] It may be suggested that Thompson somewhat loads the dice in his assessment of the role of Methodism as a religion of the oppressed by interpreting the Methodists who became politically conscious (not infrequently class conscious) and involved in Luddite activities, trade union organisation or Chartist causes, as the case may be, as examples of the 'reactive dialectic' rather than more simply as an example of an alternative formulation which, so to speak, existed in its own right. But it is sufficient here to recall the diversity of response from the working class (which on religious or secular grounds spoke of and was prepared to fight for 'the rights of man') to realise that the submissive industrial worker was only one of several types. The significance of this for the Weberian analysis is, of course, that whilst the worker who sells his labour in the best market and responds to certain incentives to increase his output might be

[1] *Ure's Philosophy of Manufacturers*, quoted *ibid.*, pp. 367–8.
[2] *ibid.*, p. 379.   [3] *ibid.*, p. 382.   [4] *ibid.*, p. 389.

described as 'rational' over and against the traditionalist worker, other forms of worker-rationality could also emerge which found expression in more solidaristic forms of behaviour of a political or economic character. This could lead either to revolutionary aspirations or to more obviously instrumental forms of behaviour, influencing the supply and quality of labour available and the amount of output produced. The dichotomy between the 'traditional' and the 'capitalistic' worker therefore leaves certain things unsaid. Secondly, one has to recall that should the attempts to internalise the belief system of the 'capitalistic' worker be inadequate or positively resisted, then more directly coercive measures could be employed to ensure compliance.

It is for these reasons that one must recognise that the congruence of values between capital and labour was of an unstable and limited kind during the period of industrialisation in England; and that the element of consensus implied in the employment contract was on the basis of necessity and force and not simply a lofty view of the virtues of team-work between masters and men. Weber, of course, was not ignorant of the role of sanctions and coercion in the employment contract. In *The Theory of Social and Economic Organisation*, for example, we find him pointing out that the risk of dismissal is an important factor in encouraging the worker to maximise production:[1] and in his *General Economic History* he writes of the difficulties which workers had in adapting themselves to factory work. Then why did they stay?

> 'The power of the possessing classes [in England] was too great; they secured the supports of the political authority through the justices of the peace, who in the absence of binding law operated on the basis of a maze of instructions and largely according to their own dictates. Down into the second half of the nineteenth century they exercised an arbitrary control over the labour force and fed the workers into the newly arising industries.[2]

What Weber does tend to stress in *The Protestant Ethic* is the importance of the skilled artisan for the success of the capitalist entrepreneur, and significantly he often speaks of this in the context of the domestic system rather than the factory system. In that context or in the context of the small family business, the

---

[1] *Theory*, p. 277.   [2] *GEH*, p. 288.

artisan could appropriately maintain an individualistic attitude to his work and rewards, conscious that he had a good chance of becoming his own boss if he worked hard and saved hard. The advent of the large factory greatly diminished the likelihood of such advancement, and indeed in many instances the basic skills which he possessed were threatened or made obsolescent by the machine. Where the resistance of skilled workers to the impact of the factory system was successful, however, it is noteworthy that the union organisation upon which it depended operated on the principle of controlling the supply of labour. Thus the individualistic notion of property rights in one's job was sustained and secured through collective action. Indeed, in the British context, as writers such as the Hammonds and G. D. H. Cole have pointed out, it was the craftsmen whose status and standards were in danger of erosion as a result of industrialisation who took the lead in organised resistance against the factory owners.[1] Such resistance, we may note, with its attempt to establish job control, implied a form of closed shop organisation which Weber recognised as part of the modern situation and necessarily conflicting with his conception of 'pure type' rational capitalism, since it interfered with the free recruitment of the labour force and potentially with the employer's powers of dismissal.[2] But such skilled workers, in so far as they remain skilled, may be distinguished from what Weber understands by the industrial proletariat. The tendency of the latter to religious indifference is made clear in *The Sociology of Religion*:

> In so far as the modern proletariat has a distinctive religious position it is characterised by indifference to or rejection of religion common to large groups of the modern bourgeoisie. For the modern proletariat the sense of dependence on one's own achievements is supplemented by a consciousness of dependence on purely social factors, economic conjunctions and power relationships guaranteed by law. Any thought of dependence upon the course of natural or meteorological processes, or upon anything that might be regarded as subject to the influence of magic or providence has been completely eliminated, as Sombart has already demonstrated in fine fashion.

[1] See G. D. H. Cole, *A Short History of the British Working Class Movement* (Macmillan, 1927); J. L. and B. Hammond, *The Skilled Labourer* (1919).
[2] See, for example, *Theory*, p. 236.

Therefore, the rationalism of the proletariat like that of the bourgeoisie of developed capitalism when it has come into the full possession of economic power, of which indeed the proletariat's rationalism is a complementary phenomenon, cannot in the nature of the case easily possess a religious character and certainly cannot easily germinate a religion. Hence in the sphere of proletarian rationalism, religion is generally supplemented by these ideological surrogates.[1]

Such ideologies, in developing a consciousness of the proletarian position, may of course vary in content and the nature of their response: some will stress the defensive need to build against the evil day of unemployment and promote benefit societies to cope with family problems caused by sickness and death; others will stress the need to develop collective bargaining arrangements to wrest a fairer share of the rewards of their industry from the owners; still others will stress one variant or another of revolutionary socialism to liberate the proletariat from the domination implied by the existing set of power relationships. The important point is that if bourgeois power is understood to be created by man (not sustained by magic or providence), it may also, in principle, be reacted to by men whether in reformist or revolutionary terms.

This central tendency of the urban proletariat to religious indifference suggested by Weber is consistent with the findings of a number of commentators on religious life in nineteenth-century[2] England.

There was an exception to this tendency:

The lowest and most economically unstable strata of the proletariat, for whom rational conceptions are the least congenial, and also the proletariat or permanently impoverished lower middle class groups who are in constant danger of sinking into

---

[1] Pp. 100-1.
[2] For ample documentation of this point see:
F. Engels: *The Condition of the Working Class in England in 1844;* Neill, 1892.
C. Booth: *Life and Labour of the People in London;* Macmillan, 1892-1903.
K. S. Inglis: *Churches and the Working Classes in Victorian England;* Routledge, 1963. E. R. Wickham: *Church and People in an Industrial City;* Clowes, 1957.

the proletarian class, are nevertheless readily susceptible to being influenced by religious missionary enterprise . . .[1]

And this, we may note, is precisely the stratum which Thompson characterises as 'the defeated and the hopeless'. Weber refers to the role of Methodism in this respect as Thompson does, and specifically to its offshoot the Salvation Army. He stresses that it promotes an emotional response in the recipient but not an ethical religion. This kind of religion, with its deliverance from present troubles through the intervention of divine grace, is seen as having some of the characteristics of magic. It is interesting to recall that one such religious group in early nineteenth-century England was in fact known as 'Magic Methodists'. Although Weber does not elaborate these observations, they are at least consistent with Thompson's view that they might serve to aid the process of 'creating' a submissive work force. Such workers, however, are clearly far removed in spirit from the active, rationally calculating, 'capitalistic' worker and it might be suggested that more accurately we are seeing in this respect the 'traditionalist' peasant metamorphosed into the 'traditionalist' worker. One deferential pattern of social relations is replaced by another.

(C) The Rationalisation Theme in Weber's Sociology

No commentator could dispute the importance of the rationalisation theme in Weber's sociology. However, the interpretation of this theme is in some respects a matter of contention. In Parsons' influential discussions of Weber we see that there is, for example, the suggestion that the rationalisation process should be described as a law: 'This conception [Parsons'] of a law of increasing rationality as a fundamental generalisation about systems of action is, of course, not new. It is the most fundamental generalisation that

---

[1] *Sociology*, p. 101.

emerges from Weber's work, his conception of the process of rationalisation.'[1] And Parsons goes on to compare the process with the second law of thermo-dynamics (and in doing so again reflects his positivist position). If the second law of thermo-dynamics led to fatalistic conclusions about the running down of the universe, it was paralleled in a similar fatalism so far as the rationalisation of the social world was concerned: '. . . in Weber's terms a stock of charismatic energy, as it were, was in process of being consumed in the course of the rationalisation process and could leave behind it at the end a "dead mechanism".'[2]

Although the analogy used here is mechanistic, it is important to recognise that Parsons elsewhere deploys organic analogies and, indeed, takes as a basic assumption that Weber is essentially an evolutionary theorist. Thus, 'Weber's perspective especially in the sociology of religion . . . was basically evolutionary'.[3] In linking the rationalisation process to this perspective, Parsons suggests that it involves the clarification, specification and systematisation of the ideas which men have concerning their reason for being. 'Such ideas imply metaphysical and theological conceptions of cosmic and world orders as well as man's position in relation to such wider orders.'[4] But such ideas he also sees as potentially placing demands on men, which may affect their practical conduct not only in terms of the external constraints placed upon them by the emerging order, but also by generating such a sense of commitment to those ideas that they might even be ready 'to put their own interests at stake in the service of the ideas'.[5] And the mechanism which Parsons stresses in his account, whereby one moves to a more developed stage of rationalisation, is the prophet, the prototype of the charismatic leader. It is not simply his opposition to the established order that Parsons notes, though that with some of the accompanying emotional fervour of the prophet and his supporters is recognised: rather it is the fact that the prophet is assessed as the bearer of a new normative order. Indeed, he explicitly compares Weber's conception of charisma 'in its condition and social aspect' to Durkheim's concept of the collective sacred.[6] Thus, through prophetic charismatic leaders, society moves from one social order

[1] T. Parsons, *Structure of Social Action* (Free Press, 1937), p. 752.
[2] *ibid.*   [3] *Sociology of Religion*, p. xxvii.   [4] *ibid.*, p. xii.
[5] *ibid.*, p. xxxiii.   [6] *ibid.*, p. xxiv.

to another, though one does not in every instance, in an evolutionary sense, necessarily move to a 'higher order'.

Perhaps the clearest overall statement of Parsons' position on Weber as an evolutionist is to be found in his paper 'Evaluation and Objectivity in Social Science, an interpretation of Max Weber's contribution'.[1]

> In the substantive sociological sense Weber's theoretical scheme is inherently evolutionary. The comparative emphasis is legitimate and essential. There is no simple linear process at the level dealt with by a Comte or a Marx and many outcomes are dependent on highly variable contingencies. Nevertheless, Weber was committed to the attempt to set forth a general picture of a modern type of social organisation, which, as it happened, emerged in its later phases primarily in the Western world, and which was qualitatively different in an evolutionary sense from anything found in other civilisations. . . .
>
> It is at the very least conceived of as a very comprehensive complex of institutional components in which universalistic law and rational-legal authority as well as profit-oriented economic enterprise played a central part.

From this we see that it is by no means a simplistic evolutionary theme that Parsons is expounding. And we may recognise in particular that if it is to be presented as an evolutionary theory it is, on Parsons' own admission (when he comments on the running down of charismatic energy), a singularly pessimistic one unlike the optimistic views usually attributed to such theorists.

There are, of course, certain grounds for regarding Weber as an evolutionary theorist: his sociology of religion does concern itself with the elementary forms of religious life and then the conditions promoting the development of religious belief systems and institutions in various civilizations; his economic history does concern itself, among other things, with the evolution of the family, the clan, the capitalistic spirit and so on; and the notion of stages occurs when he writes about the development of law. Does any problem remain, therefore, in this respect? Yes, for the following reasons.

Firstly, we find Weber himself vigorously against certain forms of evolutionary theory as applied to the social world. For example,

[2] *Int. Soc. Sc. Jnl.*, Vol. 17 (1965), pp. 58–9.

he does not regard the term 'survival of the fittest' as applicable to social relationships or actions, since the reasons leading to a change in the chances of survival of the social action or relationship may suggest so many factors that a single term is inconvenient:

> When this is done, there is always a danger of introducing uncritical value-judgements into empirical investigation. There is, above all, a danger of being primarily concerned with justifying the process of an individual case. Since individual cases are often dependent on highly exceptional circumstances, they may be in a certain sense 'fortuitous' . . . The fact that a given specific social relationship has been eliminated for reasons peculiar to a particular situation, proves nothing whatever about its 'fitness to survive' in general terms.[1]

Further, and more concretely, in *Ancient Judaism* Weber in a long footnote at the onset of his study comments on the evolutionary perspective and its limitations. He describes Welhausen's approach to Jewish religious history as 'immanent evolutionary' in that 'the developmental course of Yahwe religion is determined by its unique intrinsic tendencies, though of course under the influence of the general fate of the people.'[2] This kind of appraisal tends to play down the fact, Weber suggests, that 'Israel entered upon its historical life as a confederacy of peasants, but (like Switzerland) found itself surrounded by countries with highly developed literary cultures, urban organisation overseas and caravan trade, bureaucratic states, priestly knowledge, astronomical observations and cosmological speculations.'[3] Weber points to the work of Gunkel and others in correcting Welhausen's developmental scheme. If one accepts in the light of their work the 'actual permeation of Israelite religion with logical and animistic elements on the one hand [and] the interrelation with the circles of joint neighbouring cultures on the other', then the question which was posed for them, and for Weber, was 'what, after all, constitutes the indubitable peculiarity of Israelite religious development in comparison with those which were, in part, universally diffused, in part common traits specifically culturally determined? Moreover what are the determinants of this peculiarity?'[4]

The point which necessarily arises, then, is that to portray

---

[1] *Theory*, p. 135.   [2] *AJ*, p. 426.   [3] *ibid.*, p. 427.   [4] *ibid.*, p. 428.

Weber's position as 'evolutionary' is probably more misleading than helpful. May not one in this context simply recognise Weber as an historical sociologist—historical because he was concerned with the distinctive features of particular societies; sociological because typically he utilises the comparative method as an aid to explaining the historically specific, to account for decisive motivations, conditions and so on which led to particular social orders and situations. But we are left with more than a semantic point in so far as the linkage between the evolutionary perspective and the process of rationalisation is suggested by Parsons.

The other side of the linkage turns out on inspection not to be a unified dimension describing one social process at all. This is spelled out by Weber in the following way:

> One of the most important aspects of the process of 'rationalisation' of action is the substitution for the unthinking acceptance of ancient custom of deliberate adaptation to situations in terms of self-interest. To be sure, this process by no means exhausts the concept of rationalisation of action. For in addition this can proceed in a variety of other directions; positively in that of a conscious rationalisation of ultimate values; or negatively at the expense not only of custom but of emotional values; and finally in favour of a morally sceptical type of rationality, at the expense of any belief in absolute values.[1]

What is here implied is not simply that the content of action described as rationalised may be different depending upon whether one is examining the legal, religious, political, economic or artistic spheres of social life, but the direction of the action may be different. When the point of departure against which the rationalisation process is measured is the unthinking acceptance of ancient custom, one pursues in analysis the kinds of things which happen to individuals and social orders when action takes place on the basis of reflection. So if one examines the assumption of one's actions there may be a tendency toward consistency when contradictory forms of behaviour are recognised. This may be directed towards the means adopted to accomplish given ends so that Weber can write of the rationalisation of magic. Or one may question the ends towards which one's actions are directed so that either one ulti-

[1] *Theory*, p. 123.

mate value system is replaced by another or the notion of an ultimate value system is itself rejected. In the latter case the element of calculability in the pursuit of particular interests is the essential element of the rationalisation process. The difference from the former type of rationalisation process is well illustrated in Weber's essay 'The Meaning of Ethical Neutrality in Sociology and Economics'. He observes that: 'On the whole, people are strongly inclined to adapt themselves to what promises success, not only—as is self evident—with respect to the means or to the extent that they tend to realise their ideals, but even to the extent of giving up these very ideals.'[1]

But taking syndicalism as an example of an ultimate value position he argues that '. . . it is senseless even logically to criticise in terms of its instrumental value an action which—if consistent— must be guided by its intrinsic value. The central concern of the really consistent syndicalist must be to preserve in himself certain attitudes which seem to him to be absolutely valuable and sacred as well as to induce them in others, whenever possible.'[2]

Later in the same essay, Weber goes on to distinguish between the subjective rationalisation of conduct in which the subjective intention of the individual is planned and directed to the means which are regarded as correct for a given end, and rational behaviour which is technically correct. In the latter case right technique is equated with rationalisation: '. . . if in a single case the proposition is correct that means X is, let us say, the only means of attaining the result Y and if this proposition—which is empirically establishable—is consciously used by people for the orientation of their activity to attain the result Y then their conduct is oriented in a "technically correct" manner'.[3]

However, one is led directly on to consider the significance of conflict in human life at the level of principles, interests and ideas, which presents us with a crucial difficulty so far as Parsons' law-like formulation of Weber's position is concerned with which we opened the discussion:

Only when a specified condition is taken as a standard can we speak of progress in a given sphere of technique, for example, commercial technique or legal technique. We should make explicit that the term 'progress' even in this sense is usually only ap-

[1] *EN*, p. 23.   [2] *ibid.*, p. 24.   [3] *ibid.*, p. 35.

proximately precise because the various technically rational principles conflict with one another and a compromise can never be achieved from an 'objective' standpoint but only from that of the concrete interests involved at the time. We may also speak of 'economic' progress towards a relative optimum of want satisfaction under conditions of given resources and if it is assumed that there are given wants, that all these wants and their rank order are accepted and that finally a given type of economic order exists—and with the reservation that preferences regarding the duration, certainty and exhaustiveness, respectively of the satisfaction of these wants may often conflict with each other.[1]

Recently R. Bendix has stressed that the value of Weber's studies 'lies in analysis of the many different meanings of "rationalisation" in the various spheres of human activity'.[2] And it is mainly stemming from this position that he takes issue with Parsons' assessment of Weber as an evolutionary theorist in his paper 'Max Weber's Sociology Today'.[3] The concrete nature of the rationalisation process is highly problematic.

But does not Weber sometimes use the concept of rationalisation in a very general way to describe the contemporary human condition? Sometimes, yes. Thus: 'The fate of our times is characterised by rationalisation and intellectualisation and above all, by the "disenchantment" of the world'.[4] This process means: '. . . principally [that] there are no mysterious incalculable forces that come into play, but rather that one can, in principle, master all things by calculation. This means that the world is disenchanted. One need no longer have recourse to magical means in order to master or implore the spirits, as did the savage for whom such mysterious powers existed. Technical means and calculations perform the service. This is above all what intellectualisation means.'[5]

Bendix maintains however, and with this we agree, that in his work Weber is constantly seeking to elucidate the historical foundation of 'rationalisation', that there may be, as we have seen, conflicting forms of rationalisation. Indeed, and to a very important extent, the process of rationalisation in one sphere may have

[1] EN, pp. 35–6.
[2] R. Bendix, Max Weber (Heinemann, 1960), p. 285.
[3] Int. Soc. Sc. Jnl., Vol. 17 (1965).
[4] 'Science as a Vocation' in From Max Weber (Kegan Paul, 1948), p. 155.
[5] ibid., p. 139.

irrational concomitants or consequences in another. Whereas Parsons emphasises the normative order which the rationalisation process imposes on individuals, Bendix points to the instabilities existent in even the most rationalised orders—and not simply, we may note, accounted for by charismatic leaders who break with an established order. Bendix, as do Rheinstein and Freund[1], places more significance in his expository comments on the distinction widely found in Weber's writing between formal and substantive rationality, and the counter-poised concepts of formal and substantive irrationality as summarised in the matrix below:

	Formal	*Substantive*
Rationality	I	2
Irrationality	3	4

These categories are further refined when particular sociological problems are confronted. This is very well illustrated in the following passage from Weber's *Law in Economy and Society*:

Both law making and law finding may be either rational or irrational. They are 'formally irrational' when one applies in law making or law finding means which cannot be controlled by the intellect. For instance, when recourse is had to oracles or substituted therefore. Law making and law finding are 'substantively irrational' on the other hand to the extent that decision is influenced by concrete factors of the particular case as evaluated upon an ethical, emotional or political basis rather than by general norms. 'Rational' law making and law finding may be of either a formal or a substantive kind. All formal law is, formally at least, relatively rational. Law, however, is 'formal' to the extent that in both substantive and procedural matters, only unambiguous general characteristics of the facts of the case are taken into account. This formalisation can again be of two different kinds. It is possible that the legally relevant characteristics are of a tangible nature, i.e. that they are perceptible as sense data. This adherence to external characteristics of the facts, for

[1] See Max Rheinstein's introductory essay to Weber's *Law*, and Julien Freund, *The Sociology of Max Weber* (Allen Lane, 1968).

instance, the utterance of certain words, the execution of a sig-
nature, or the performance of a certain symbolic act with a fixed
meaning, represents the most rigorous type of legal formalism.
The other type of formalistic law is found where the legally relevant characteristics of the facts are disclosed through the logical
analysis of meaning and where accordingly definitely fixed legal
concepts in the form of highly abstract rules are formulated and
applied. This process of 'logical rationality' diminishes the significance of extrinsic elements and thus softens the rigidity of
concrete formalism. But the contrast to 'substantive rationality'
is sharpened, because the latter means that the decision of legal
problems is influenced by norms different from those obtained
through logical generalisation of abstract interpretations of
meaning. The norms to which substantive rationality accords
predominance include ethical imperatives, and other expediential
rules, and political maxims, all of which diverge from the formalism of the 'external characteristics' variety as well as from that
which uses logical abstraction.[1]

Any one legal system may in actuality be composed of different
'mixes' of rational/irrational, formal/substantive elements, and
whatever the actual mix or however far one form of legal procedure
may appear to dominate, antagonisms of many kinds, either latent
or overt, are to be found. It is the task of the sociologist to locate
them and to account for them. Therefore if one wishes to describe
a trend towards the formal rationalisation of a legal system one
may note in Western societies the disappearance of, for example,
trial by ordeal, but formal irrationality does not totally disappear
as Rheinstein points out.[2] Thus, the oath, the conditional self-
curse is maintained, not all possible rational methods of truth finding are admissible as a basis for furnishing evidence in a case and
charismatic law creators like Hitler, Lenin and Stalin still emerge
from time to time. Weber himself speaks of 'the insoluble conflict
between the formal and substantive principles of justice'.[3] In his
penetrating discussion of the emergence of specifically occidental
forms of legal systems, Weber shows how a formalistic approach to
rational law making and law finding, with its emphasis on logical
deduction from abstract concepts as the basis for making judgement in particular cases, has been eroded by a process of substan-

[1] *Law*, pp. 63–4.   [2] *ibid.*, Introduction, p. lv.   [3] *ibid.*, p. 319.

tive rationalisation. This is reflected in the emergence of special branches of law—commercial law, labour law and so on—often with special courts and procedures of their own. The general explanation which Weber propounds is worth noting here since it is parallel in form to his explanation of why it was that modern capitalism emerged in the West (and, since it confronts similar data, intermeshes with that explanation):

> Only the Occident has witnessed the fully developed administration of justice of the folk community and the status group stereotyped form of patrimonialism; and only the Occident has witnessed the rise of the rational economic system, whose agents first allied themselves with the princely powers to overcome the estates and then turned against them in revolution; and only the West has known 'Natural Law', and with it the complete elimination of the system of personal law, and of the ancient maxim that special law prevails over general law. Nowhere else, finally, has there occurred any phenomenon resembling Roman law and anything like its reception. All these events have to a very large extent been caused by concrete political factors which have only the remotest analogies elsewhere in the world. For this reason, the stage of decisively shaping law by trained legal specialists has not been fully realised anywhere outside the Occident. Economic conditions have . . . everywhere played an important role, but they have nowhere been decisive alone and by themselves.[1]

Yet these distinctive developments contain within them, in Weber's view, 'tendencies favourable to the dilution of legal formalism'.[2]

> . . . the development of the formal qualities of the law appears to have produced peculiar antimonies. Rigorously formalistic and dependent on what is tangibly perceivable as far as it is required for security to do business, the law has at the same time become informal for the sake of business loyalty in so far as required by the logical interpretation of the intention of the parties or by the 'good usage' of business intercourse, which is understood to be tending toward some 'ethical minimum'.

The law is driven into anti-formal directions and moreover by

---

[1] *Law*, p. 304.   [2] *ibid.*, p. 305.

all those powers which demand that it be more than a mere means of pacifying conflicts of interests. These forces include the demand for substantive justice by certain social class interests and ideologies: they also include the tendencies inherent in certain forms of political authority of either authoritarian or democratic character concerning the ends of law which are respectively appropriate to them; and also the demand of the 'laity' for a system of justice which would be intelligible to them; finally . . . anti-formal tendencies are being promoted by the ideologically rooted power aspirations of the legal profession itself.[1]

These anti-formal tendencies are in part rational and in part irrational at the substantive level in Weber's definition of these terms. In the main Weber notes the ethical rationalisations which operate to anchor certain legal systems and which are derived from particular interest groups, such as business or labour. But there is alongside this the notion of 'value irrationalism' which may be interpreted, for example, not only by the demand for lay participation in legal procedures—juries, justices of the peace and so on—but also by the *reductio ad absurdum* of the lawyers who first appeal to the superiority of case law over formal legal principles and then proceed to maintain that no precedent should be regarded as binding in reaching legal decisions, since each case is different. Thus in each case there is, so to speak, a free balancing of values. Eventually Weber points to the development of law in Western societies as 'a rational technical apparatus which is continually transformable in the light of expediental considerations and devoid of all sacredness of content'.[2] One is sharply reminded of an older contention that justice is that which operates in the interests of the stronger.

The conceptual distinctions utilised by Weber in his sociology of law operate in similar ways elsewhere in his work. In his sociology of economic life, for example, he describes as formally rational a system of economic activity 'according to the degree in which the provision for needs, which is essential to every rational economy, is capable of being expressed in numerical calculable terms and is so expressed'.[3]

There arises from this the technical question of how one may

---

[1] *Law*, pp. 320–1.   [2] *ibid.*, p. 32.   [3] *Theory*, p. 185.

most efficiently make this calculation. Here Weber points to the method of capital accounting: 'Capital accounting is the valuation and verification of opportunities for profit and of the success of profit-making activity. It involves the valuation of the total assets of the enterprise, whether these consist in goods in kind or in money, at the beginning of a period of activity; and the comparison of this with a similar valuation of the assets still present, or newly acquired, at the end of the process.'[1] And he attached great importance to double-entry book-keeping as a device for estimating the profitability of enterprises. But there arises also the sociological question, namely, under what conditions could the formal rationality of economic activity be realised? And it is here we reach a paradox, since Weber explains that both the emergence of a money economy (the prerequisite for capital accounting) and capital accounting itself depends upon quite specific substantive conditions. And however else they are viewed they are the outcome of particular struggles for power and to that extent are irrational and transient (we should recall that as actual outcomes in the real world they were in any case only imperfectly realised). So, for example, the formal rationality of money calculation is dependent on a price system, but 'money prices are the product of conflicts of interest and compromise; they thus result from systems of power relationships . . .' And again, money is 'primarily an instrument in the competitive struggle . . . a means of quantitative expression of estimated opportunities and risks met in the pursuit of competitive advantages'.[2]

Likewise capital accounting is dependent upon market freedom 'in the sense both of the absence of monopolistic limitations which are imposed or are economically irrational, and of those which are voluntary and economically rational through orientation to the securing of market advantages'; and upon 'the social conditions of a disciplined organisation and the appropriation of the means of production. This implies the existence of a system of imperatively co-ordinated relationships.'[3]

Further, while a formally rational economic system may exist to meet certain demands in the technically most successful manner, Weber argues: 'it is not wants as such but effective demand for utilities which regulates the production of goods by profit-making enterprises oriented to capital accounting. What is to be produced

[1] *Theory*, pp. 191–2.   [2] *ibid.*, p. 211.   [3] *ibid.*

is thus determined by the structure of marginal utilities in the income group which has both the inclination and the resources to purchase a given utility. This will depend on the distribution of wealth in a particular society.'[1]

For these kinds of reasons Weber alludes to the 'unavoidable element of irrationality in economic systems'[2] which he sees as a product of the conflict between formal and substantive rationality. He treats substantive rationality as a generic concept:

> It conveys only one element common to all the possible empirical situations; namely that it is not sufficient to consider only the purely formal fact that calculations are being made on grounds of expediency by the methods which are among those available technically the most nearly adequate. In addition it is necessary to take account of the fact that economic activity is oriented to ultimate ends of some kind: whether they be ethical, political, utilitarian, hedonistic, the attainment of social distinction, of social equality, or of anything else. Substantive rationality cannot be measured in terms of formal calculation alone, but also involves a relation to the absolute values or to the content of the particular ends to which it is oriented. In principle, there is an indefinite number of possible standards of value which are 'rational' in this sense. . . . In addition, it is possible to criticise the attitude toward the economic activity itself or toward the means used, from ethical, ascetic or aesthetical points of view.[3]

The irrationality of the modern economic order for Weber arises both from the fact that the substantive conditions which promoted profit-oriented industrial enterprise—the epitome of rational bourgeois capitalism—were, in so far as they existed, the outcome of power struggles; and from the fact that other forms of substantive rationality impeded the ability of individual enterprises to calculate their profits efficiently or to operate independently. Among the more important factors 'interfering' with the question of a formally rational economy which Weber cites are the following:

1. Speculation. 'The influence exercised on the market situation, especially that for capital goods and in turn on the orientation

of production of goods for profit by speculative interests outside the producing organisations themselves, is one of the
sources of the phenomena known as the "crises" of the modern market economy.'[1]

2. Job control by workers. 'This means that workers cannot be
selected solely on the grounds of their technical efficiency and
to this extent there is a limitation on the formal rationalisation
of economic activity.'[2]

3. Movements promoting planned economies. 'A planned economy oriented to want satisfaction must, in proportion as it is
radically carried through, weaken the incentive to labour so
far as the risk of lack of support is involved. For it would, at
least so far as there is a rational system of provision for wants,
be impossible to allow a worker's dependents to suffer the full
consequences of his lack of efficiency in production. Furthermore, autonomy in the direction of organised production
units would have to be greatly reduced or, in the extreme case,
eliminated. Hence it would be impossible to retain capital
risk and proof of merit by a formally autonomous achievement. The same would be true of autonomous power over
other individuals and important features of their economic
situation... A preliminary step in the direction of the budget-
ary planned economy is to be found wherever consumption is
rationed or wherever measures are taken to control the
spontaneous distribution of goods'.[3]

In so far as the economic and political spheres interpenetrated,
this formal economic rationalisation was hampered. Conflicts then
centre around what policies (encompassing means and ends) shall
be implemented in the rational reorganization of economic life at
the substantive level.

In the light of the above discussion we may perhaps the more
safely consider the phenomenon of bureaucratisation as an important manifestation of the process of rationalisation. In Weber's
multi-faceted work on bureaucracy there is a basic type distinction
drawn between bureaucratic and non-bureaucratic forms of administration (such as the collegiate, honorific or avocational). The
advantages of 'precision, speed, unambiguity, knowledge of the

---

[1] *Theory*, p. 250.   [2] *ibid.*, p. 236.   [3] *ibid.*, pp. 214–15.

files, continuity, discretion, unity, strict subordination, reduction of friction and of material and personal costs'[1] must, of course, be treated as a comparative statement between these two basic types of administration and not as an absolute one. Bureaucratisation has to be understood in its 'pure' type as a mode of formal (not substantive) rationalisation since essentially the discussion centres around the notion of calculability and efficiency: 'Bureaucratic administration is, other things being equal, always from a formal technical point of view, the most rational type.'[2]

For Weber it was this form of administration which characterised modern Western society:

> The development of the modern form of the organisation of composite groups in all fields is nothing less than identical with the development and continual spread of bureaucratic administration. This is true of church and state, of armies, political parties, economic enterprises, organisations to promote all kinds of causes, private associations, clubs and many others. Its development is, to take the most striking case, the most crucial phenomenon of the modern Western state.[3]

However, just as market capitalism was based on irrational foundations, so too is the bureaucratic apparatus whose permanent existence is dependent upon fully developed money economies. Weber notes the conjunction of capitalism and bureaucracy in the West, and of course the bureaucratic administration's usefulness as a vehicle for capital accounting is fully recognised. The paradox is that the bureaucratic apparatus, by virtue of the fact that its controllers want to increase their knowledge of the environment the better to predict outcomes, tended in practice to interfere with the free market conditions of classical capitalism. The capitalistic entrepreneur could, in Weber's view, retain some freedom of action over and against the bureaucratic machine, but his actions could be circumscribed and his future was threatened. The point was later developed by Joseph Schumpeter:

> Since capitalist enterprise, by its very achievements, tends to automatic progress, we conclude that it tends to make itself superfluous and to break to pieces under the pressure of its own

---

[1] *From Max Weber*, p. 214.   [2] *Theory*, p. 337.   [3] *ibid.*

success. The perfectly bureaucratised giant industrial unit not only omits the small or medium-sized firm and 'expropriates' its owners, but in the end it also ousts the entrepreneur and expropriates the bourgeoisie as a class which in the process stands to lose not only its income but what also is infinitely more important, its function.[1]

In similar fashion the modern politician was seen by Weber as being thrown up by the party bureaucratic machine, and the Cabinet Minister, if he has only dilettante and not specialist knowledge, would be effectively constrained in his decision-making by the advice of his permanent officials. One possible alternative was the emergence of charismatic (irrational) leaders to counter this process of rationalisation. Such leaders could appeal to the masses, so to speak, over the heads of the bureaucrats. In so far as they were genuinely representative men they could be described as plebiscitary leaders and Weber saw parliamentary institutions and regular elections as devices for ensuring that they did not turn into dictators. Another possibility (and one which was distasteful to Weber) was that the bureaucratic machine (a technical means for obtaining specified ends efficiently) might be presided over by a technician: 'The question is always who controls the existing bureaucratic machinery. And such control is possible only in a very limited degree to persons who are not technical specialists.'[2]

It is as though a technique for achieving ends becomes an ultimate value in itself. Yet of course some substantive goals will be pursued, however 'pragmatically' they are defined and conceived: and necessarily one is talking about the exercise of power. Now, of course, a competitive situation may still remain where there are bureaucracies and counter-bureaucracies and consequently conflicts at the level of substantive rationality. (This is the model which informs Schumpeter's analysis of democracy in modern states and Galbraith's discussion of American capitalism). But where the state bureaucracy achieves monolithic dominance through the interpenetration of the political and economic spheres, an unopposed and deeply entrenched form of rationalisation is to be discerned. Thus:

[1] J. Schumpeter. *Capitalism, Socialism and Democracy*, p. 134. (Allen and Unwin 1943.)
[2] *Theory*, p. 338.

If private capitalism were to be eliminated, the sovereign state bureaucracy would rule supreme. The private and the public bureaucracies would merge into one hierarchy instead of balancing each other. The social structure would be similar to that of Egypt in antiquity, but it would take an incomparably more rational and hence inescapable form.[1]

To what, then, are action and policy oriented? There now remains only one answer: reasons of state. And what is the state?

'The modern state is a compulsory association which organises domination. It has been successful in tending to monopolise the legitimate use of physical force as a means of domination within a territory.'[2]

This, then, is the ultimate irrational foundation of bureaucratic rationalisation: a system of domination in the service of the political power struggle between nation states. It is at this point that one may note the force of Marcuse's comment:

The very concept of technical reason is perhaps ideological. Not only the application of technology but technology itself is domination (of nature and man)—methodical, scientific, calculated, calculating control. Specific progress and interests of domination are not foisted upon technology 'subsequently' and from the outside; they enter the very construction of the technical apparatus. Technology is always a historical–social *project*: in it is projected what a society and its ruling interests intend to do with man and things. Such a purpose of domination is 'substantive' and to this extent belongs to the very form of technical reason.[3] . . .

We have sought in this introductory essay to indicate in some measure the richness of Weber's thought. The continuing relevance of his ideas in helping us more clearly to understand many social issues of our day can scarcely be doubted. The readings

[1] *Gesemmelte Politische Schriften*, (Munchen, 1921), p. 151, trans. Fred H. Blum.
[2] 'Politics as a Vocation' in *From Max Weber*, pp. 82–3.
[3] 'Industrialisation and Capitalism in Max Weber' in *Negations* (Allen Lane, 1968), pp. 223–4.

which now follow will help us to recognise the importance of his contribution in a range of substantive areas, and to the task of creating a satisfactory science of society. A founding father of sociology certainly, but also, as Aron engagingly put it—'our contemporary'.[1]

[1] See R. Aron *Main Currents of Sociological Thought*, Vol. 2. Basic Books 1967.

Part One

Sociological Analysis and Research Methodology

INTRODUCTION

The first four passages in this section are taken from *The Theory of Social and Economic Organisation* and serve to illustrate and amplify what is entailed in the action frame of reference, which, as we have seen, constitutes the decisive element of Weber's sociology. There is no need to recapitulate the previous discussion, but we might appropriately add to it here with specific reference to the passage on social stratification.

Weber continually refers to social groups that are 'positively' or 'negatively' privileged, and it is this interest in privilege which gives unity to his approach to the study of social stratification. At the same time the fact that privilege embodies many different considerations and arises from many different sources implies a multi-dimensional theory of social stratification. This Weber clearly recognises. He draws what has now become a familiar distinction between class and status, retaining for the former, as Marx had done before him, strictly economic connotations: 'the control or lack of it which the individual has over goods and services and existing possibilities of their exploitation for the attainment of incomes or receipts within a given economic order.' The attempt to depict who controls what necessarily demands further differentiation. This is the significance of his observation that 'in principle, control over different combinations of consumer goods, means of production, investments, capital funds or marketable abilities constitutes class statuses which are different with each variation and combination'. That is why, for Weber, class situation is defined ultimately by one's market situation (position in the labour market, or power in the commodities market, as the case may be).

Status groups are composed of individuals who share with others a distinctive life style. 'In contrast to the purely economically determined "class situation" we wish to designate as "status situation" every typical component of the life fate of men that is

73

determined by a specific, positive or negative, social estimation of *honour*.'[1] The implication of this is that theories of social stratification necessarily involve a complex analysis of the interrelations between class (in its various economic dimensions) and status (with its manifold bases and claims to privilege). Failure to do just that was the ground of Mills' critique of Warner's *Social Life of a Modern Community*.[2]

It is as well to point out that in this key area of Weber's sociology great importance is attached to 'objective' structural considerations over and above the knowledge that people may have of their situation. The attempt to describe precisely who has command over what resources, which groups (the negatively privileged) are controlled by others, and so on may be fraught with empirical difficulties, but it serves to remind us forcibly that Weber can never be finally classified as a phenomenologist. This point is well made by Gerth and Mills:

> Class situations are determined by the relations of the market; in the last analysis they go back to the differences between the propertied and the non-propertied. Weber thus shares with the objective school the emphasis upon the economic order and the strict distinction between objectively characterised positions and a variety of shifting and subjective attitudes that *may* be related to such positions. . . . Only when subjective opinions can be attributed to men in an objective class-situation does Weber speak of 'class consciousness'; and when he focuses upon problems of 'conventions', 'styles of life', of occupational attitudes, he prefers to speak of prestige or 'status groups'.[3]

The final passage in this chapter has here been translated for the first time and brings to our attention a little known aspect of Weber's research interests. It is a briefing document which he prepared for field workers who were going to participate in a study of industrial workers in Germany (1908–11). This was organised under the auspices of a reform organisation, the Verein für Sozialpolitik. The project as a whole was never completed, although Weber did publish his own contribution, 'The Psycho-

---

[1] Gerth and Mills, op. cit., pp. 186–7.
[2] See the reprinted review in *Power, Politics and People*, O.U.P., 1963.
[3] Op. cit., p. 69.

physics of Industrial Work'.[1] The document reproduced here is truly fascinating. We may enumerate some of the reasons for saying this:

1. It provides a practical example of what Weber understood by ethical neutrality in a research programme with which he was identified.

2. It reveals a lively awareness of the usefulness of economic data, even in research work that is primarily sociological in character. The economic determinants of technical innovation and the operation of labour markets are seen as cases in point. This is because he is interested in the sources of recruitment and the career patterns of workers in industry: 'from our point of view, the occupational career of the workers would appear as a kind of "military road" on which, from particular geographical, ethnic, social, and cultural starting-points . . . they have advanced to their qualification for the job they finally obtain.'

3. A similar awareness of the importance of physiological and psychological data in relation to performance, learning, fatigue and so on is revealed. He himself shows great familiarity with the methodological problems of experimental psychology and the conceptual difficulties involved in studying psychological aspects of work. But he warns the research team not to lose themselves in secondary problems, and to enlist the help of experts in related disciplines where possible.

4. There is a vigorous and impressive advocacy of the virtue of first asking sociological questions when seeking to explain industrial behaviour: 'always examine first the influences of social and cultural background, upbringing and tradition and . . . proceed as far as possible with this principle of explanation.' This point is made over and against explanations which begin by postulating differences in inherited characteristics of workers. This, Weber argues, is the last question to ask not the first.

5. Weber shows a thorough acquaintance with the phenomenon of output restriction and notes the fear that many workers had that if they produced high outputs, their piece-rates would be cut. He is sensitive to the social factors which determine ideas of appropriate effort among workers, and points not only to ethnic, social and cultural background but to the wage system itself as a significant consideration. The discussion of this and related

[1] In *Gesammelte Aufsätze zur Soziologie und Sozialpolitik* (Tübingen, 1924).

matters, including the effects of shift systems and breaks, on fatigue and output, pre-dates by many years that more familiar landmark in industrial sociology, the Hawthorne plant studies at Western Electric, Chicago. He notes, for example, that 'the whole internal structure of the working process and the formation of social groups, into which the working class falls, the predominantly monarchic, authoritarian, or voluntaristic division of labour and of discipline within these groups . . . are intimately connected with the system of remuneration.'

6. There is some very practical advice about the collection of data, the approach to the interviewing programme, handling the problem of confidentiality and so on, much of which can still be read today with profit.

7. Finally, Weber's methodological sophistication and his concern with matters of detail are never seen as ends in themselves but as throwing light on the process of social change in contemporary society. What is the impact of industrial production in an advanced economy upon those who are touched by it? What is the cultural significance of industrial change? Does the effect of the industrial system on the workers 'transcend even the scope of the question of "capitalist" or "socialist" organisation of production in its significance for their fate'? Does not the system encourage a purely pecuniary involvement with work? Is the system leading towards the increasing economic and social differentiation of the working class, or the converse?

(A) Social Action and its Classification[1]

THE CONCEPT OF SOCIAL ACTION

Social action, which includes both failure to act and passive acquiescence, may be oriented to the past, present, or expected future behaviour of others. Thus it may be motivated by revenge

[1] Source: *Theory of Social and Economic Organisation*, pp. 112–18 *passim*.

for a past attack, defence against present, or measures of defence against future aggression. The 'others' may be individual persons, and may be known to the actor as such, or may constitute an indefinite plurality and may be entirely unknown as individuals. Thus 'money' is a means of exchange which the actor accepts in payment because he orients his action to the expectation that a large but unknown number of individuals with whom he is personally unacquainted will be ready to accept it in exchange on some future occasion. . . .

Not every type of contact of human beings has a social character; this is rather confined to cases where the actor's behaviour is meaningfully oriented to that of others. For example, a mere collision of two cyclists may be compared to a natural event. On the other hand, their attempt to avoid hitting each other, or whatever insults, blows, or friendly discussion might follow the collision, would constitute 'social action'. . . .

Mere 'imitation' of the action of others, such as that on which Tarde has rightly laid emphasis, will not be considered a case of specifically social action if it is purely reactive so that there is no meaningful orientation to the actor imitated. The borderline is, however, so indefinite that it is often hardly possible to discriminate. The mere fact that a person is found to employ some apparently useful procedure which he learned from someone else does not, however, constitute, in the present sense, social action. Action such as this is not oriented to the action of the other person, but the actor has, through observing the other, become acquainted with certain objective facts; and it is these to which his action is oriented. His action is then *causally* determined by the action of others but not meaningfully. On the other hand, if the action of others is imitated because it is 'fashionable' or traditional or exemplary, or lends social distinction, or on similar grounds, it is meaningfully oriented either to the behaviour of the source of imitation or of third persons or of both. There are, of course, all manner of transitional cases between the two types of imitation. Both the phenomena discussed above, the behaviour of crowds and imitation, stand on the indefinite borderline of social action. The same is true, as will often appear, of traditionalism and charisma. The reason for the indefiniteness of the line in these and other cases lies in the fact that both the orientation to the behaviour of others and the meaning which can be imputed to the actor himself, are by no means always capable of clear determination and are often altogether unconscious and seldom fully self-conscious. Mere 'influence' and meaningful orientation cannot therefore always be clearly differentiated on the empirical level. But conceptually it is essential to distinguish them, even though merely 'reactive' imitation may well have a degree of sociological importance at least equal to that of the type which can be called social action in the strict sense. Sociology, it goes without saying, is by no means confined to the study of 'social action'; this is only, at least for the kind of sociology being developed here, its central subject-matter, that which may be said to be decisive for its status as a science. But this does not imply any judgement on the comparative importance of this and other factors.

Social action, like other forms of action, may be classified in the following four types according to its mode of orientation: (1) in terms of rational orientation to a system of discrete individual ends (*zweckrational*), that is, through expectations as to the behaviour of objects in the external situation and of other human individuals, making use of these expectations as 'conditions' or 'means' for the successful attainment of the actor's own rationally chosen ends; (2) in terms of rational orientation to an absolute value (*wertrational*); involving a conscious belief in the absolute value of some ethical, aesthetic, religious, or other form of behaviour, entirely for its own sake and independently of any prospects of external success; (3) in terms of affectual orientation, especially emotional, determined by the specific affects and states of feeling of the actor; (4) traditionally oriented, through the habituation of long practice.[1]

---

[1] The two terms *zweckrational* and *wertrational* are of central significance to Weber's theory, but at the same time present one of the most difficult problems to the translator. Perhaps the keynote of the distinction lies in the absoluteness with which the values involved in *Wertrationalität* are held. The sole important consideration to the actor becomes the realisation of the value. In so far as it involves ends, rational considerations, such as those of efficiency, are involved in the choice of means. But there is no question either of rational weighing of this end against others, nor is there a question of 'counting the cost' in the sense of taking account of possible results other than the attainment of the absolute end. In the case of *Zweckrationalität*, on the other hand, Weber conceives action as motivated by a plurality of relatively independent ends, none of which is absolute. Hence, rationality involves on the one hand the weighing of the relative importance of their realisation, on the other hand, consideration of whether undesirable consequences would outweigh the benefits to be derived from the projected course of action. It has not seemed possible to find English

1. Strictly traditional behaviour, like the reactive type of imitation discussed above, lies very close to the borderline of what can justifiably be called meaningfully oriented action, and indeed often on the other side. For it is very often a matter of almost automatic reaction to habitual stimuli which guide behaviour in a course which has been repeatedly followed. The great bulk of all everyday action to which people have become habitually accustomed approaches this type. Hence, its place in a systematic classification is not merely that of a limiting case because, as will be shown later, attachment to habitual forms can be upheld with varying degrees of self-consciousness and in a variety of senses. In this case the type may shade over into number two (*Wertrationalität*).

2. Purely affectual behaviour also stands on the borderline of what can be considered 'meaningfully' oriented, and often it, too, goes over the line. It may, for instance, consist in an uncontrolled reaction to some exceptional stimulus. It is a case of sublimation when affectually determined action occurs in the form of conscious release of emotional tension. When this happens it is usually, though not always, well on the road to rationalisation in one or the other or both of the above senses.

3. The orientation of action in terms of absolute value is distinguished from the affectual type by its clearly self-conscious formulation of the ultimate values governing the action and the consistently planned orientation of its detailed course to these values. At the same time the two types have a common element, namely that the meaning of the action does not lie in the achievement of a result ulterior to it, but in carrying out the specific type of action for its own sake. Examples of affectual action are the

terms which would express this distinction succinctly. Hence the attempt has been made to express the ideas as clearly as possible without specific terms.

It should also be pointed out that, as Weber's analysis proceeds, there is a tendency of the meaning of these terms to shift, so that *Wertrationalität* comes to refer to a system of ultimate ends, regardless of the degree of their absoluteness, while *Zweckrationalität* refers primarily to considerations respecting the choice of means and ends which are in turn means to further ends, such as money. What seems to have happened is that Weber shifted from a classification of ideal types of action to one of elements in the structure of action. In the latter context 'expediency' is often an adequate rendering of *Zweckrationalität*. This process has been analysed in Parsons' *Structure of Social Action*, chap. xvi.

The other two terms *affektuell* and *traditional* do not present any difficulty of translation. The term affectual has come into English psychological usage from the German largely through the influence of psychoanalysis. [Parsons' footnote.]

satisfaction of a direct impulse to revenge, to sensual gratification, to devote oneself to a person or ideal, to contemplative bliss, or, finally, toward the working off of emotional tensions. Such impulses belong in this category regardless of how sordid or sublime they may be.

Examples of pure rational orientation to absolute values would be the action of persons who, regardless of possible cost to themselves, act to put into practice their convictions of what seems to them to be required by duty, honour, the pursuit of beauty, a religious call, personal loyalty, or the importance of some 'cause' no matter in what it consists. For the purposes of this discussion, when action is oriented to absolute values, it always involves 'commands' or 'demands' to the fulfilment of which the actor feels obligated. It is only in cases where human action is motivated by the fulfilment of such unconditional demands that it will be described as oriented to absolute values. This is empirically the case in widely varying degrees, but for the most part only to a relatively slight extent. Nevertheless, it will be shown that the occurrence of this mode of action is important enough to justify its formulation as a distinct type; though it may be remarked that there is no intention here of attempting to formulate in any sense an exhaustive classification of types of action.

4. Action is rationally oriented to a system of discrete individual ends (*zweckrational*) when the end, the means, and the secondary results are all rationally taken into account and weighed. This involves rational consideration of alternative means to the end, of the relations of the end to other prospective results of employment of any given means, and finally of the relative importance of different possible ends. Determination of action, either in affectual or in traditional terms, is thus incompatible with this type. Choice between alternative and conflicting ends and results may well be determined by considerations of absolute value. In that case, action is rationally oriented to a system of discrete individual ends only in respect to the choice of means. On the other hand, the actor may, instead of deciding between alternative and conflicting ends in terms of a rational orientation to a system of values, simply take them as given subjective wants and arrange them in a scale of consciously assessed relative urgency. He may then orient his action to this scale in such a way that they are satisfied as far as possible in order of urgency, as formulated in the principle of

'marginal utility'. The orientation of action to absolute values may thus have various different modes of relation to the other type of rational action, in terms of a system of discrete individual ends. From the latter point of view, however, absolute values are always irrational. Indeed, the more the value to which action is oriented is elevated to the status of an absolute value, the more 'irrational' in this sense the corresponding action is. For the more uncondi-tionally the actor devotes himself to this value for its own sake, to pure sentiment or beauty, to absolute goodness or devotion to duty, the less is he influenced by considerations of the conse-quences of his action. The orientation of action wholly to the rational achievement of ends without relation to fundamental values is, to be sure, essentially only a limiting case.

5. It would be very unusual to find concrete cases of action, especially of social action, which were oriented *only* in one or another of these ways. Furthermore, this classification of the modes of orientation of action is in no sense meant to exhaust the possibilities of the field, but only to formulate in conceptually pure form certain sociologically important types, to which actual action is more or less closely approximated or, in much the more common case, which constitute the elements combining to make it up. The usefulness of the classification for the purposes of this investigation can only be judged in terms of its results.

(B) Social Relationships and the Concept of Conflict[1]

The term 'social relationship' will be used to denote the behaviour of a plurality of actors in so far as, in its meaningful content, the action of each takes account of that of the others and is oriented in these terms. The social relationship thus *consists* entirely and exclusively *in* the existence of a *probability* that there will be, in some meaningfully understandable sense, a course of social action.

[1] Source: *Theory of Social and Economic Organisation*, pp. 118–20, 132 *passim*.

For purposes of definition there is no attempt to specify the basis of this probability.

1. Thus, as a defining criterion, it is essential that there should be at least a minimum of mutual orientation of the action of each to that of the others. Its content may be of the most varied nature; conflict, hostility, sexual attraction, friendship, loyalty or economic exchange. It may involve the fulfilment, the evasion or the denunciation of the terms of an agreement; economic, erotic or some other form of 'competition'; common membership in national or class groups or those sharing a common tradition of status. In the latter cases mere group membership may or may not extend to include social action; this will be discussed later. The definition, furthermore, does not specify whether the relation of the actors is 'solidary' or the opposite.

2. The 'meaning' relevant in this context is always a case of the meaning imputed to the parties in a given concrete case, on the average or in a theoretically formulated pure type—it is never a normatively 'correct' or a metaphysically 'true' meaning. Even in cases of such forms of social organisation as a state, church association or marriage, the social relationship consists exclusively in the fact that there has existed, exists or will exist a probability of action in some definite way appropriate to this meaning. It is vital to be continually clear about this in order to avoid the 'reification' of these concepts. A 'state', for example, ceases to exist in a sociologically relevant sense whenever there is no longer a probability that certain kinds of meaningfully oriented social action will take place. This probability may be very high or it may be negligibly low. But in any case it is only in the sense and degree in which it does exist or can be estimated that the corresponding social relationship exists. It is impossible to find any other clear meaning for the statement that, for instance, a given 'state' exists or has ceased to exist.

3. The subjective meaning need not necessarily be the same for all the parties who are mutually oriented in a given social relationship; there need not in this sense be 'reciprocity'. 'Friendship', 'love', 'loyalty', 'fidelity to contracts', 'patriotism', on one side, may well be faced with an entirely different attitude on the other. In such cases the parties associate different meanings with their actions, and the social relationship is to that extent objectively 'asymmetrical' from the points of view of the two parties. It may

nevertheless be a case of mutual orientation in so far as one party presumes a particular attitude toward him on the part of the other even though this may be partly or wholly erroneous and orients his action to this expectation. This can, and usually will, have consequences for the course of action and the form of the relationship. A relationship is objectively symmetrical only as, according to the typical expectations of the parties, the meaning for one party is the same as that for the other. Thus the actual attitude of a child to its father may be at least approximately that which the father, in the individual case, on the average or typically, has come to expect. A social relationship in which the attitudes are completely and fully corresponding is in reality a limiting case. But the absence of reciprocity will, for terminological purposes, be held to exclude the existence of a social relationship only if it actually results in the absence of a mutual orientation of the action of the parties. Here as elsewhere all sorts of transitional cases are the rule rather than the exception.

4. A social relationship can be of a temporary character or of varying degrees of permanence. That is, it can be of such a kind that there is a probability of the repeated recurrence of the behaviour which corresponds to its subjective meaning, behaviour which is an understandable consequence of the meaning and hence is expected. In order to avoid fallacious impressions, let it be repeated and continually kept in mind, that it is *only* the existence of the probability that a certain type of action will take place, corresponding to a given subjective meaning complex, which constitutes the 'existence' of the social relationship. Thus, that a 'friendship' or a 'state' exists or has existed means this and only this: that we, the observers, judge that there is or has been a probability that on the basis of certain kinds of known subjective attitude of certain individuals there will result in the average sense a certain specific type of action. For the purposes of legal reasoning it is essential to be able to decide whether a rule of law does or does not carry legal authority, hence whether a legal relationship does or does not 'exist'. This type of question is not, however, relevant to sociological problems.

5. The subjective meaning of a social relationship may change, thus a political relationship, once based on solidarity, may develop into a conflict of interests. In that case it is only a matter of terminological convenience and of the degree of continuity of the

change whether we say that a new relationship has come into existence or that the old one continues but has acquired a new meaning. It is also possible for the meaning to be partly constant, partly changing.

6. The meaningful content which remains relatively constant in a social relationship is capable of formulation in terms of maxims which the parties concerned expect their partners to adhere to, on the average and approximately. The more rational in relation to values or to given ends the action is, the more is this likely to be the case. There is far less possibility of a rational formulation of subjective meaning in the case of a relation of erotic attraction or of personal loyalty or any other affectual type than, for example, in the case of a business contract.

7. The meaning of a social relationship may be agreed upon by mutual consent. This implies that the parties make promises covering their future behaviour, whether toward each other or toward third persons. In such cases each party then normally counts, so far as he acts rationally, in some degree on the fact that the other will orient his action to the meaning of the agreement as he (the first actor) understands it. In part, they orient their action rationally to these expectations as given facts with, to be sure, varying degrees of subjectively 'loyal' intention of doing their share. But in part also each one is motivated by the value to him of his 'duty' to adhere to the agreement in the sense in which he understands it. This much may be anticipated. . . .

A social relationship will be referred to as 'conflict'[1] in so far as action within it is oriented intentionally to carrying out the actor's own will against the resistance of the other party or parties. The term 'peaceful' conflict will be applied to cases in which actual physical violence is not employed. A peaceful conflict is 'competition' in so far as it consists in a formally peaceful attempt to attain control over opportunities and advantages[2] which are also desired by others. A competitive process is 'regulated' competition to the extent that its ends and means are oriented to an order. The struggle, often latent, which takes place between human individuals or types of social status, for advantages and for survival, but without a meaningful mutual orientation in terms of conflict,

[1] *Kampf.*
[2] *Chancen.* This usage of the term is to be distinguished from that translated as probability or likelihood. [Parsons' footnote.]

will be called 'selection'. In so far as it is a matter of the relative opportunities of individuals during their own lifetime, it is 'social selection'; in so far as it concerns differential chances for the survival of inherited characteristics, 'biological selection'. . . .

Not every process of social selection is, in the present sense, a case of conflict. Social selection, on the contrary, means only in the first instance that certain types of behaviour, and hence of the corresponding personal qualities, are more favourable than others in procuring differential advantages in attaining to certain social relationships, as in the role of 'lover', husband', 'member of parliament', 'official', 'contractor', 'managing director', 'successful business man', and so on. But the concept does not specify whether this differential advantage in selection for social success is brought to bear through conflict or not, neither does it specify whether the biological chances of survival of the type are affected one way or the other. It is only where there is a genuine competitive process that the term 'conflict' will be used.

It is only in the sense of 'selection' that it seems, according to our experience, that conflict is empirically inevitable, and it is furthermore only in the sense of *biological* selection that it is inevitable in principle. Selection is inevitable because apparently no way can be worked out of eliminating it completely. It is possible even for the most strictly pacific order to eliminate means of conflict and the objects of and impulses to conflict only in that it deals with each type individually. But this means that other modes of conflict would come to the fore, possibly in processes of open competition. But even on the utopian assumption that all competition were completely eliminated, conditions would still lead to a latent process of selection, biological or social, which would favour the types best adapted to the conditions, whether their relevant qualities were mainly determined by heredity or by environment. On an empirical level the elimination of conflict cannot go beyond a point which leaves room for some social selection, and in principle a process of biological selection necessarily remains.

From the struggle of individuals for personal advantages and survival, it is naturally necessary to distinguish the 'conflict' and the 'selection' of social relationships. It is only in a metaphorical sense that these concepts can be applied to the latter. For relationships exist only as systems of human action with particular subjective meanings. Thus a process of selection or a conflict between them means only that one type of action has in the course of time been displaced by another, whether it is action by the same persons or by others. This may occur in various ways. Human action may in the first place be consciously aimed to alter certain social relationships—that is, to alter the corresponding action—or it may be directed to the prevention of their development or continuance. Thus a 'state' may be destroyed by war or revolution, or a conspiracy may be broken up by savage suppression; prostitution may be suppressed by police action; 'shady' business practices, by denial of legal protection or by penalties. Furthermore, social relationships may be influenced by the creation of differential advantages which favour one type over another. It is possible either for individuals or for organised groups to pursue such ends. Secondly, it may, in various ways, be an unanticipated consequence of a course of social action and its relevant conditions that certain types of social relationships (meaning, of course, the corresponding actions) will be adversely affected in their opportunities to maintain themselves or to arise. All changes of natural and social conditions have some sort of effect on the differential probabilities of survival of social relationships.

(C) Social Stratification and Class Structure[1]

THE CONCEPTS OF CLASS AND CLASS STATUS

The term 'class status'[2] will be applied to the typical probability that a given state of (a) provision with goods, (b) external conditions of life, and (c) subjective satisfaction or frustration will be

---

[1] Source: *Theory of Social and Economic Organisation*, pp. 424-9.
[2] Weber uses the term 'class' (*Klasse*) in a special sense, which is defined in this paragraph and which, in particular, he contrasts with *Stand*. There seems no other alternative translation of *Klasse*, but it should be kept in mind that it is being used in a special sense. [Parsons' footnote.]

possessed by an individual or a group. These probabilities define class status in so far as they are dependent on the kind and extent of control or lack of it which the individual has over goods or services and existing possibilities of their exploitation for the attainment of income or receipts within a given economic order.

A 'class' is any group of persons occupying the same class status. The following types of classes may be distinguished: (*a*) a class is a 'property class' when class status for its members is primarily determined by the differentiation of property holdings; (*b*) a class is an 'acquisition class' when the class situation of its members is primarily determined by their opportunity for the exploitation of services on the market; (*c*) the 'social class' structure is composed of the plurality of class statuses between which an interchange of individuals on a personal basis or in the course of generations is readily possible and typically observable. On the basis of any of the three types of class status, associative relationships between those sharing the same class interests, namely, corporate class organisations, may develop. This need not, however, necessarily happen. The concepts of class and class status as such designate only the fact of identity or similarity in the typical situation in which a given individual and many others find their interests defined. In principle, control over different combinations of consumer goods, means of production, investments, capital funds or marketable abilities constitutes class statuses which are different with each variation and combination. Only persons who are completely unskilled, without property and dependent on employment without regular occupation, are in a strictly identical class status. Transitions from one class status to another vary greatly in fluidity and in the ease with which an individual can enter the class. Hence the unity of 'social' classes is highly relative and variable.

The primary significance of a positively privileged property class lies in the following facts: (i) Its members may be able to monopolise the purchase of high-priced consumer goods. (ii) They may control the opportunities of pursuing a systematic monopoly policy in the sale of economic goods. (iii) They may monopolise opportunities for the accumulation of property through unconsumed surpluses. (iv) They may monopolise opportunities to accumulate capital by saving, hence, the possibility of investing property in loans and the related possibility of control over

D

executive positions in business. (v) They may monopolise the privileges of socially advantageous kind of education so far as these involve expenditures.

Positively privileged property classes typically live from property income. This may be derived from property rights in human beings, as with slave-owners, in land, in mining property, in fixed equipment such as plant and apparatus, in ships, and as creditors in loan relationships. Loans may consist of domestic animals, grain, or money. Finally, they may live on income from securities.

Class interests which are negatively privileged with respect to property belong typically to one of the following types: (a) they are themselves objects of ownership, that is they are unfree; (b) they are 'outcasts', that is 'proletarians' in the sense meant in antiquity; (c) they are debtor classes and, (d) the 'poor'.

In between stand the 'middle' classes. This term includes groups who have all sorts of property, or of marketable abilities through training, who are in a position to draw their support from these sources. Some of them may be 'acquisition' classes. Entrepreneurs are in this category by virtue of essentially positive privileges; proletarians, by virtue of negative privileges. But many types such as peasants, craftsmen and officials do not fall in this category. The differentiation of classes on the basis of property alone is not 'dynamic', that is, it does not necessarily result in class struggles or class revolutions. It is not uncommon for very strongly privileged property classes, such as slave-owners, to exist side by side with such far less privileged groups as peasants or even outcasts without any class struggle. There may even be ties of solidarity between privileged property classes and unfree elements. However, such conflicts as that between landowners and outcast elements or between creditors and debtors, the latter often being a question of urban patricians as opposed to either rural peasants or urban craftsmen, may lead to revolutionary conflict. Even this, however, need not necessarily aim at radical changes in economic organisation. It may, on the contrary, be concerned in the first instance only with a redistribution of wealth. These may be called the 'property revolutions'.

A classic example of the lack of class antagonism has been the relation of the 'poor white trash', originally those not owning slaves, to the planters in the Southern States of the United States. The 'poor whites' have often been much more hostile to the Negro than the planters who have frequently had a large element of patriarchal sentiment. The conflict of outcast against the property classes, of creditors and debtors, and of landowners and outcasts are best illustrated in the history of Antiquity.

THE SIGNIFICANCE OF ACQUISITION CLASSES

The primary significance of a positively privileged acquisition class is to be found in two directions. On the one hand it is generally possible to go far toward attaining a monopoly of the management of productive enterprises in favour of the members of the class and their business interests. On the other hand, such a class tends to ensure the security of its economic position by exercising influence on the economic policy of political bodies and other groups.

The members of positively privileged acquisition classes are typically entrepreneurs. The following are the most important types: merchants, shipowners, industrial and agricultural entrepreneurs, bankers and financiers. Under certain circumstances two other types are also members of such classes, namely, members of the 'liberal' professions with a privileged position by virtue of their abilities or training, and workers with special skills commanding a monopolistic position, regardless of how far they are hereditary or the result of training.

Acquisition classes in a negatively privileged situation are workers of the various principal types. They may be roughly classified as skilled, semi-skilled and unskilled.

In this connexion as well as the above, independent peasants and craftsmen are to be treated as belonging to the 'middle classes'. This category often includes in addition officials, whether they are in public or private employment, the liberal professions, and workers with exceptional monopolistic assets or positions.

Examples of 'social classes' are: (a) the 'working' class as a whole, which approaches this type the more completely mechanised the productive process becomes; (b) the 'lower middle' classes;[1] (c) the 'intelligentsia' without independent property and

[1] Like the French 'petite bourgeoisie', the German term *Kleinbürgertum* has a somewhat more specific meaning than the English 'lower-middle class'. It refers particularly to economically independent elements not employed in large-scale organisations. The typical examples are the small shopkeeper and the proprietor of a small handicraft workshop. [Parsons' footnote.]

the persons whose social position is primarily dependent on technical training such as engineers, commercial and other officials, and civil servants. These groups may differ greatly among themselves, in particular according to costs of training. (*d*) The classes occupying a privileged position through property and education.

The unfinished concluding section of Karl Marx's *Kapital* was evidently intended to deal with the problem of the class unity of the proletariat, which he held existed in spite of the high degree of qualitative differentiation. A decisive factor is the increase in the importance of semi-skilled workers who have been trained in a relatively short time directly on the machines themselves, at the expense of the older type of 'skilled' labour and also of unskilled. However, even this type of skill may often have a monopolistic aspect. Weavers are said to attain the highest level of productivity only after five years' experience.

At an earlier period every worker could be said to have been primarily interested in becoming an independent small bourgeois, but the possibility of realising this goal is becoming progressively smaller. From one generation to another the most readily available path to advancement both for skilled and semi-skilled workers is into the class of technically trained individuals. In the most highly privileged classes, at least over the period of more than one generation, it is becoming more and more true that money is overwhelmingly decisive. Through the banks and corporate enterprises members of the lower middle class and the salaried groups have certain opportunities to rise into the privileged class.

Organised activity of class groups is favoured by the following circumstances: (*a*) the possibility of concentrating on opponents where the immediate conflict of interests is vital: thus workers organise against management and not against security holders who are the ones who really draw income without working; similarly peasants are not apt to organise against landlords; (*b*) the existence of a class status which is typically similar for large masses of people; (*c*) the technical possibility of being easily brought together. This is particularly true where large numbers work together in a small area, as in the modern factory. (*d*) Leadership directed to readily understandable goals. Such goals are very generally imposed or at least are interpreted by persons, such as intelligentsia, who do not belong to the class in question.

SOCIAL STRATA AND THEIR STATUS

The term 'social status'[1] will be applied to a typically effective claim to positive or negative privilege with respect to social prestige so far as it rests on one or more of the following bases: (*a*) mode of living, (*b*) a formal process of education which may consist in empirical or rational training and the acquisition of the corresponding modes of life, or (*c*) on the prestige of birth, or of an occupation.

The primary practical manifestations of status with respect to social stratification are connubium, commensality, and often monopolistic appropriation of privileged economic opportunities and also prohibition of certain modes of acquisition. Finally, there are conventions or traditions of other types attached to a social status.

Stratificatory status may be based on class status directly or related to it in complex ways. It is not, however, determined by this alone. Property and managerial positions are not as such sufficient to lend their holder a certain social status, though they mey well lead to its acquisition. Similarly, poverty is not as such a disqualification for high social status though again it may influence it.

Conversely, social status may partly or even wholly determine class status, without, however, being identical with it. The class status of an officer, a civil servant, and a student as determined by their income may be widely different while their social status remains the same, because they adhere to the same mode of life in all relevant respects as a result of their common education.

A social '*stratum*' *stand* is a plurality of individuals who, within a larger group, enjoy a particular kind and level of prestige by virtue of their position and possibly also claim certain special monopolies.

The following are the most important sources of the development of distinct strata: (*a*) the most important is by the development of a peculiar style of life including, particularly, the type of occupation pursued; (*b*) the second basis is hereditary charisma arising from the successful claim to a position of prestige by virtue of birth; (*c*) the third is the appropriation of political or hierocratic authority as a monopoly by socially distinct groups.

[1] *Ständische Lage.*

The development of hereditary strata is usually a form of the hereditary appropriation of privileges by an organised group or by individual qualified persons. Every well-established case of appropriation of opportunities and abilities, especially of exercising imperative powers, has a tendency to lead to the development of distinct strata. Conversely, the development of strata has a tendency in turn to lead to the monopolistic appropriation of governing powers and of the corresponding economic advantages.

Acquisition classes are favoured by an economic system oriented to market situations, whereas social strata develop and subsist most readily where economic organisation is of a monopolistic and liturgical character and where the economic needs of corporate groups are met on a feudal or patrimonial basis. The type of class which is most closely related to a stratum is the 'social' class, while the 'acquisition' class is the farthest removed. Property classes often constitute the nucleus of a stratum.

Every society where strata play a prominent part is controlled to a large extent by conventional rules of conduct. It thus creates economically irrational conditions of consumption and hinders the development of free markets by monopolistic appropriation and by restricting free disposal of the individual's own economic ability. This will have to be discussed further elsewhere.[1]

(D) Verification in Sociological Analysis[2]

Understanding may be of two kinds: the first is the direct observational understanding of the subjective meaning of a given act as such, including verbal utterances. We thus understand by direct observation, in this sense, the meaning of the proposition $2 \times 2 = 4$

[1] This chapter breaks off at this point but is obviously incomplete. There is, however, no other part of Weber's published work in which the subject is systematically developed, although aspects of it are treated in different connexions at many points. [Parsons' footnote.]

[2] Source: *Theory of Social and Economic Organisation*, pp. 94–100, 107–12 *passim.*

when we hear or read it. This is a case of the direct rational understanding of ideas. We also understand an outbreak of anger as manifested by facial expression, exclamations or irrational movements. This is direct observational understanding of irrational emotional reactions. We can understand in a similar observational way the action of a woodcutter or of somebody who reaches for the knob to shut a door or who aims a gun at an animal. This is rational observational understanding of actions.

Understanding may, however, be of another sort, namely explanatory understanding.[1] Thus we understand in terms of *motive* the meaning an actor attaches to the proposition twice two equals four, when he states it or writes it down, in that we understand what makes him do this at precisely this moment and in these circumstances. Understanding in this sense is attained if we know that he is engaged in balancing a ledger or in making a scientific demonstration, or is engaged in some other task of which this particular act would be an appropriate part. This is rational understanding of motivation, which consists in placing the act in an intelligible and more inclusive context of meaning.[2] Thus we understand the chopping of wood or aiming of a gun in terms of motive in addition to direct observation if we know that the woodchopper is working for a wage or is chopping a supply of firewood for his own use or possibly is doing it for recreation. But he might also be 'working off' a fit of rage, an irrational case. Similarly we understand the motive of a person aiming a gun if we know that he has been commanded to shoot as a member of a

[1] Weber here uses the term *aktuelles Verstehen*, which he contrasts with *erklärendes Verstehen*. The latter he also refers to as *motivationsmaessig*. 'Aktuell' in this context has been translated as 'observational.' It is clear from Weber's discussion that the primary criterion is the possibility of deriving the meaning of an act or symbolic expression from immediate observation without reference to any broader context. In *erklärendes Verstehen*, on the other hand, the particular act must be placed in a broader context of meaning involving facts which cannot be derived from immediate observation of a particular act or expression. [Parsons' footnote.]

[2] The German term is *Sinnzusammenhang*. It refers to a plurality of elements which form a coherent whole on the level of meaning. There are several possible modes of meaningful relation between such elements, such as logical consistency, the æsthetic harmony of a style, or the appropriateness of means to an end. In any case, however, a *Sinnzusammenhang* must be distinguished from a system of elements which are causally interdependent. There seems to be no single English term or phrase which is always adequate. According to variations in the context, 'context of meaning', 'complex of meaning', and sometimes 'meaningful system' have been employed. [Parsons' footnote.]

firing squad, that he is fighting against an enemy, or that he is doing it for revenge. The last is affectually determined and thus in a certain sense irrational. Finally we have a motivational understanding of the outburst of anger if we know that it has been provoked by jealousy, injured pride, or an insult. The last examples are all affectually determined and hence derived from irrational motives. In all the above cases the particular act has been placed in an understandable sequence of motivation, the understanding of which can be treated as an explanation of the actual course of behaviour. Thus for a science which is concerned with the subjective meaning of action, explanation requires a grasp of the complex of meaning in which an actual course of understandable action thus interpreted belongs.[1] In all such cases, even where the processes are largely affectual, the subjective meaning of the action, including that also of the relevant meaning complexes, will be called the 'intended' meaning.[2] This involves a departure from ordinary usage, which speaks of intention in this sense only in the case of rationally purposive action.

In all these cases understanding involves the interpretative grasp of the meaning present in one of the following contexts: (a) as in the historical approach, the actually intended meaning for concrete individual action; or (b) as in cases of sociological mass phenomena the average of, or an approximation to, the actually intended meaning; or (c) the meaning appropriate to a scientifically formulated pure type (an ideal type) of a common phenomenon. The concepts and 'laws' of pure economic theory are examples of this kind of ideal type. They state what course a given type of human action would take if it were strictly rational, unaffected by

[1] On the significance of this type of explanation for causal relationship, see paras. below in the present section.
[2] The German is *gemeinter Sinn*. Weber departs from ordinary usage not only in broadening the meaning of this conception. As he states at the end of the present methodological discussion, he does not restrict the use of this concept to cases where a clear self-conscious awareness of such meaning can be reasonably attributed to every individual actor. Essentially, what Weber is doing is to formulate an operational concept. The question is not whether, in a sense obvious to the ordinary person, such an intended meaning 'really exists', but whether the concept is capable of providing a logical framework within which scientifically important observations can be made. The test of validity of the observations is not whether their object is immediately clear to commonsense, but whether the results of these technical observations can be satisfactorily organised and related to those of others in a systematic body of knowledge. [Parsons' footnote.]

errors or emotional factors and if, furthermore, it were completely and unequivocally directed to a single end, the maximisation of economic advantage. In reality, action takes exactly this course only in unusual cases, as sometimes on the stock exchange; and even then there is usually only an approximation to the ideal type.[1]

Every interpretation attempts to attain clarity and certainty, but no matter how clear an interpretation as such appears to be from the point of view of meaning, it cannot on this account alone claim to be the causally valid interpretation. On this level it must remain only a peculiarly plausible hypothesis. In the first place the 'conscious motives' may well, even to the actor himself, conceal the various 'motives' and 'repressions' which constitute the real driving force of his action. Thus, in such cases even subjectively honest self-analysis has only a relative value. Then it is the task of the sociologist to be aware of this motivational situation and to describe and analyse it, even though it has not actually been concretely part of the conscious 'intention' of the actor; possibly not at all, at least not fully. This is a borderline case of the interpretation of meaning. Secondly, processes of action which seem to an observer to be the same or similar may fit into exceedingly various complexes of motive in the case of the actual actor. Then even though the situations appear superficially to be very similar we must actually understand them or interpret them as very different, perhaps, in terms of meaning, directly opposed.[2] Third, the actors in any given situation are often subject to opposing and conflicting impulses, all of which we are able to understand. In a large number of cases we know from experience it is not possible to arrive at even an approximate estimate of the relative strength of conflicting motives and very often we cannot be certain of our interpretation. Only the actual outcome of the conflict gives a solid basis of judgement.

More generally, verification of subjective interpretation by comparison with the concrete course of events is, as in the case of all hypotheses, indispensable. Unfortunately this type of verification is feasible with relative accuracy only in the few very

[1] The scientific functions of such construction have been discussed in Weber's article in the *Archiv für Sozialwissenschaft*, Vol. xix, pp. 64 ff.
[2] Simmel, in his *Probleme der Geschichtsphilosophie*, gives a number of examples.

special cases susceptible of psychological experimentation. The approach to a satisfactory degree of accuracy is exceedingly various, even in the limited number of cases of mass phenomena which can be statistically described and unambiguously interpreted. For the rest there remains only the possibility of comparing the largest possible number of historical or contemporary processes which, while otherwise similar, differ in the one decisive point of their relation to the particular motive or factor the role of which is being investigated. This is a fundamental task of comparative sociology. Often, unfortunately, there is available only the dangerous and uncertain procedure of the 'imaginary experiment', which consists in thinking away certain elements of a chain of motivation and working out the course of action which would then probably ensue, thus arriving at a causal judgement.[1]

For example, the generalisation called Gresham's Law is a rationally clear interpretation of human action under certain conditions and under the assumption that it will follow a purely rational course. How far any actual course of action corresponds to this can be verified only by the available statistical evidence for the actual disappearance from circulation of under-valued monetary units. In this case our information serves to demonstrate a high degree of accuracy. The facts of experience were known before the generalisation. which was formulated afterwards; but without this successful interpretation our need for causal understanding would evidently be left unsatisfied. On the other hand, without the demonstration that what can here be assumed to be a theoretically adequate interpretation is also in some degree relevant to an actual course of action, a 'law', no matter how fully demonstrated theoretically, would be worthless for the understanding of action in the real world. In this case the correspondence between the theoretical interpretation of motivation and its empirical verification is entirely satisfactory and the cases are numerous enough for verification to be considered established. But to take another

---

[1] The above passage is an exceedingly compact statement of Weber's theory of the logical conditions of proof of causal relationship. He developed this most fully in his essay *Die Objektivität sozialwissenschaftlicher Erkenntnis*, op. cit. It is also discussed in certain of the other essays which have been collected in the volume, *Gesammelte Aufsätze zur Wissenschaftslehre*. The best and fullest secondary discussion is to be found in Von Schelting's book, *Max Webers Wissenschaftslehre*. There is a briefer discussion in chap. xvi of T. Parsons' *Structure of Social Action*.

example, Eduard Meyer has advanced an ingenious theory of the causal significance of the battles of Marathon, Salamis, and Platea for the development of the cultural peculiarities of Greek, and hence, more generally, Western civilisation.[1] This is derived from a meaningful interpretation of certain symptomatic facts having to do with the attitudes of the Greek oracles and prophets towards the Persians. It can only be directly verified by reference to the examples of the conduct of the Persians in cases where they were victorious, as in Jerusalem, Egypt, and Asia Minor, and even this verification must necessarily remain unsatisfactory in certain respects. The striking rational plausibility of the hypothesis must here necessarily be relied on as a support. In very many cases of historical interpretation which seem highly plausible, however, there is not even a possibility of the order of verification which was feasible in this case. Where this is true the interpretation must necessarily remain a hypothesis.

A motive is a complex of subjective meaning which seems to the actor himself or to the observer an adequate ground for the conduct in question. We apply the term 'adequacy on the level of meaning'[2] to the subjective interpretation of a coherent course of conduct when and in so far as, according to our habitual modes of thought and feeling, its component parts taken in their mutual relation are recognised to constitute a 'typical' complex of meaning. It is more common to say 'correct'. The interpretation of a sequence of events will, on the other hand, be called *causally* adequate in so far as, according to established generalisations from experience, there is a probability that it will always actually occur in the same way. An example of adequacy on the level of meaning in this sense is what is, according to our current norms of calcula-

[1] See Eduard Meyer, *Geschichte des Altertums* (Stuttgart, 1901), Vol. iii, pp. 420, 444 ff.
[2] The expression *sinnhafte Adäquanz* is one of the most difficult of Weber's technical terms to translate. In most places the cumbrous phrase 'adequacy on the level of meaning' has had to be employed. It should be clear from the progress of the discussion that what Weber refers to is a satisfying level of knowledge for the particular purposes of the subjective state of mind of the actor or actors. He is, however, careful to point out that *causal* adequacy involves in addition to this a satisfactory correspondence between the results of observations from the subjective point of view and from the objective; that is, observations of the overt course of action which can be described without reference to the state of mind of the actor. For a discussion of the methodological problem involved here, see *Structure of Social Action*, chaps. ii and v. [Parsons' footnote.]

tion or thinking, the correct solution of an arithmetical problem. On the other hand, a causally adequate interpretation of the same phenomenon would concern the statistical probability that, according to verified generalisations from experience, there would be a correct or an erroneous solution of the same problem. This also refers to currently accepted norms but includes taking account of typical errors or of typical confusions. Thus causal explanation depends on being able to determine that there is a probability, which in the rare idea case can be numerically stated, but is always in some sense calculable, that a given observable event (overt or subjective) will be followed or accompanied by another event.

A correct causal interpretation of a concrete course of action is arrived at when the overt action and the motives have both been correctly apprehended and at the same time their relation has become meaningfully comprehensible. A correct causal interpretation of typical action means that the process which is claimed to be typical is shown to be both adequately grasped on the level of meaning and at the same time the interpretation is to some degree causally adequate. If adequacy in respect to meaning is lacking, then no matter how high the degree of uniformity and how precisely its probability can be numerically determined, it is still an incomprehensible statistical probability, whether dealing with overt or subjective processes. On the other hand, even the most perfect adequacy on the level of meaning has causal significance from a sociological point of view only in so far as there is some kind of proof for the existence of a probability[1] that action in fact normally takes the course which has been held to be meaningful. For this there must be some degree of determinable frequency of approximation to an average or a pure type.

Statistical uniformities constitute understandable types of action

[1] This is the first occurrence in Weber's text of the term *Chance* which he uses very frequently. It is here translated by 'probability', because he uses it as interchangeable with *Wahrscheinlichkeit*. As the term 'probability' is used in a technical mathematical and statistical sense, however, it implies the possibility of numerical statement. In most of the cases where Weber uses *Chance* this is out of the question. It is, however, possible to speak in terms of higher and lower degrees of probability. To avoid confusion with the technical mathematical concept, the term 'likelihood' will often be used in the translation. It is by means of this concept that Weber, in a highly ingenious way, has bridged the gap between the interpretation of meaning and the inevitably more complex facts of overt action. [Parsons' footnote.]

in the sense of this discussion, and thus constitute 'sociological generalisations', only when they can be regarded as manifestations of the understandable subjective meaning of a course of social action. Conversely, formulations of a rational course of subjectively understandable action constitute sociological types of empirical process only when they can be empirically observed with a significant degree of approximation. It is unfortunately by no means the case that the actual likelihood of the occurrence of a given course of overt action is always directly proportional to the clarity of subjective interpretation. There are statistics of processes devoid of meaning such as death rates, phenomena of fatigue, the production rate of machines, the amount of rainfall, in exactly the same sense as there are statistics of meaningful phenomena. But only when the phenomena are meaningful is it convenient to speak of sociological statistics. Examples are such cases as crime rates, occupational distributions, price statistics and statistics of crop acreage. Naturally there are many cases where both components are involved, as in crop statistics.

Processes and uniformities which it has here seemed convenient not to designate as (in the present case) sociological phenomena or uniformities because they are not 'understandable', are naturally not on that account any the less important. This is true even for sociology in the present sense which restricts it to subjectively understandable phenomena—a usage which there is no intention of attempting to impose on anyone else. Such phenomena, however important, are simply treated by a different method from the others; they become conditions, stimuli, furthering or hindering circumstances of action. . . .

It is customary to designate various sociological generalisations, as for example 'Gresham's Law', as scientific 'laws'. These are in fact typical probabilities confirmed by observation to the effect that under certain given conditions an expected course of social action will occur, which is understandable in terms of the typical motives and typical subjective intentions of the actors. These generalisations are both understandable and definite in the highest degree in so far as the typically observed course of action can be understood in terms of the purely rational pursuit of an end, or where for reasons of methodological convenience such a theoretical type can be heuristically employed. In such cases the relations of means and end will be clearly understandable on grounds of experience, particularly where the choice of means was 'inevitable'. In such cases it is legitimate to assert that in so far as the action was rigorously rational it could not have taken any other course because for technical reasons, given their clearly defined ends, no other means were available to the actors. . . .

It has continually been assumed as obvious that the science of sociology seeks to formulate type concepts and generalised uniformities of empirical process. This distinguishes it from history, which is oriented to the causal analysis and explanation of individual actions, structures, and personalities possessing cultural significance. The empirical material which underlies the concepts of sociology consists to a very large extent, though by no means exclusively, of the same concrete processes of action which are dealt with by historians. Among the various bases on which its concepts are formulated and its generalisations worked out, is an attempt to justify its important claim to be able to make a contribution to the causal explanation of some historically and culturally important phenomenon. As in the case of every generalising science, the abstract character of the concepts of sociology is responsible for the fact that, compared with actual historical reality, they are relatively lacking in fullness of concrete content. To compensate for this disadvantage, sociological analysis can offer a greater precision of concepts. This precision is obtained by striving for the highest possible degree of adequacy on the level of meaning in accordance with the definition of that concept put forward above. It has already been repeatedly stressed that this aim can be realised in a particularly high degree in the case of concepts and generalisations which formulate rational processes. But sociological investigation attempts to include in its scope various irrational phenomena, as well as prophetic, mystic, and affectual modes of action, formulated in terms of theoretical concepts which are adequate on the level of meaning. In *all* cases, rational or irrational, sociological analysis both abstracts from reality and at the same time helps us to understand it, in that it shows with what degree of approximation a concrete historical phenomenon can be subsumed under one or more of these concepts. . . . Theoretical analysis in the field of sociology is possible only in terms of such pure types. It goes without saying that in addition it is convenient for the sociologist from time to time to employ average types of an empirical statistical character. There are concepts which do not require methodological discussion at this point. But when reference is made to 'typical' cases, the term should always be understood, unless otherwise stated, as meaning *ideal* types, which may in turn be rational or irrational as the case may be (thus in economic theory they are always rational), but in any case are always constructed with a view to adequacy on the level of meaning.

It is important to realise that in the sociological field as elsewhere, averages, and hence average types, can be formulated with a relative degree of precision only where they are concerned with differences of degree in respect to action which remains qualitatively the same. Such cases do occur, but in the majority of cases of action important to history or sociology the motives which determine it are qualitatively heterogeneous. Then it is quite impossible to speak of an 'average' in the true sense. The ideal types of social action which, for instance, are used in economic theory are thus 'unrealistic' or abstract in that they always ask what course of action would take place if it were purely rational and oriented to economic ends alone. But this construction can be used to aid in the understanding of action not determined purely economically, but which involves deviations arising from traditional restraints, affects, errors and the intrusion of other than economic purposes or considerations. This can take place in two ways. First, in analysing the extent to which in the concrete case, or on the average for a class of cases, the action was in part economically determined along with the other factors. Secondly, by throwing the discrepancy between the actual course of events and the ideal type into relief, the analysis of the non-economic motives actually involved is facilitated. The procedure would be very similar in employing an ideal type of mystical orientation with its appropriate attitude of indifference to worldly things, as a tool for analysing its consequences for the actor's relation to ordinary life; for instance, to political or economic affairs. The more sharply and precisely the ideal type has been constructed, thus the more abstract and unrealistic in this sense it is, the better it is able to perform its methodological functions in formulating the clarification of terminology, and in the formulation of classifications, and of hypotheses. . . .

The theoretical concepts of sociology are ideal types not only from the objective point of view, but also in their application to subjective processes. In the great majority of cases actual action goes on in a state of inarticulate half-consciousness or actual unconsciousness of its subjective meaning. The actor is more likely to 'be aware' of it in a vague sense than he is to 'know' what he is doing or be explicitly self-conscious about it. In most cases his action is governed by impulse or habit. Only occasionally, and, in the uniform action of large numbers, often only in the case of a few individuals, is the subjective meaning of the action, whether rational or irrational, brought clearly into consciousness. The ideal type of meaningful action where the meaning is fully conscious and explicit is a marginal case. Every sociological or historical investigation, in applying its analysis to the empirical facts, must take this fact into account. But the difficulty need not prevent the sociologist from systematising his concepts by the classification of possible types of subjective meaning. That is, he may reason as if action actually proceeded on the basis of clearly self-conscious meaning. The resulting deviation from the concrete facts must continually be kept in mind whenever it is a question of this level of concreteness, and must be carefully studied with reference both to degree and kind. It is often necessary to choose between terms which are either clear or unclear. Those which are clear will, to be sure, have the abstractness of ideal types, but they are none the less preferable for scientific purposes.

(E) A Research Strategy for the Study of Occupational Careers and Mobility Patterns

METHODOLOGICAL INTRODUCTION FOR THE SURVEY OF THE SOCIETY FOR SOCIAL POLICY CONCERNING SELECTION AND ADAPTATION (CHOICE AND COURSE OF OCCUPATION) FOR THE WORKERS OF MAJOR INDUSTRIAL ENTERPRISES. (1908)[1] [Translated by D. Hÿtch.]

Contents:

I. *General character of the survey:* socio-political neutrality. Restriction to self-contained industry. Elimination of merely 'morphological' problems. Significance for the construction of the survey of the mode of composition of production costs. The technique and the formulation of questions of the survey. The learning process and the 'skill' of the worker in their significance for the questions of the survey.

II. *The scientific problems of the survey:* the physiological and psychological basis of occupational aptitude. Problems of 'heredity'. Fundamental methodological difficulties in the understanding of differences in occupational aptitude determined by hereditary factors. Aim of the inquiry.

III. *The methodology of the survey:* its subject. Significance for the inquiry of shifts, allocation of breaks and systems of remuneration. Wage-accounting, calculation of wage costs and efficiency in their relevance to the survey: selection of workers. Use of factory rolls for the survey. Questioning of the workers themselves. The two types of execution of the survey: factory survey and survey of trade union statistics. Details concerning the inquiries in both cases. Aim of the survey.

[1] Source: J. C. B. Mohr, *Gesemmelte Aufsatze zur Soziologie und Sozialpolitik* (Tübingen, 1924).

GENERAL CHARACTER OF THE SURVEY

The present survey is trying to establish, on the one hand, what effect self-contained industry has on the individual personality, the career and the extra-occupational style of living of the workers, what physical and mental qualities it develops in them, and how these are expressed in the total behaviour of the workers; and on the other hand, to what extent industry on its side, in its capacity for development and in the direction of its development, is governed by given qualities arising out of the ethnic, social and cultural background, the tradition, and the circumstances of the workers. There are therefore two distinct questions combined here, which the theoretician can and must separate, but which, in practical examination, almost invariably occur intertwined, so that, in the *final* analysis at least, the one cannot be answered without the other.

With this survey, the Society for Social Policy enters the domain of works serving exclusively scientific purposes. The proposed publications, and likewise any debate that may arise therefrom, have no directly practical 'socio-*political*' intention; their goal is a purely sociological one. The issue is *not* how social conditions in industry are to be 'assessed' or, in particular, whether the situation in which self-contained industry places the workers today is satisfactory or not, whether anyone, and if so, who, should take the 'blame' for any unsatisfactory aspects of the same, or what should or could be done to improve it and in what way. No; it is exclusively a matter of the unbiased, objective statement of facts and the ascertainment of their causes in industrial conditions and the individual character of its workers. Similarly these facts, which it is our aim to establish, do not lie in areas, and do not lead to problems, which can be tackled by means of legislation. That is not to say that they could offer no practical interest. There is the question of whether the efficiency of our major industries is related to qualities determined by cultural level and the intrinsic character of the people, or, to put it the other way round, what characteristics, useful, physical or mental, engendered in our workers by the ceaseless progress of our industrial development, shall we have to reckon with in future because they are essential for industry; and we must also ask to what general living conditions the workers, thus formed, are and will be committed. These questions are certainly of considerable significance for extremely important general problems, not simply of a commercial-political nature, but also in the 'cultural-political' sphere (e.g. educational policy also). The spread of enlightenment concerning those issues could be of considerable practical interest to those involved, industrialists and workers alike. Eventually, more light than is available today could be shed on questions such as the following: In view of the given conditions obtaining in industry, what may and what may not be considered 'attainable' by way of legislation?

However, these potential practical side-effects of the survey are not its aim. It is *not* the intention of the Society to bring up for discussion, by means of this survey, any practical issues, as was, and had to be, the case with many of its previous surveys. More-over, the Society has no thought of sitting in moral judgement over those involved, be they employers or employed: the scientific objectivity of the examinations would be in no way enhanced by such intentions. The whole problem at issue (it does not seem superfluous to stress this to my colleagues too) is, socio-politically speaking, a totally neutral one by its very nature. From this it follows, for example, that when a researcher, working on one aspect, meets complaints from the workers about any conditions (system of remuneration, conduct of foremen, etc.) in factories, this circumstance would *not*, within the terms of the present survey, concern him as the symptom of a practical 'issue' on which he would have to pronounce judgement; rather it would be taken into consideration simply as the phenomenon attendant upon certain transformations (technical, economic or psychological) whose progress it is his business objectively to *explain*. Considered in this sense, such evidence of the state of mind of the workers could be of significant interest to the present survey. However, the researcher would then have to view such complaints not with regard to their 'justification', but purely with regard to their occurrence. And, naturally, to expressions of irritation concerning the workers, on the part of the employers, the same principle applies: they are to be ascertained as *symptoms* of friction in development and analysed where necessary.

The present survey, then, is pursuing 'theoretical' goals, in the sense just mentioned, and it appears pertinent to make clear the nature of these goals more explicitly than can have been evident from the 'plan of work',[1] which was forwarded earlier.

The objectives of the survey are limited firstly inasmuch as they are concerned with *major self-contained industry*—that is, concerns which carry on solely, or at least chiefly, large-scale self-contained commercial enterprise; any attached out-work should, of course, be compared in terms of the characteristics and origin of the workers, with those employed in self-contained industry. In general a comparison with conditions in cottage industry (if there be any) could be fruitful. Furthermore, the ultimate aim of the survey does *not* lie in the analysis of the 'morphological' issues: the organisation of production and turnover and the internal structure of the concern, according to their limitation by technical and economic considerations. Of course, it is absolutely indispensable, in the very nature of the survey, that the researcher procure for himself a thorough knowledge of these matters for his own field, as is required in the first paragraph of the 'plan of work'. The crucial points are dealt with for a particular industry, for example, in Dr G. Ephraim's treatise[2] and the study of this appraisal is to be recommended. However, theses of this kind could not be considered as answers to the questions raised by the present survey, however indispensable they may be as a preparation for tackling such questions. Thus, for example, the true object of the report would never be the division of the individual concern into working units (e.g. of so-called 'plant', to use the conventional expression, by which is meant, in more precise terminology, one production enterprise such as the iron industry, under one management, within one geographically connected complex of buildings, divided into *technical* working units—the foundry, boiler-shop, machine-shop, etc.—or a weaving-mill, again with technical working units, the dressing department, reel department, weaving and hemming departments, etc.) and the methods of interdepartmental contact and accounting.

The interest of this survey begins rather at questions like the following: To what extent does an interchange of manpower occur between those 'working units' within the concern, however they may be separated or combined physically or on paper (for purposes of assessment) or by the technicalities of production? Is there

---

[1] Not included in the present volume.
[2] *Organisation and Running of a Textile Mill* (Tübingen, 1906).

'promotion' from one to the other, or, on the other hand, is there more or less strict segregation? And has this any consequences with regard to social intercourse? In this, for example, moulding-shop and boiler-shop, reel and weaving departments, weaving and hemming departments, behave totally differently to one another. It is just the same with the organisation of sales, so important in itself. It is *not*, for its own sake, the object of this survey. On the other hand, it not infrequently enters *indirectly* into the issues of this survey in most incisive fashion; for example, inasmuch as distribution by wholesalers, as is familiar to England's textile industry, favours the most thoroughgoing specialisation of individual firms, and thus of their workers, and consequently their constant occupation with the same task, which is of importance both for the career of the workers, which concerns us, and for the possibility it affords of gaining some reasonably accurate data concerning their efficiency (see below). Where a strong degree of direct trade with retailers occurs, as it frequently does in Germany, specialisation is impeded, therefore the changing mode of employment of the individual worker, or at least the changing varieties he produces (as in many branches of the textile industry), is characteristic of his situation and makes it very difficult to obtain clear figures which could distinguish the measure of his output, its variation, and its comparability with that of other workers in the same factory.

If, then, problems of sales and actual factory organisation are called upon to play only an indirect role in this survey, although a very important one in certain circumstances, on the other hand the researchers should be counselled to heed some preliminary *economic* questions, in the stricter sense, in addition to such organisational ones. Thus it seems especially important that the researcher should endeavour to obtain as clear a picture as possible of the scale of the *capital requirement* (for 'technical' working units of particular sizes) and of the 'organic' *composition* of the requisite capital, that is, the relation of building and machine capital on the one hand to the cost of raw materials and wages on the other, for the industries with which he is dealing. Doubtful though it is how far the individual employer will be inclined to give precise details about his own position in this respect, it has nevertheless been found by experience that serviceable average values can probably be established relatively easily. It would be no less important to ascertain how the *periods of return* on capital have altered in recent times in the course of technical and economic development in the industry concerned, and what the current situation is.

The mode of composition of an industry's capital, and that means decomposition of the elements of its production costs, manifests itself chiefly in the direction in which its propensity for labour-saving is moving. The installation of a new, technically improved machine always means the elimination of a series of processes which were necessary with the tools previously employed; and that means the redundancy of certain hitherto essential qualities in the workers, but, on the other hand, the employment of men to work the newly installed machines who must, for their part, develop certain other qualities in order to fit themselves for the task.

Now it is one of the crucial requirements of this survey that it be established, firstly, what *kind* of workers with what *kind* of qualities are being excluded on the one hand and bred on the other by such technical changes; and, secondly, to what extent is this determined by the general economic basis of the industry concerned, which depends on the amount and *type* of capital required. Owing to the scarcity of capital available at the moment, technical transformation is following fairly exactly the path marked out by the current maximum in possible cost saving. Where this lies at any given time is determined to a high degree by the capital composition of individual economic units under the same direction. For example, where the cost of uneconomic material consumption, of machine wear or of flaws and irregularities in the product, or the bare wage-costs as such, carry particularly heavy weight, *relatively*, within such a unit, its propensity for technical development varies accordingly. Consequently, as is well known, industry strives not simply for the absolute elimination of highly-paid workers as such by technical innovations, but rather it seeks to obviate them when, for instance, wage-costs in the relevant section of the production process take up by *comparison* a particularly high fraction of the total capital, because the workers concerned are at the same time highly qualified, i.e. expensive, and relatively very numerous. Here the question which concerns this survey is this: to what extent, in individual cases, are they being ousted in favour of a smaller class of workers, perhaps with even higher qualifications; or by less well qualified and easily replaceable workers? Such fluctuations are, however, by no means always due to simple calculations of wage-costs; rather it is precisely our task to examine to what extent, and in what direction, technological changes, and thereby the composition of the labour force, are determined by these demands, and to what extent by other requirements such as regularity of the product, economy of materials, etc.

Such changes can also be a special function of the industry's interest in the *acceleration of capital return*. The ability to increase the speed of return on total capital at the same time, not only in spite of but by means of the constant increase of standing capital, particularly of machine capital, typically governs extensive technical innovations. Those sections of production in which the most time is saved by mechanisation, and thereby there is the most saving of workers, are therefore those which are most open to these processes of change-over. Furthermore, large sections of the ready-made and half-finished article industry are subject to the law of increasing 'standardisation' of their products. In order to eliminate the costly multiplicity of their production and marketing machinery, they are endeavouring to reduce their products to a minimum number of types, standardised as far as possible, and to 'mechanise' production from this point of view. Accordingly, technical innovations and processes of elimination and incorporation which result from the pressure of this interest, occur most intensively at that point in the production process where there is most to be gained in *type* of products.

These and other economic determinants of technical innovations, which vary according to the nature of individual industries, are *not* to be established by the survey for their own sake. Rather they are primarily, for our present purposes, of purely methodological importance, namely for the question: which individual industries and, within each, which sections of their labour force present a particularly suitable subject for the determination of differences of aptitude among the workers, their causes and consequences; that is: Where would a thorough examination of this point, with the aid of means to be discussed later, have the greatest chances of success? This will be the case where (1) wage-costs represent a particularly high fraction of the total capital expenditure and therefore the rational utilisation of the labour force is especially urgent for the maintenance of profit; (2) and this commonly but by no means always coincides with the first, where the *qualification* of the workers is of paramount importance for technical success in production, in terms of quantity and quality, i.e. where the industry is to a particularly high degree *dependent* on the aptitude of the workers; and finally where (3) 'standardisation' of products, and with it the continuity of the similar occupation of the workers, is particularly great and permits the most accurate possible measurement of the workers' output (see below)—which again often, but by no means always, coincides with the two first-named points. Standardised products, a highly skilled labour force, and the relatively great importance of wage-*costs*, produce, when they all occur together, a particularly favourable field for the success of all inquiries pertinent to the '*selection*' of workers. However, it goes without saying that the survey, quite apart from the fact that it does not focus exclusively on this question, absolutely must not omit to consider industries also in which the conditions of study are not so favourable in this respect. The prospects of obtaining results from the latter are by no means necessarily worse; for it must not be forgotten that, apart from pure aptitude, which can be measured directly by the output, purely historical conditions also determine the employment of particular sources in particular jobs.

Objectively speaking, those economic bases of the realisation of capital and their transformations are of interest for the question: To what extent, in the measurable past, have those peculiarities of capital composition, of return on capital, and of 'standardisation' in the individual industries led to changes in the *internal structure* of the labour force, in the men's careers, and in their professional and 'human' qualities? Which *individual* changes of this type are to be ascribed to the *individual* developmental trends in capital realisation? On the other hand it should also be asked whether, and in what sense, the *industry* concerned for its part finds itself (or imagines itself) restricted in the manner of its realisation of capital, e.g. in the trend to increasing capital invest-ment in general, to standardisation, to increasing speed of turn-over, etc., by given qualities of its labour force, because these qualities *impede* technical innovations of a certain type. If so, one must go on to ask: whether this restriction obtains (or obtained) universally for the industry, or perhaps only locally and by contrast with other economic areas, i.e. to what extent it depends (or depended) on the characteristics of the *locally* available labour forces. Lastly, in what way is (or was) the industry concerned desirous of, or forced to, adapt itself to this section of the factors governing production in the extent, structure and turnover of its capital expenditure? The comparison of *different* industries drawing on the *same* labour market, and equally the comparison of geographically separate factories of the *same* industry, which draw on *different* labour markets, could be particularly instructive here: indeed it is of vital importance for the whole situation of the textile industry and its labour force that the Silesian textile industry, which attracts cheap labour from the inexhaustible reservoirs of manpower of Eastern Europe, is embraced in one and the same economic area with the firms of the West which are founded on a (relatively) highly paid labour force. All the contrasts of the social structure of East and West make their contribution here.

The question of the manner in which the individual industries procure their labour force obviously belongs equally in this context. If the natural course would be to start by asking what *technical* form does the advertisement of vacancies, recruitment, and provision of work take in the individual industry and for the individual categories of workers, nevertheless the real task is to find out how far the individual industries are to a greater or lesser extent tied to the labour available locally or in particular areas, or how far they were, and are, in a position to attract workers from outside, and what difficulties they encounter in doing so. To ascertain as accurately as possible from *which* other *jobs* the individual categories of workers in the factories concerned were recruited, would be of quite special interest, especially in industries where vast expansion or rapid technical transformation is taking place. From our point of view, the occupational career of the workers would appear as a kind of 'military road' on which, from particular geographical, ethnic, social and cultural starting-points (which should be more closely examined), they have advanced to their qualification for the job they finally attain. Characteristic results would naturally be most easily obtained for workers whose specific qualities, according to the technical character of the industry concerned, are to a particularly high degree indispensable.

The role which *technology* is called upon to play in this survey follows from what has been said. As thorough a knowledge as possible of the technology of the industry under consideration is the obvious prerequisite to the possibility of its being carried out. The study of one of the numerous text-books may well afford the most elementary knowledge, but of course, never more than that. Therefore, where my colleagues are not themselves technicians, or (which would be particularly welcome) perhaps teachers at technical schools which prepare for the understanding and operation of machines, they cannot be too urgently advised constantly to avail themselves of the assistance of technicians intimately acquainted with the operation and requirements of the machines concerned and their historical development. A *description* of the technology of the individual industries is desirable naturally only as far as it is essential for the understanding of the questions which are the objective of this survey. For in view of the vast, easily accessible technological literature, it would of course be pointless to treat such descriptions as ends in themselves. Naturally it is the 'technical' peculiarity of the production process, especially of the machines, which *directly* determines in the workers all the qualities the individual industry needs, and their potential career as well. In the investigation of the manner of this connection, however, the end is in no way the description of the machines, but *purely* the thorough analysis of the *manipulations* which the workers have to carry out *on* the machines: and that *solely* in order to find out what quite special capabilities have to be brought to bear in the physical operations of the individual category of workers. *This* analysis, indeed, can certainly never be too thorough.

The researcher will not uncommonly be most easily alert to the crucial points if he makes a thorough study of the details of the *learning* process, and seeks in particular to find out which of the individual components into which the manipulation of the individual worker can be broken down, is, according to the evidence of the workers themselves as well as of the employers, technicians, and foremen, found to be the *most difficult* at the beginning of apprenticeship, presents the most obstacles to learning, and is most rarely achieved to absolute perfection. In this connection the variety of geographical, ethnic, social and cultural *background* of the workers should be studied with regard to any effect it may have on the *ability* to learn.

It is well known that the learning process, the thorough examination of which can in these respects be of considerable importance for the objectives of this survey, takes widely differing forms in the individual categories of worker. In the case of certain very simple tasks it is reduced to very simple processes of practice. Even the most elementary unskilled labour cannot be carried out without the influence of habit-formation. These very simple, least skilled jobs can be of a 'physical' as well as a 'mental' nature, to use the conventional terminology. The counting and checking of quantities of finished products, for instance, can be of such a purely mechanical nature that it requires almost no practice at all, and, in contrast to the operation of machines, can be carried out by individuals of very limited capabilities, provided only that a minimum of personal reliability, i.e. a trait of personality, is present. From the lowest ranges of 'unskilled' labour to skill which approaches artistry there is potentially, in theory, an almost unbroken continuum of performances and categories of workers. A simple division into 'skilled' and 'unskilled' workers is by no means always practically possible either. Rather, it will have to be particularly determined how the labour force in factories of a certain type and size is spread numerically over the individual degrees of skill required, and further, how this composition has changed in the recent past, what changes are likely in the foreseeable future, and why. Industries often divide very characteristically into those where a more or less broad class of almost completely 'unskilled' labour stands next to a nucleus of highly-skilled quality workers, and those where such differences, within the individual categories of the labour force, are only differences of degree. Owing to technical evolution, which for its part is connected with the above-mentioned trends in capital realisation, these conditions are in a process of constant development, whose direction should be described.

In the investigation of this matter, '*skill*' is of course to be distinguished above all by its *type*. It will be found advisable, in accordance with normal usage, to understand by a 'skilled' worker one who has followed a real, in some sense multilateral course, after the fashion of the old craft guilds' trade apprenticeship or at least similar to this, be it in the guild, in special apprentice shops, or in the factory itself. From these should be distinguished, as 'trained' workers, those who are immediately placed at machines of the same, or similar, type as those which they have to operate permanently, and trained on these until their output reaches the minimum or norm necessary for the viability of their employment, naturally taking into account the transitional stages which may occur between the two categories. Above all else the task here is to find out *why* the individual industry or factory necessitates one form of learning or another, i.e. whether, and for what reason, a special course is required even today, instead of direct training, for particular categories of workers but not for others, owing to the nature of their task; or to find out to what extent the employment of such 'skilled' (in the old sense) labour is *not* the consequence of the technical character of the demands which the work makes by its very nature on the workers concerned, but is essentially a historical relic. In order to clarify the reasons for such differences, it will also be desirable in every case to ascertain the approximate *cost* arising directly or indirectly from training, for instance, owing to certain machines and foremen being made available especially for this, or owing to underproduction against a guaranteed minimum wage during apprenticeship, etc. Then it would be very important to establish what level of achievement must be demanded in individual cases for the *completion* of training, that is to say, for employment as a fully-fledged worker; and finally, above all, in what *period of time* this level is reached by the workers of individual categories, according to age, sex, their geographical, ethnic, social and cultural background, their earlier work in different occupations, and what underlies the differences which may emerge in this respect. Any reliable results on this particular point, based on sufficiently comprehensive and carefully interpreted data, could become especially important for the survey, since it might be possible to trace them back to differences in the *learning* ability of the workers according to differences in their backgrounds. This naturally applies only when apprenticeship takes place under roughly similar conditions. For it makes, for instance, a great deal of difference whether a worker has to learn his manipulations at a new machine, piece by piece, according to the instructions of a master, or is constantly near already fully practised workers carrying out the same manipulations, and by imitating them can 'feel' his way into his work. The experience in factories is that the training period for many jobs can be cut to almost one-sixth by the influence of this 'empathy'. On the other hand, even under identical conditions, the requisite training period varies greatly in individual cases, and the causes of such differences should be investigated, especially in so far as they arise from differences of background.

Besides this, the influence of the internal structure of the labour force, determined by the character of their output, the degree of skill required for it, and the type of learning or training, would of course be one of the points with which the analysis (1) of the professional career, (2) of social relations among the workers, and lastly (3) of the general 'characterological' qualities of the working class, as developed by large-scale industry, should begin. The essential questions to consider here are obviously (a) how far the evolution of the working class is moving in the direction of qualitative distinction (and, influenced by this, economic and social distinction) of its various classes, or conversely, in the direction of increasing uniformity; (b) how far the utility of the individual industrial worker appears increasingly *specialised*, tailored to the exclusive use of quite special individual qualities, or conversely, *universalistic*; (c) to what extent individual industries are correspondingly *emancipating* themselves increasingly from certain qualities of their workers, be they due to practice or training, and how far any 'standardisation' of products means a 'standardisation' of the workers as well, or conversely how far specialised equipment means a multiplicity of qualities in the workers. Furthermore, the following questions belong here: (d) what the chances of promotion for the workers are within particular types of occupation, both economically (according to the possible shape of their earnings curve), and organisationally (according to the degree of relative responsibility or even *superiority* which may in the course of their careers succeed the subordination which was inevitable at first); and 'psychologically' (according to their subjective *inclination* with regard to the individual posts they have the opportunity to hold), the important point of view of 'job satisfaction' (H. Herkner) and, for example, also the assessment of the pertinent question of under what conditions may the 'operation' of the machine be felt by the workers to be 'mastery' of it; and lastly (e) how the result of all these influences affects the psychophysical and characterological individuality of the workers of an industry, and their 'style of living'. These crucially important questions of the survey must of course all take as their *starting-point* the simple process of the acquisition by practice of particular capabilities which the industry demands, but also they must take into account the general physical and mental requirements and consequences of the acquisition and possession of such skills.

Now it cannot be expected of my colleagues, in so far as they are not physiologists or experimental psychologists by profession or training, that they should be in possession of the expert knowledge required to deal with such findings of those disciplines as could be at all relevant to the purposes of this survey. Any attempt to evaluate such results *without* strict expert supervision would only too easily lead to dilettantism. If, nevertheless, these problems are examined a little more closely, then this is done in order to gain a rough perspective, which should *in principle* be aimed at as the ultimate goal in a survey of this kind, but not for the purpose of inducing colleagues who are chiefly just state economists—who will probably constitute the majority—to venture into spheres with which they are not conversant as experts. It would also seem useful that the individual should be clear about which problems he has *not* broached with *his* inquiry. Incidentally, nothing would be more welcome than any assistance from experts in the relevant disciplines themselves.

II

THE SCIENTIFIC PROBLEMS OF THE SURVEY

It must be stated right at the outset that, owing to the enormous difficulty of experimental control, the significant progress which has certainly been made in the analysis of the processes now under consideration has for the time being led only partially to results which, even where there is a complete command of the data, can be directly utilised for the purposes of this survey.

This is valid to a considerable degree even for the sphere of purely *muscular activity*. In so far as changes in the technique of predominantly physical labour are to be considered, it is recommended that the help of an expert physiologist be enlisted. On the basis of observations made, one should then examine *to what extent* the course of technological development, taking place under the pressure of private industrial economy of cost, is at the same time moving towards physiological economy of effort (saving on 'energy loss', i.e. on the physical output of the muscular system not realised in the form of work). It is established, for instance, that 'learning' to execute particular tasks is always essentially an 'automation' of voluntary impulses that were originally consciously articulated; and likewise, that this means a physiological saving of energy in the muscular or nervous system. However, it remains to be discovered how far, in individual cases, this principle holds in the particular industry. Furthermore, it is also established that the acquisition of a 'working rhythm' renders a similar service, in part directly, in part as a means of mechanisation. In the individual case it could well be worth the trouble of finding out the position with regard to rhythm-acquisition under the influence of machines; in this it should be borne in mind that, according to experimental investigations already carried out, these effects seem to vary according to whether they conform to the rhythm which is most efficient for the individual's psychophysical equipment, or are forced upon it from outside against its resistance. Essentially more complex problems, only to be tackled with the help of physiologists, would on the other hand be touched on, for example, with questions like how far in fact (as has been maintained), (1) the elimination of muscular effort and (2) continued working at machines go hand in hand with (1) the elimination of the use of the larger muscles in favour of the smallest ones possible, and (2) the growing restriction of the co-operation of muscles not directly required. Finally, there is the question (3) to what extent the increase of machine *speed*, and with it the increase in working intensity, has run, and is still running, parallel with the contended (and, in theory at least, probably also experimentally demonstrable) exploitation of the sum-total of stimulus-effects, in such a way that, for this reason, a saving of energy in the *physiological* sense of the word results in effect. Many of the crucial physiological assumptions here are disputed among the experts themselves. Nevertheless, the analysis of the technical evolution of vital industries, from these and related points of view, could produce valuable results, but only if it is carried out under the supervision of experts. It would therefore be very welcome if physiologists, or doctors thoroughly conversant with physiology, would participate as colleagues in the work of this survey. In any case it could be the business of the physiological expert alone to judge, according to the state of physiological knowledge, how far one would be on firm ground *today* in carrying out such investigations, and to what concrete points attention should be paid in so doing. One must never lose sight of the fact, however—in the face of the sometimes almost irresistible temptation for the individual scientific disciplines to try to trace sociological phenomena purely from the point of view of their own subject, e.g. to interpret industrial evolution entirely as a function of individual laws of economy of physiological energy—that the aim of industry as such is not economy of *energy* but economy of cost, and that the possible ways of achieving it *by no means* always coincide with evolution towards the *physiologically* rational; that rather, for a wide variety of reasons, the development towards the *economic* optimum of return on capital may deviate from the *physiological* optimum of return on *effort*. In such cases, however, where technological development does, in fact, show a persistent and unambiguous characteristic process of transformation in the demands on the workers (how frequently this may be the case is by no means established *a priori*) the task is to ask, firstly, what part, in these actual cases, the individual economic trends arising from the interests of economic viability (saving on wages, economic use of raw materials and machines, increase in turnover rate, standardisation, etc.) play in this physiological development, and *only then* what parts of the muscular or nervous systems are selected for use, which others rejected, and what consequences this has, has had, or may yet have, for the physiological condition. It is in no case sufficient merely to point out that technical development may have corresponded to particular postulates of the economy of physiological effort.

In the nature of things it would be far more important still to this survey (to find out what basic mental conditions and consequences, if any, the evolution of the workings of modern industry has had and still has), if adequately explained, acknowledged and accurate findings of the discipline of experimental psychology could be applied to this end. Unfortunately, at the moment, this is so only to a limited degree. The very far-reaching investigations of that discipline into the problem of labour have been orientated, in so far as they have been influenced at all by current problems, chiefly towards the intellectual purity of the school. On the one hand it has become clear that, in contrast to many hopes which were cherished at the outset, there is, at least at present (perhaps permanently, in the view of many researchers) no kind of mass method which is accurate and at the same time suitable for *mass* investigations of a type which could yield perfect results concerning the course of the curves of individual practice and fatigue differences in this respect, and their limitation by qualities of temperament and character. Neither the system of so-called 'mental tests', practised particularly in France and America, nor attempts to measure the mental after-effects of work with aesthesiometers and similar instruments, are considered by the circle of authoritative German experts to be a sufficiently sure means of establishing individual differences. Rather, such investigations always demand continual experiments, often for weeks on end, with one individual, under carefully prepared and maintained conditions. For this reason those investigations have hitherto been inherently incapable of dealing with, in particular, the mental and psychophysical conditions of factory work. Because of their mainly doctrinal orientation, but also for reasons which lie in the principles of their methodology and the nature of their instruments, they are concerned predominantly with the investigation of feats of memory and processes of association; secondarily—and the results of *these* investigations would naturally come up most prominently for consideration—with the influence of fatigue and habit in the case of 'intellectual' work. The concept 'intellectual' here embraces a fairly wide area, inasmuch as it includes highly typical, often purely mechanical performances of the psychophysical equipment (learning of meaningless syllables, etc.). In investigating the efficiency of industrial workers, the contrast 'physical work—intellectual work' would be largely or totally irrelevant, if one were to understand 'intellectual' in its strictest sense of exclusively *combinatory* activity. Indeed the opportunity for such activity occurs, for machine workers at least, only exceptionally and more coincidentally, and then mostly only on a small scale. On the other hand, any less rigorous interpretation of the concept of 'intellectual' work admits broad areas of industrial labour. And above all, the *differences* in the type of performance which industry demands of its labour force are, when measured by the contrast 'intellectual-physical', very great, greater at any rate than the contrast between the most 'intellectually' active sector of the working class and their superiors in the social scale. Indeed, the concept 'in-

E

tellectual' has here been totally omitted and is useless for any classification. The question is rather this: to what extent and in what direction do particular types of operation make demands on the *central* nervous system, and what type of reaction by this forms the basis of the operation concerned? It has been said, for example, not entirely incorrectly, that the activity of a worker operating a cylinder-borer, in the preparation of the material for the machine, resembles *in essence*—that is to say, in the functions which are required of the psychophysical system—that of a surgeon during an operation. The qualification of a female worker, for instance, acquainted with the operation of mechanical looms, finally depends by no means on chiefly 'physical' qualities, but essentially on whether she possesses the 'presence of mind' and 'perspective' to control such a large number of looms *simultaneously*—so that the use of *this* type of machine, and at the same time the employment of the worker herself, becomes *economic* for the employer.

There is, strictly speaking, no such thing as *exclusively* 'physical' work, i.e. work which makes demands only on certain muscles and the appropriate innervation mechanism. To be sure, however, in the case of a worker occupied with the excavation of earth, certain muscles and their attendant innervation mechanism are called into action, exhausted and exercised, in preference to all others, while those functions of the psychophysical equipment which we associate primarily with 'intellectual' work (speed of association, ability to concentrate the attention, etc.) play relatively little part, so little that 'fatigue' through work and 'habit-formation' due to work impinge less upon them. If therefore, in view of the fluidity of the border between the individual kinds of work, one wishes to make general distinctions at all, one can only ask what faculties and functions of the worker's psychophysical equipment are the objects of preferential selection for a particular job, and hence of *fatigue* on the one hand, *practice* on the other.

This, then, would be the crucial viewpoint, for the purposes of this survey, for a classification of the workers as well. It appears certain that, in many industries, technical evolution is moving towards an increasing demand on nervous functions, especially those of concentration and similar brainwork, that is, towards work which is distinguished from that of the 'intellectual' (in the conventional sense of the word) working classes essentially by the uniformity of its content and the absence of the values we habitually associate with the ends of 'intellectual' work. How far this is so, and what consequences, if any, it has in psychophysical, ethical and 'human' terms, disputed as these questions are, perhaps only the survey itself can tell us. To this end, colleagues are strongly recommended, in so far as they are not trained neurologists themselves, to get in touch with experienced doctors who are completely *au fait* with neuropathology, in order to discover the immediate nervous effect of factory work and—which in many views at least is equally important as an ethological force—of the attendant circumstances of that work (e.g. of machine noise), that is, the kind of energy consumption which is determined by them: with the reservation, of course, that *this* survey, whose concern is to establish *developmental* trends, is not thereby pushed into the mainstream of practically pure sociological discussions.[1] A systematic inquiry among general practitioners into the tendency to worker neuroses within the individual categories of industry and workers would be well worth considering. Similarly, the co-operation of people with experience in these spheres would be especially welcome for the present survey.

The individual results brought to light by the work of *experimental* psychology on the course of processes of fatigue and practice, important as they are in themselves, may perhaps not be of great *direct* benefit to the special aims of this survey, for the reasons mentioned above. Nevertheless, it is possible that an acquaintance with some of the simplest *concepts* customarily used in more recent investigations of this type could be of use, however contested the content of many of them unfortunately still is at present. However, concepts like that of 'exhaustibility' (measured in terms of the pace and extent of the progress of fatigue), 'recuperability' (in terms of the rate of recovery of efficiency after exhaustion has taken place), 'capacity for habit-formation' (in terms of increase in output as work progresses), 'habit stability' (in terms of the degree of 'extinction' occurring after breaks and interruptions in the work), 'capacity for stimulation' (in terms of the degree to which the 'psychomotor' influence of the very action of working increases output), 'capacity for concentration' and

[1] Upon this side of the question cf. e.g. the essay of Dr G. Heilig, 'Factory Work and Nerve Damage', in *Wochenschrift für soziale Medizin* (1908, No. 31 ff.) and the work of Dr W. Hellpach and others quoted therein.

'distractability' (in terms of the presence or absence, and, in the former case, the extent of a decline in output due to unaccustomed 'milieu' or 'disturbances'), 'facility of adaptation' (to an unaccustomed environment, disturbances, and, theoretically the most important, to the scheme of work)—these and similar concepts are sufficiently unambiguous in content, represent measurable values, are of proven utility, and may very probably afford the researcher a synopsis of certain simple components of personal work qualification and if necessary a handy terminology. For they can be used even where the degree to which the components they stand for influence output is not arithmetically certain.

Furthermore, issues concerning, for example, the relationships between fatigue and change of work, the subjective and objective consequences of being 'focused' on a particular job, the way in which, in the learning of complicated tasks and schemes of work, adaptation of their individual psychophysical elements takes place, the differences of the sensory and motor bases of reaction in their consequences for the quantity and quality of output, and on the other hand, how they are determined by differences in the psychophysical basis of 'personality'—these and similar issues within the specialist field of psychology, however little of ultimate certainty they may have furnished up to now on many points, would in themselves be well able to widen perspectives on a series of general problems, which extend into the extremely complex questions of the factors of industrial efficiency and the effects of technical evolution, especially of the 'breakdown' of work and similar processes. In particular, it would be highly important if any precise psychophysical data could be found relating to the question of *change of work* in its effects and presuppositions. Naturally one should not, in the process, lose sight of the idea that in the present survey this problem, too, is to be attacked wholly from the standpoint of economic viability. This point of view is mostly opposed to the changing of work, since on the whole this is, of course, a process which has a detrimental influence, often to a highly incisive degree, on the uninterrupted use of plant. On the other hand, however, where there is, for example, extensive specialisation, it may provide an opportunity for the individual production-line worker, where necessary, to acquaint himself personally with the consequences of his errors by working on the following stage of the production process. At all events, in every case where job-changing takes place, one should ask first what has been the experience of factory managers in individual industries and in individual types of employment with change of job within the factory, in its effect on output? Furthermore, what differences are observed in aptitude according to the type of work done by the worker immediately before placement in his present job, or earlier, or even in his youth? These differences are often very considerable and also arithmetically ascertainable (see below). In addition, however, the experience and the subjective attitude of the workers themselves would come into consideration. The latter is, of course, determined to a very great extent by rational causes: differences in wages, ease of work, etc. Where these causes are plainly decisive, it is naturally not a matter of taking a position with regard to the question of whether, purely in itself, uniformity or change of work is preferred, and whether, and how, this could be determined by physiological or psychological influences.

Even the attitude of the workers to change of job as such—i.e. in cases where the different types of work display no significant differences in amenity or financial reward—is nevertheless determined to a large extent by rational economic factors. Wherever it persistently impairs output within a factory, as a result of 'loss of habit' and the need to accustom oneself to a new job, it depresses earnings (when wages are for piece-work). In industries with diverse production (low standardisation), in times of depression when individual orders are smaller and therefore multiplicity of production (calculated against a unit of time) increases, the crisis falls, in the form of more frequent change in the mode of employment, on the earning potential of the labour force. Naturally, one cannot speak of a physiological or psychological basis for their attitude to these processes in these cases either; nor when one observes that older married workers prefer the regular wages of a continuous job, even if it is monotonous, while younger single men (in the interest of furthering their skill and with it the market value of their labour) prefer change. Yet besides these and many similar cases, whose significance should be thoroughly studied, in which considerations of financial objectives determine the behaviour of the workers, there are numerous others in which their behaviour does not appear to be dictated unequivocally by such considerations, and seems sometimes even to run counter to these motives. It seems plausible, and has on occasion been observed, that a change of job purely as such, i.e. in cases where financial opportunities and the amenity or unpleasantness of the work are not the deciding factors, is felt by them to be desirable. Yet it is equally certain that other cases are attested where it was not wanted, not even when the workers were given full guarantees that it could in no way entail financial disadvantage for them; that not merely coincidental circumstances or general inner adherence to tradition were at work here seems probable since sometimes that reluctance occurred even in workers who readily, indeed by preference even, changed firm and place of employment, as long as they could only move out into another job of the same type. Whether the concept of being 'accustomed' and 'attuned' to a concrete performance, which is apparently measurable even in terms of experimental psychology in its significance for the work curve, would be useful as an explanation here, cannot be decided *a priori*.

In these and many similar cases, it always seems possible that no purely psychophysical considerations would permit an unequivocal answer, as the other motives involved are far too complex. This situation will recur repeatedly. On the whole, almost wherever the researcher has cause to depict differences in the general 'spiritual' qualities of the workers, according to their type of employment and background, i.e. differences of their 'character', 'temperament', and their 'intellectual' and 'moral' state—things which, without a shadow of doubt, have often an important, sometimes a decisive, influence on their suitability for the individual types of industrial work—he will still, in the present state of psychological work, fairly frequently have to rely on his own efforts. Admittedly the old 'four humours' are today replaced most often by the four possible combinations of (1) intensity and (2) duration of the respective 'emotional state'. However, the qualitative content present in the old concepts is thus lost. Attempts, in 'differential psychological', 'characterological', 'ethological', or specifically 'psychological' terms (or by whatever other names they are known), to replace this last by a different classification of the 'humours', and to classify completely those numerous and from a psychological standpoint highly complex, qualitative differences of mental condition we term 'character', have so far met with no success—because of easily understandable, general methodological difficulties which lie in the task itself. There is at present no generally acknowledged classification of differences of this kind, in particular none which would be suitable, as it stands, to serve as a basis for the purposes of the present survey. Moreover, the psychological distinctions with which psychiatry is working today are, for reasons arising out of the peculiar nature of this discipline, in part too simple, in part, conversely, too specific. Therefore the researcher can only be counselled to observe, accurately and as far as possible in concrete terms, the form of expression of traits of character in so far as they occur truly unambiguously, that is to say the differences in the reactions of individuals which can be observed in their external behaviour, in which he believes he recognises such traits, and to describe them in everyday language in as simple and generally comprehensible a manner as possible.

In general, however, in the interest of the aim of this survey, colleagues should, from the outset, be urgently warned of one thing: in case they have occasion, through reading or stimulation by an expert, trained physiologist, psychologist, biologist or anthropologist, to become conversant with the general theoretical debates of those disciplines, *not* to (1) 'lose' themselves in these problems, interesting as they must appear to all, and moreover (2) under no circumstances to 'align' themselves with any of the conflicting general theories of a psychological, biological or anthropological nature. Not that those very general scientific problems could not ultimately affect even the inquiries with which this survey is concerned. Nor that the facts which these our inquiries will (if successful) bring to light could not possibly be of interest for those general theories as well. Both are possible. But plainly there could be nothing more detrimental to the objectivity of the examination of *facts*, which is the basic prerequisite for the success of this survey, and above all, its principal objective, than that the determination of those facts should be undertaken from the outset from the point of view of the verification of the validity or the fallaciousness of one of those general scientific hypotheses. If it sometimes leads to errors when scientific experts undertake such experiments without accurate knowledge of economic problems, then, were the same to be done by non-experts, owing to the then inevitable dilettantism the interests of science would scarcely be furthered, but the aims of this survey, especially owing to the ever-present temptation to construct from a single hypothetical viewpoint, would be seriously impaired. For, even where the work is carried on with great conscientiousness, the danger is always there that facts which will not fit that hypothetical interpretation may be ignored, or at any rate not established and recorded with the desirable zeal and in the desirable amplitude. Therefore it cannot be too strongly urged that (1) where the support of scientific knowledge is desirable, expert help should always be enlisted, (2) the results of specialist scientific work should *only* be used when it is a matter of connections between acknowledged facts resting on a firm basis of observation, and (3) general scientific theories and terminologies should only be employed where, for once in a way, this really would be of directly tangible advantage to the aim of this survey, *and* it is backed up by general acceptance among experts.

These principles hold especially where the inquiry, whenever it employs the concept of 'natural mechanisms' (this will be scarcely avoidable) enters the realm of questions of *biological inheritance*. If the reasons for differing aptitudes are to be investigated at all, it can hardly avoid reference to them. Neither should it avoid such reference, inasmuch as one plainly *must*, in some study of the investigation, put to oneself the question of how far it is possible to trace back obtaining differences of this kind to inherited differences of stock. However, the question is how far the investigation can be trained upon the solution of *these* problems with the means of *this* survey. In theory no one should doubt the possibility, the probability even, that 'racial differences' might be significant for aptitude for industrial labour, as has at present emerged most clearly in the well-known results of the employment of Negroes in the textile industry of North America, but as also appears to be manifest, for example, in Spain and Belgium. Very many factory managers will confirm that experience varies with the individual German 'tribes' as regards their utility. Bavarian and north-west German iron-workers, Silesian and Westphalian weavers, Rhenish-Belgian and North German sheet-metal workers, all enjoy widely differing reputations, and the list will expand prodigiously in the hands of the researchers, if they turn their attentions to it at all. That the *inherited* differences of importance for working aptitude are to be found chiefly in the field of the nervous and mental make-up, in the mode of reaction, as it differs in pace, steadiness and reliability, and in the differences of 'temperament' partially due to the latter, which for

their part influence the capacity for discipline which is essential
for large-scale industry, should likewise not be disputed in theory.
Now the task is, firstly, to winnow critically and present the chaos
of unverifiable assertions on these points which doubtless the
researcher will meet with, and then, as far as is at all possible, to
examine further how far in the individual case the existence of
'inherited' differences, in the biological sense, can be substan-
tiated—and not merely differences of tradition, which are certainly
very often, if not most frequently, encountered: the woolly
conventional concept of the 'folk character' as the 'source' of
particular qualities of the working class inextricably unites these
two vastly different conceptions. There is notoriously scarcely an
inquiry as hard to answer unequivocally and exhaustively in almost
every particular—indeed there is one tenable point of view from
which it is apparently never answerable unequivocally, in the
last analysis, and in any case the struggle of conflicting biological
'theories' rages over the interpretation even of relatively certain
facts. For that very reason this mistake must in any case be
avoided, besides those mentioned above—that of thinking that,
from the data collected *here*, which at best can only embrace a
few generations, *any* inferences can be drawn in support of one
or other of those theories, such as Darwinism, in its orthodox or
Weismann's interpretation, 'neo-Lamarckism', the Hering-Semon
theory, etc., and that it is one's job, or even merely desirable, in
the processing of the data, to turn the same to account in this
direction. This is, of course, not the case. Suppose, for example,
that the observation which has been made from time to time were
confirmed, that the populations of areas which have been centres
of industry (e.g. cottage industry) for long periods of time show,
in general, not merely a particularly strong inclination towards
industrial work, but also—and this must be carefully distinguished
from the former—they are better qualified than other populations
for industrial work, that is to say more adaptable, and that even
for work of a different type from the kind traditionally handed
down: then, in the event of failure of all attempts to trace this fact
back to influences of tradition, education, imitation, etc., so that
the 'inheritance' of that qualification becomes likely, it could still
be interpreted in a great variety of ways, both as the consequence
of original embryonic mechanism bred by 'selection', and as the
result of constant practice, whose consequences for the evolution

of physical equipment have been inherited, and as the consequence of 'hereditary mechanisms', and perhaps in many other ways as well. However, only biological experts could decide which way would be the easiest, and the data which our survey might possibly be able to offer would, beyond all doubt, seem to them totally inadequate for such a decision.

A consideration of the facts of the case 'from first principles' would doubtless bear in mind that (1) *every* act of human expression can be seen as a particular manner, determined by present circumstances, of the 'functioning' of inherited 'dispositions', which for their part were 'developed' in a particular way by past circumstances, and that (2) the question of whether, *in general*, inherited mechanisms or acquired qualities are the 'crucial mainspring' or of chief 'importance', is *a priori* misguided and therefore fruitless. It is misguided because the question of whether anything is 'important' or not as a causal motive depends on what it is supposed to be 'important' or 'unimportant' *for*; that is, from what special point of view is its significance being looked at in the individual case. The inquiries of this survey would never concern themselves—even if one should ever succeed in reaching such problems on *any* point—with the 'solution' of that general question, but always purely and simply with the question of whether those special qualities, which render economic the employment of the workers who possess them for the physical execution of particular tasks of specific character, may be founded in the individual cases chiefly on the influence of environment on the workers concerned, or not. Here, however, one would have to reckon, from the outset, with the possibility that this question might not admit of a different answer for each individual category of workers in each individual industry; one would also have to reckon with the indubitable fact that, owing to environment, the effects of differences of make-up can undergo different developments, and vice versa, to a considerable extent. Plainly the totally vague concept of 'milieu', which incorporates the most heterogeneous elements, would need breaking down in each individual case into the various types of conditions embraced by it. The degree of development or atrophy of existing inherited 'mechanisms' without doubt depends particularly strongly on the influence of youth. This is rendered probable by both general considerations and experimental observations, admittedly uncertain and few in number, which have been made to date, for instance concerning the connection between qualitative exactitude of motor performance and level of intellectual development, or that between fatigue, associative capabilities and social background. Such influences of youth are exerted, among other things, by type of nourishment and upbringing, degree of incentive, and opportunity for intellectual activity, and the richness of experience offered by the milieu of the youthful years. The wealth or poverty of material circumstances and the 'spiritual horizon' of the home, determined chiefly by the social class of the parents, school education and military service, the population and economic and cultural character of the home town, or town where youth was spent, and then early experiences at work, exert, in all probability, such a tenacious influence on the direction followed by development, and on the development or suppression of individual capabilities, that (as has been shown experimentally to be likely, e.g. for artistic talent) only gifts for particular activities that are very above-average seem to have the ability to make themselves felt to any recognisable extent in the face of the conditions, determined by the social and cultural class-structure, which held sway during the period of maximum plasticity. Those general 'dispositions' which may become important for working aptitude are also without doubt partially capable of being acquired, on the one hand being enhanced by 'training', on the other being inhibited or directly harmed by the way of life of the populace, both intra- and extra-uterine. The differences between country and town extraction (by 'town' is here meant places, however small, which manifest the business life peculiar to towns and its consequences) occasionally make themselves, on close inspection of the wage-cost accounts of industrial concerns, extremely clearly apparent (see below).

These considerations would make it appear methodologically advisable, when analysing differences of working aptitude, and their causes, not to take as one's starting point hypotheses of heredity, but, ever conscious that the 'ancestral estate' may play a part at any point, always to examine *first* the influences of social and cultural background, upbringing and tradition, and to proceed as far as humanly possible with this principle of explanation. In the example used earlier of the (apparent) specific qualification of old industrial communities for industrial work (N.B. by this is meant, in every case, even work of a different nature from that traditionally handed down) it could emerge, for instance, that different old industrial communities behave differently in this respect; that one shows a propensity for a relatively easy transition to other types of industrial work, while another does not (such as Silesia, as opposed to the Central German cottage-industry communities). In this case the suspicion fairly obviously arises that it is a matter of inherited differences. Nevertheless, in such cases one would first have to examine in detail the possible influences of tradition and the social and cultural 'environment', and take into account the possibility that not both aptitude and propensity for the transition to a profession would be lacking. In order to proceed as meticulously as possible one should ask to what extent the previous type of industrial occupation of the communities under comparative examination is related, physiologically and psychologically, to any industrial openings which may, for economic reasons, come into consideration as substitutes; or conversely, to what extent the 'habits' of the old occupation and being 'attuned' to the earlier type of work can have an 'inhibitive' effect vis-à-vis adaptation to requirements of a different nature. However, in the first instance the analysis would hardly be able to proceed this far, and perhaps have no cause to do so either. For *before* these difficult problems are broached it is necessary to have examined how far social stratification in general and economic structure, density of municipal centres, uniformity or multiplicity of production methods in general, traditional historical customs, and factors determined by the manner of upbringing, which affect those regions in which these processes of transformation are coming about, favour adherence to tradition or, conversely, a capacity for adaptation to innovations, and finally—as can likewise occur—how far a situation obtains whereby the old working community, as it migrates, is replaced by a constant influx of new ones, stemming from a different cultural milieu, and thus 'adherence to tradition' in the one case and change of occupation in the other only apparently represent mainfestations of the same masses of population. Only after consideration of such influences and their possible bearing, and in the event of these not furnishing a sufficient explanation, would one come on to those questions of psychophysical 'predisposition', and *lastly*, if necessary, to the influence of inherited characteristics.

This course seems the more advisable since, for the sphere of *mental* performances at least, it is apparently by no means so simple to formulate just *what*—in the relevant area for psycho-physical working aptitude—is always, or at least regularly, the object of hereditary transfer, according to data furnished by biology and psychiatry. If one wished to say, for instance, that not mental 'content' but just 'formal' attributes of the completion of mental processes, or that not spiritual 'activating mechanisms' but merely general 'capabilities', or that not 'actual' qualities of personal behaviour, but only more or less determined 'predispositions' to same, or that only the psychophysical 'equipment', but not the function it evolves in a person's lifetime, is inherited—then all these and similar contrasts are, by their nature, fluid within fairly wide limits. In any event they can only serve as a vigorous warning against attributing complex qualities and 'characteristics' of a community to 'heredity' without close inspection. At present there are no scientific aids to enable the inheritability of any qualities vital for industry to be precisely ascertained. No attempt has been made to undertake anthropological measurements or examinations of broad sections of the population, taking as a basis classification in terms of 'professions' or rather—since indeed (which could perhaps well be borne in mind) this alone is really decisive—in terms of technical performance, as expressed in the mode of employment in the production process, and it would be very hard to carry out on a large scale, most of all for private surveys. Only military courts could carry out surveys here, and only on recruits, i.e. workers, whose 'occupational career' is only just beginning. The same goes for the mass surveys of experimental psychology, quite apart from the fact that, as emphasised above, they are for the time being at any rate not developed for the purpose. As far as judgments concerning the working aptitude of broader masses and its causes are at issue, therefore, one can at present only be in a position to posit *direct* conditioning by heredity (in the biological sense of the word) with a degree of plausibility where physiological differences between individual categories of workers are absolutely obvious, or where ethnic differences go hand in hand with a clear differentiation, observable through generations, of the mode of employment, and with obvious differences of 'temperament' and 'character' which recur generation after generation, and which cannot be explained by the nature of the culture of the home town.

Furthermore, where a labour force is being analysed which is not principally derived from a few ethnically and culturally clearly discrete areas, but is very mixed, one will not be in a position to investigate the manner and degree of influence of home environment for all these different backgrounds. Yet even where conditions are particularly favourable, in the present survey the researcher will probably do well, in all cases where conspicuous and constantly recurring differences of working aptitude cannot with certainty be traced back *either* to reasons of economics or tradition arising from the workers' background *or* to manifestly inherited physical qualities—and these, unfortunately, will probably be the overall majority—simply to set out, and demonstrate in detail, the fact of the existence of those differences, but to make *no attempt* to construe the reasons for them of heredity, tradition, or other circumstances.

This the more so since a further circumstance enters the arena, making it extremely difficult to ascribe differences of working aptitude unequivocally to simple basic qualities founded on 'inherited mechanisms', wherever these differences are not of a purely physical, but also of a mental, nature. A glance at the work of experimental psychology shows how extraordinarily complex are the components of a work curve observed in the laboratory, and how difficult can be the interpretation of its course and ultimately the tracing of differences back to (for the present) 'basic' differences in the character of the subjects: and this is in experiments carried out under the strictest supervision and, above all, with the most assiduous co-operation of the persons being examined themselves (who, for the purposes of the examination, have also been subjected to a particular training and control of their behaviour). However, all the finer nuances of talents for particular actions which are thereby established—with greatly varying certainty—as ultimately decisive, will almost always be hidden in the reality of factory work by factors which have a greater or lesser coarsening effect, and which influence the height and path of the work curves. The effect of eating habits (which are in part connected with the domestic qualifications of the workers' wives), alcohol consumption, sometimes the effects of type of sexual life, but above all—as has already been mentioned and will be discussed later in greater detail—the degree of *financial interest* which links the worker and the level of his

earnings, and thus the measure of his output: these things influence the growth of potentiality in a labour force to such an
enormous extent that, where there are significant differences
between these cruder determinants of efficiency, there is frequently
no chance of detecting those differences in mental make-up which
are expressed far more subtly and indirectly. Differences in the
extent of specific 'predisposition', and therefore of any inherited
gifts, for a particular job, naturally only emerge really definitely
and distinctly at an *equal* degree of intensity of concentration.
Since there is no means of measuring with objective certainty this
purely subjective motive, because of its very nature, experimental
psychology starts in many cases from the principle that only when
several people achieve the same performance, provided that their
actual output is their absolute maximum potential output, can an
experiment on their greater or lesser predisposition (i.e. on any
inherited mechanisms as well) with regard to this performance
yield any reasonably certain information.

Such provisions are easily made in the laboratory, where the
persons under examination have a spurious interest in the success
of the experiment, and the latter only lasts quite a short time.
However, in the case of the continual work of a lifetime in the
factory, those workers who, by virtue of their optimum efficiency,
can achieve, and seek to achieve, a wage considerably in excess of
the normal measure, and who are therefore very often employed
as foremen—the so-called 'runners'—are usually compelled,
directly or indirectly, by the solidarity of their fellow-workers, to
'put the brake on', i.e. remain within the limits of average effort
which will permit the others to 'keep up', and which eliminates
the danger, always in the workers' minds, of increases in earnings
due to particularly high output possibly causing the employer to
reduce the piece-rate. That methodological principle of experimental psychology may lead us, in the present survey, to subject, if
possible, just such 'model workers' to a particularly thorough
examination of the factors determining their specific capabilities,
and in particular of their ethnic, social and cultural background,
but above all to look for results concerning differences of working
aptitude only where the system of remuneration and its administration carry a sufficient incentive to maximum effort. And in order to
ascertain the influence of the inherited psychophysical equipment
and the social and cultural tradition and environment of the

workers separately, in such a way as to get beyond general hypotheses which cannot be validated, it would need the careful examination of such cases as are as far as possible similar in respect of all those factors just mentioned whose effect is palpably more crude and direct, and in which the working effort is not held within the traditional limits by the system frequently still accepted of the (in reality) fixed 'price limit'. Thus, only in one section of the labour force of one division of major industry is there a chance, even by means of such close examination of performance, of obtaining an accurate picture of the extent of working aptitude.

In view of these many difficulties, the question could well be raised of why the 'scientific' side of the problems being tackled by this survey is being so thoroughly discussed at all at this point. This came about for diverse reasons. Firstly, it appears right in principle, in carrying out a survey like the present one, to give an account of the *existence* of such 'basic' questions to which, owing to the lack of the necessary data, no reliable answer can be given at present in the vast majority of cases, but which would *have* to be answered in order to achieve really definitive results. It is therefore both one's bounden duty to be clear about where the 'ideal' goal of the scientific analysis would lie, and also desirable that the probable gaps (in terms of that goal) in the knowledge that has been attained to date, and perhaps will be attainable in the foreseeable future, be made entirely apparent to the researcher himself and to his readers, both the fact of their existence and the reasons therefor. Furthermore, however, the Society is not turning with its appeal for co-operation only to researchers of purely economic training, but just as much to the representatives of scientific disciplines. If the time may still be far away when definitive answers can be given to questions like those touched upon above, nevertheless—as will be discussed in what follows—the way is completely open for making an initial beginning in tackling them also from the direction of those instruments of research which are at our command in our specialist field, and it is to be hoped that the present cleft between the tools of the two disciplines will slowly be resolved in common work.

III

THE METHODOLOGY OF THE SURVEY

From everything which has been said up to now, my respected colleagues will glean to what extent, in the present case, something *other* than a representation of the 'morphology' and the technical and business organisation of the individual industries is being aimed at in crucial points. This 'other' can perhaps be formulated thus: *the points to be examined are, on the one hand, the type of 'selection processes' carried out by large-scale industry, in accordance with its intrinsic needs, on the community whose careers are tied to it, and on the other hand, the manner of 'adaptation' of the 'physically' or 'intellectually' working personnel of large-scale industries to the living conditions presented to them.* In this way an approach will gradually be made to answering the question: what sort of people are produced by modern large-scale industry, by virtue of its inherent characteristics, and *what fate* does it prepare for them professionally and thus indirectly extra-professionally as well?

The purpose of the 'plan of work' is first and foremost to provide colleagues with a temporary aid to inform them about such points as will probably be of importance *in any event* for the purposes of this survey.

Included among the questions of the 'plan of work' are a considerable number which require answering, not for their own sake but because it would be impossible otherwise to proceed to the real tasks of the survey.

Thus, for example, research into the *length of the day's shift* and its significance is by no means, in view of the voluminous literature on this subject, an aim of the survey *in itself*. However, the length of shift naturally means, on the one hand, a very important part of the workers' careers; on the other hand, it is a significant symptom of the type of performance, and hence of the qualities, which the industry concerned requires of its workers, in particular of the degree of qualitative working intensity, or the reverse, which it demands. An industry with very prolonged shifts will not be able to expect high degrees of purely physical, muscular performance, nor high degrees of nervous performance either. On the other hand, where workers whose capacity for

135

intensive work, natural or induced by training, is small, for reasons of their innate or induced qualities, or qualities lacking due to heredity and upbringing—where these constitute the sole labour force available to an industry, that industry will attempt to remain viable by long shifts. It cannot be our task here to elucidate these well-known conclusions. However, the question of how in practice, from the point of view of economic *viability*, the problem of the relationship between shift length and performance has taken on its present form in *individual* industries, may indeed very well come into consideration for the purposes of this survey. A state of affairs came about, for instance, about fifty years ago in the mining industry, when the work was done very largely by hand and opportunities for making money were greatly on the increase, whereby the workers in fact achieved just as much in six hours of rationally calculated piece-work as they had previously done in ten at traditional rates of pay (admittedly with differing degrees of fatigue), and whereby enormous increases in production were achieved in four shifts. These opportunities do not exist in the same form for workers tied to a machine, and therefore it should be ascertained as far as accurate information is available, for *every* industry, how output and wage-costs are related to the technical conditions peculiar to each, according to the length of the working shift. But above all, the question which should be put here is, *to what extent* in individual cases is the length of shift a 'symptom' of certain *qualities* of the labour force? (That this is by no means always the case may be taken as an acknowledged fact.) Similarly, the length of *breaks* and the way in which they are apportioned are almost always determined by the effect they have on output—where there are any rational motives and not, as is probably the general rule, purely traditional ones. For breaks just as for length of shift, therefore, it should be ascertained as accurately as possible whether, and if so *what*, empirical results have been found in this sphere for the individual categories of workers, divided according to their geographical and social origin, upbringing and position in the production process. (This should, of course, be done when changes have recently been made in the length of shift or in the allocation of breaks.) How, for example, has 'working freshness' evolved at different times of day, what is the workers' attitude to the 'English' division of the working day, etc.—questions which, owing to the fact that these circumstances are determined most frequently by habit alone, will admittedly be, in very many cases, of only limited fruitfulness.

The inquiry into *wage structure* is destined to play a similar role. It may be taken that my respected colleagues are acquainted with current literature on this (for instance with Schlop-Bernhard's book). Incidentally, a comprehensive publication of the Society for the Wellbeing of the Working Classes, which they are strongly urged to read, and which examines this very point in great detail, primarily as it affects the iron and machine industry, is at present in preparation. If, then, an analysis of the wage system purely for its own sake does *not* feature in the plan of this survey, it goes without saying that my respected colleagues will have no choice but to acquaint themselves most thoroughly with this point, as it affects their sphere, before they do anything else. For on the one hand the influence of the remuneration system on output, and with it on the qualities—especially those of a physical nature— developed by the workers, is the most decisive imaginable. In an extraordinarily large number of cases where it was thought one was dealing with unchangeable qualities in a particular labour force, were they inbred or determined by tradition and environment, in particular with mentally or physically determined limits of their working *capability* which were laid down once and for all, changes in the remuneration system have shown, after sufficient time has elapsed for their effects to become apparent, that in fact the manner of their *interest* in the quantity or quality of their work was the decisive factor. In addition there are the far-reaching consequences which the differences in the remuneration systems entail for the degree of incentive for the individual classes of workers in a factory, in their relationship to one another, to works managers, foremen, comrades engaged in the same piece-work, and others. The whole internal structure of the working process and the formation of 'social' groups into which the working class falls, the predominantly monarchic, authoritarian, or voluntaristic nature of the division of labour and of discipline within these groups (facts which are of major importance for the answering of many of the questions of the 'plan of work') are intimately connected with the system of remuneration.

The general types involved here are known from literature, but it is of course essential that these be determined for each individual case before the 'occupational psychology' of an actual labour force can be explored. Where various industries are in competition in the same labour market, but also where different types of work are executed by categories of workers of equal social standing within the same factory, the 'wages policy' is one of the most important of the firm's problems, and should be studied as thoroughly as possible, as far as any precise information is obtainable on the subject. On the other hand, however, the nature of the remuneration system in use, at least where it is *not* simply handed down by tradition but is rationally arranged for optimum working effort, is one of the most important symptoms, very often a direct indication, of which *qualities* of its labour force the industry concerned must stress decisively, and which it can endeavour to inculcate by means of direct or indirect bonuses to its individual workers or groups. Indeed, both the system of remuneration and the rate of pay are frequently by no means rationally controlled, but rather by traditions which are sometimes totally irrational. Therefore it will in every case be necessary, not only to establish the existence of a particular system of remuneration, but also how far tradition, and how far rational considerations, determined it, and, in the latter case, how far it can provoke effort or 'putting the brake on', and also above all whether any changes have been made recently, as a result of what findings, for what purposes, and with what results. Here it should obviously be established as carefully as possible whether, contemporaneously with the changing of the remuneration system or—as may be equally characteristic—in the *wake* of this change, a sudden or gradual change in the personnel of the labour force has taken place, and for what reasons. Perhaps any total or partial 'failure' of the introduction of a new system of remuneration will be particularly instructive for the researcher here, within the framework of this survey. For however far-reaching the consequences of the systems of remuneration may be, their effect is nevertheless not all-powerful. Even where the circumstances are otherwise absolutely identical, by no means every new system of remuneration achieves the same results with every labour force. Of especial interest to the inquiry of this survey are just such limitations of the effect of the incentive to work lying in the remuneration system, as well as any differences there may be in the reactions of workers of *different* ethnic, geographical, cultural, social or religious background to the *same* systems of remuneration.

It follows from this that the question of what form is taken by *wage accounting*, the *calculation of wage costs*, and the mathematical checking of the workers' 'effective power', by reason of the remuneration system, is of immediate practical interest for the *methodology* of this survey. Where it is a question of securing reasonably accurate figures for personal differences in efficiency, determined by ethnic, social, and cultural background, the researcher will draw on this source in the first instance, wherever it is accessible to him. Now, whether wage accounting in an industrial firm promises results for the purposes of this survey depends primarily on whether it is arranged so as to make the output of each *individual* worker directly or indirectly open to calculation and constant checking, and whether, at the same time its *application*, in view of 'maximum potential', is appropriate for favouring *optimum* output. Then it would depend on how far accounting relating to wage-*costs* (especially for purposes of retrospective calculation) exists, establishing in every case the piece-rate, calculated hours and actual output, based on the individual pay chits made out for the individual job, or on similar detailed documents. This is most often necessary in firms which work with systems of payment by individual bonuses. However, many firms using a simple piece-work system have also, in their own interest, prepared such statistics, embracing every single worker. And they are trying accurately to establish, further, not only wage costs, but also the effective output of every single worker, and the most diverse equipment exists for checking the individual workers' exploitation of the machines. Where book-keeping is sufficiently precise, the variation in output from day to day can be ascertained from the relevant entries—in theory, even hourly checking would be possible in the case of many such pieces of apparatus (for example, shuttle-stroke counters in a textile mill). Only where the economic viability of the employment of each individual worker is established in such a way, *exactly* corresponding to the viability of implementing individual types of machine, coal, and raw materials—and this is possible and appropriate only in certain sections of industry (it remains to be established in which) for a wide variety of reasons—will the researcher be able to reap the maximum possible result in exactitude of data. Where systems of group piece-work obtain, one should investigate in every single case what important information, if any, for the purposes of this survey, according to the manner of formation of the groups and the calculation of wages, can be derived from wage accountancy. It is by no means because the mere existence of the group remuneration system made it impossible to procure suitable information. Where each individual worker receives his share of the group earnings in the form of an assessed 'hourly rate', varying according to the degree of efficiency he has developed, which then forms the basis for the division of earnings within his group, it is admittedly only 'relatively' accurate and time-consuming, but by no means impossible, to obtain a *mathematical* basis for the determination of individual efficiency. In any event, wherever the researcher can gain insight into information of this kind, it is of first-class value for the purposes of this survey and should in every case be thoroughly checked from all relevant points of view.

Now presumably each of my respected colleagues will devise his own method of turning to good account the information yielded by wage accountancy, and in so doing he will have to weigh and test how far the inquiry he has chosen promises to be fruitful for the purposes of the survey. Only let it be noted that it would probably depend in any case, among other things, on the following points of inquiry: (1) any differences of remuneration methods determined by differences of background and their reasons; (2) differences in the level and consistency of output among workers of various backgrounds at static piece-rates, on the one hand; differences in the effect of changes in the latter (introduction of new remuneration systems, especially piece-work systems, increase of piece-rate in the event of insufficient earnings or—far more commonly—reduction due to high earnings) on the other; furthermore (3) differences in the rate of increase in the workers' efficiency, measured by the development of their piece-wages (where these cannot be established from the books, by the frequency and degree of reduction of the piece-rate or, in the case of group piece-work, of the change in the assessed hourly rate, as a substitute), (4) comparison of the path of the earnings curves of workers of different background and identical type of occupation on the one hand, identical background and different type of occupation on the other, paying particular attention to (*a*) ascertainment of the time elapsing until *peak* earning power is reached, and then (*b*) the period during which the worker maintains that peak level, noting the age at which the latter was reached and when it began to decline, and also those changes in the mode of payment and occupation which determine the loss of efficiency with increasing age. All this *may* afford clues towards answering the question of how quickly maximum efficiency is reached by the workers, and for how long it is maintained (and thus answer the crucial questions of this survey), (1) according to the nature of the job and (2) according to the geographical, ethnic, social and cultural background and character of the workers.

Only experience will tell *how far* wage accounts and wage-cost calculations will prove to be suitable documentation for such reckonings in the individual industries. Furthermore, understandably, it is by no means to be taken for granted that any industrial firm one cares to choose will show itself ready to let an unknown third party inspect its wage accounts. However, on the other side, there is no reason to suppose that industry in general should think that the use for the purposes of this survey of the statistics they have prepared for their own private ends should give cause for misgivings. It goes without saying that neither in this special case, nor under normal circumstances, are the directors to be required to reveal any trade secrets, nor (extremely desirable though it would be *per se* to have such information) their cost-price figures. The researcher will, in very many cases, run up against the reservation that the inspection of wage-*cost* figures might in fact afford insight into actual cost-price calculations, thus endangering important trade secrets. However, if there is goodwill on both sides, it is possible in *all* cases, to arrange the excerpts and, even more, any figures ultimately to be published, and to restrict them firmly to such data, so that there is not the slightest possibility of a competitor working out a useful figure for the effective cost price of *one* particular quality of goods. For it is obvious that the researcher may not cull extracts from, or publish any part of, the contents of order chits made out for purposes of subsequent calculation, and also that he has not the slightest interests in being allowed to do so; and for the most important matters (such as extracts from wage accounts and effective power calculations) it would be sufficient to establish *relative* figures. It would not even be necessary to publish the absolute level of wage earnings and piece-rate tables (as is nevertheless carried out voluntarily by major industries on a very considerable scale, in part by way of exchange between competitors). In every case it would be very welcome indeed if as large a number of colleagues as possible could gain the personal confidence of directors of major concerns to such an extent that such information would be entrusted to them. It is possible that many boards of directors would prefer to have the requisite extracts and calculations carried out by the firm's own employees. However, colleagues cannot be urgently enough enjoined to sit down at the wage books *themselves*, wherever possible, to carry out at least some of the largely mechanical work of making extracts. In my personal experience a few dozen pads of pay chits or effective power tables carefully gone through and worked out by the researcher himself, and discussed in every detail with the director or his representative, are far more satisfactory than the most comprehensive set of statistics and the sight of a row of figures, fine though they might be, compiled for him by someone else. He will have formed a far more accurate opinion of coefficients of output, especially to what extent power over the very different and often complicated incentives contained in the form of remuneration is influenced by materials, machines, change in type of occupation, interruption of work, 'braking' on the part of the worker or (in times of sales stagnation) on the part of the factory (by means of the practice, so common nowadays in this event, of fixing a maximum output quota), and finally of the degree and direction in which, after all these circumstances have been taken into account, the individual personality of the worker actually determines the path of his earnings curve. Nevertheless, in many cases the researcher, if he can obtain any information at all, will only be able to get what has been selected by the factory itself; and *after* he has formed a fairly certain impression, from a series of his own calculations, of the way in which the figures came into being, it is naturally subject to no methodological scruples whatsoever if he gratefully accepts the help of the firm's officials, if this is to be had for the production of such extracts. In the quiet season of the firms concerned, such assistance, indeed, could yield a small supplement to their accountants' earnings and perhaps also, in its results, information of interest to the firm's director. The current period of depression would be particularly favourable for plying managerial boards with such questions—even if it is highly improbable that the example of a printing works which, in a similar period, once kept a few machines running for the benefit of a certain psychophysical experiment, will be followed in large-scale industry.

For all this, in not a few cases, whether because suitable figures do not exist, or because they can be made only partially available or not at all, the researcher will be constrained to draw on less exact sources for the examination of workers' efficiency in its development and differences. In every case he should find out first *in what way the selection of the efficient* is carried out, in detail, within the industry or class of workers concerned. That a constant process of selection of workers it is profitable to employ should take place by some means or other is a basic essential to the existence of every single industry under the control of capitalism; and the same can be said of all the other factors of production from the point of view of economic viability, irrespective of what remuneration system or what other economic bases of working conditions they may possess. In every case the question is simply, how does the selection take place? Where the factory trains apprentices, it may begin during training, in gross cases of inefficiency. Where there is piece-work, workers are dismissed if, after a suitable period of training, they show themselves to be manifestly incapable of attaining the assessed earnings which are the basis of the calculation of the piece-rate (it is well-known that such a figure lies behind the fixing of *every* piece-rate), and thus of utilising their machines to the calculated average. It is well known that in England the trade union may play the same role, inasmuch as it makes the ability to attain certain minimum earnings at piece-rates a condition of admission to membership—and that frequently means a condition of being allowed to work at all. In every case it would be worth the trouble of investigating the extent to which German workers' organisations exercise a similar 'selection' of their members in other ways, and, indirectly, in the same way. Wherever this may be the case, a comparison of the character and background of the organised workers with that of the 'non-organised' workers would naturally be of significance for the survey. In other cases it is the gang and its foreman, whether he be freely elected or appointed, which decides its own composition within certain limits and thus practises the selection of men efficient at a particular task. The management is compelled to demote inefficient members by reducing their hourly rate (which constitutes the divisor for the distribution of earnings) and ultimately to dismiss them. The task of obtaining really reliable and above all representative information about the type and trend of this selection is, of course, always a rather difficult one; but the attempt should invariably be made. The observations and evidence of master craftsmen, works managers and inspectors concerning the qualities of the workers will usually form the basis of the allocation of work to the individual workers and, if necessary, of the composition of gangs. It will depend on the state of affairs in individual industries and factories, and also on the skill of my respected colleagues, as to how far it is possible to make the often very great wealth of experience, uniquely acquired by these officials of industry in the course of their work—concerning differences in efficiency and factors affecting them—directly or indirectly serviceable for the purposes of this survey. How far this would be possible by means of a personal, systematic and thorough questioning of these employees about how that selection is carried out (which would of course always be the most worthwhile method) naturally depends in the first instance on the express agreement of the employers. The success of the survey, then, relies very heavily on the employers' being sufficiently impartial and far-sighted to feel firmly convinced that no information is being 'elicited' here to whose publication they could not agree, and furthermore, on the researcher's personality inspiring them with confidence in his impartiality, and finally, on their realising that the goal is a really valuable one scientifically. Where one meets with resolute, insurmountable mistrust, the survey has no prospect of success. Incidentally, the researcher, for his part, will always have to record everything which he did not see for himself, nor was able to authenticate by inspecting wage accounts or by some other means, with the express observation that this was information supplied to him and not ascertained by himself.

What a trustworthy researcher will obtain without difficulty from every not excessively anxious firm is permission to examine and extract information from the *factory roll* (workers' book). Every factory must be in possession of the facts shown on health cards, namely, date of birth, place of birth, and in addition (which can be important as indicating distance from place of work) the current address of its workers, as their minimum credentials. Of great importance for the survey is the very fact

that, in this way, the workers' background and division by age
and sex can be ascertained, set alongside their current mode of
employment (which can probably be found out without difficulty
as well), and if necessary (since almost all firms keep such books)
traced back historically in relation to frequency of change of firm;
furthermore, when a substantial number of firms in different
industries in the same region, or in the same industry in different
regions, has been investigated, differences of age classification and
background can be worked out. The factory rolls usually contain,
over and above this, information concerning marital status,
religion (often), and occasionally the type of domicile (rented
property or own cottage); moreover, the factory itself can be
investigated. In this way, one can always determine the characteristic contrast between industries with local working stock
(often found alongside a group of 'outsiders', very unsettled
precisely because of this close-knit local group, which decreases
the *average* length of stay with the firm) and those with free
recruitment of workers, as well as their evolution in one direction
or another, and shed light on their causes and effects by judicious
inquiries. In general, one should always *begin* by sifting through
this information which is sometimes more instructive than the
researcher—and frequently the firm's director—at first expects.

The *questioning of the workers* should now be combined with
the information gleaned from the employers or their staff. In
this matter considerable difficulties of theory and method are
likely to arise, although these will probably not lie in the gleaning
of information from the workers in itself. The workers' organisations have shown, in their own publications as well as in those of
various official and private surveys from time to time, not only
that they are willing to co-operate whenever they are convinced of
the scientific value of a survey, but that their members are often
very well versed in the art of answering questionnaires in the
correct manner for statistical purposes, which is by no means
always easy. The difficulty is more likely to lie in gaining information from the workers which could be *integrated* with that collected
from the employers. The *ideal* in this respect, of course, would
be the thorough study of as large a number of *firms* as possible,
analysing the data given by their rolls and wage accounts, examining the evidence of the employers and their officials on the one
hand, and on the other carrying out a fully comprehensive

questioning of the entire labour force of the *same* firms, with regard to their geographical, ethnic, social and cultural background, occupational career, position, and all the other objective and subjective facts to be considered by the survey. Wherever this can be achieved, even if it is only for a single (sufficiently extensive) firm, it should be aimed at in the first instance. But if it comes up against insurmountable technical difficulties, it would of course not be absolutely necessary to *interview* the *entire* labour force of the categories concerned in order to ascertain their determination by any ethnic, social or cultural factors, if the examination of the factory rolls and the information culled from wage accounts, or other figures or serviceable facts made the existence of characteristic differences in working aptitude seem likely. The examination of a certain number of workers (as large a number as possible, nevertheless) who appear more than others to be characteristically differentiated, quantitatively or qualitatively, could in some circumstances fulfil this purpose. However, even within this limitation, because of this state of affairs one cannot completely rely on these cases being numerous enough to afford, in their entirety, a sufficiently accurate impression of what the working class as a whole has to say about the situation. Even if the firm's management were to show the utmost co-operation with regard to permitting direct intercourse with the workers and the direct distribution to them of questionnaires, it is still not always guaranteed that the working classes, for their part, will promote a survey sanctioned or supported by the management. It will not always be possible to overcome this mistrust, despite the express request, which in my experience is usually advisable, that the names of those being questioned be omitted, and despite the express guarantee that the information supplied by both sides will be made available exclusively to the scientific investigators engaged in its assimilation and processing.

In many cases, then, one will have to manage without using the method here described of obtaining information from the workers themselves, and the survey, based on data and facts given by the directors and their staffs, will then frequently express only their point of view, complemented by the researcher's personal observations. Supplementing this by distributing questionnaires to the local organisations, in the regions concerned, of the trade unions and trade associations of various types—desirable as it is—cannot, in the nature of things, really constitute a total substitute for this lack. Workers' organisations extend right across the firms in their field. They do not regularly embrace whole categories of workers within a factory. On the other hand, they often include workers in factories with different types of production. If, then, not all the firms in which members of the organisation are employed are analysed, and if nowhere near all the categories of workers in these factories are organised—as they hardly ever are—then for these reasons the information to be processed is not coincident. Above all, however, even the most strongly developed organisations only represent, as a rule, a selection of the total labour force of the category concerned, which often has little personal contact with, and is sometimes in direct opposition to, the non-organised workers, so that the attempt (which should always be considered) to have the questionnaires distributed to the non-organised workers in the factories concerned by their mediation would probably not always hold very good prospects. More or less exhaustive information for the assessment of the typical career of *one* category of workers may be soonest expected, in the nature of things, from certain highly-qualified 'skilled' workers, where the workers' organisations sometimes embrace very nearly the whole of the category of workers concerned.

From this it follows that in many cases the survey must be divided into two distinct types of survey:

(1) The one will take as its starting point, wherever it can, the analysis of *firms*, paying attention primarily to the questions of the 'plan of work'. It will first establish, *in numerical terms*, the internal structure of the labour force in terms of categories of workers, i.e. the need for manpower of a particular type, required for the operation of each particular machine and for a technical unit of a particular size, and then the remuneration system in its provisions and effects. Furthermore, it will seek to analyse factory rolls and, wherever possible, wage account books; then to assess the experience of directors and staff and that of technical experts acquainted with the demands made on the workers by the development of machines in the recent past; and finally to complement their results as far as possible by means of personal surveys among the workers in the factory. Where it turns with its questionnaires to the local labour organisations, the survey will have in addition, where possible, to attempt personal research into the perhaps

very diverse situations of the non-organised workers. The suggestion that information from professional associations and other workers' security organisations be used to ascertain the frequency with which workers change firms, and other points on which only estimates were available, seems well worth bearing in mind.

(2) The other type of survey will, with the aid of the questionnaire, turn its attention to the *workers' organisations*; since, in this case, the value of the information increases with the number of surveys completed, it will take areas of greatest possible size as a basis, in some cases the entire Reich: that is, it will ask not the local, but in the first instance at least, the central offices of the workers' organisations for their co-operation, in particular in mediating with the smaller organisations, which would then be requested, for their part to take over the addressing of the questionnaires to be delivered to them—in a stamped envelope, with a stamped addressed envelope for return. Here the project of considering the non-organised workers as well will, as a general rule, be excluded. Rather, this type of survey would set out to enumerate the information as comprehensively as possible, from many single viewpoints and combinations of viewpoints, and then, as far as it could, it would interpret the figure thus obtained in the light of the development trends of the industry concerned, by then known or to be determined with the help of experienced technicians.

Of course, there are other conceivable combinations of points of departure besides these two types, and any piece of work, even if it only deals with an important side problem of the survey from a viewpoint of the researcher's own choice, may be welcome, as long as it remains within the scope of its essential objectives: the determination of the influence of the technical and economic characteristics of large-scale self-contained industry and their adaptation to the characteristics of their workers and vice versa. Where, because of the geographical concentration of an industry, the two principal avenues of approach to the survey to be taken into consideration can be combined in the hands of one researcher, this is particularly satisfactory. However, this cannot always be the case. And since *under no circumstances* should the survey fail to be applied to the maximum information possible from the workers' organisations, type no. 2 (representations based on trade union and trade association *statistics*) will in many cases occur in its own right in the hands of special researchers, in *addition* to type no. 1 (representations based on surveys of factory or industry, perhaps taking into account information supplied by workers' security organisations), and it will be very welcome if there are colleagues who wish to look after this side of the survey only. On the other hand it will be just as welcome if a piece of work limits itself to the processing of information from the factory rolls and wage accounts of large firms, from all the relevant viewpoints, and it would be useful if, at the same time, the changes in the internal structure of the working class, in the demands made on aptitude, and in the typical 'professional careers' of the workers, were analysed by someone closely acquainted with the changing shape of the technology of an industry.

A great deal has already been said above about points to be considered in carrying out the first type of survey, and the essentials are contained in the 'plan of work'. In case researchers should, in the process, succeed in establishing personal sympathy with the workers, let it be simply added here that in addition to the points principally dealt with above (because they offer more complex problems—the aptitude and the career of the workers, considered objectively) their *subjective* attitude to their work is naturally of equal importance. Here belong such questions as: what jobs are held by them to be relatively more desirable, and why? i.e. whether—this is the crux—besides the obvious financial interest, other motives have a decisive effect, and what are they? Do they differ according to the geographical, ethnic, social, and cultural background of the workers, that is, to what extent are any differences in the distribution of workers of different backgrounds in individual jobs based on differences, not merely of aptitude, but also of inclination and the social prestige of the type of work involved? (One from scores of examples: seamstresses in textile firms, whose work, owing to its cleanliness and probably also to its similarity to housework, seems to them to be socially superior to the higher-paid work of weavers, and thus brings about marked social and geographical variations in recruitment, in particular strong recruitment in towns.) Furthermore, what *subjective* results physical and mental, of the different type of work do the workers feel, or think they feel, i.e. in what way does fatigue due to work, machine noise or other working conditions, make itself felt subjectively, and what effect does it have in extra-occupational life?

Do the workers have definite ideas about desirable changes such as in breaks or remuneration systems, and what are they (always for individual categories, of course)? Furthermore, why did they take up this work and no other—of their own accord or at their parents' instigation? To what extent did their allotment to the occupation correspond to their inclinations, or was this dictated by financial interest or other objective causes? Still more important, to what career did they introduce their children, or do they intend to, with what preparation, and for what reason? Last but not least, the question touched on earlier: what is the *subjective* attitude of the workers to the two possibilities, either uniform occupation with one and the same working routine, or alternation between different kinds (naturally excluding those cases where attitude is predetermined purely by the matter of wages)? Can the workers give reasons for apparent differences in their attitude in this respect? Do these seem to derive from their ethnic, social and cultural background and differences of character due to these? Or are they, on the other hand, due to the nature of the work involved? In what direction is this attitude developing in individual industries, if a development is discernible at all? To what extent and under what circumstances (if at all) are the workers increasingly bound, apparently mentally as well, as can sometimes be observed, to their current occupation (as long as the factors mentioned earlier, age and family circumstances, do not stand in the way)?

Workers will very often not be able to answer directly, and frequently not at all with certainty, these and similar questions contained in the 'plan of work'. However, the fact that they cannot do this appears to be characteristic in itself of their whole mental condition, even if the developmental trends concerned can be confirmed, and is also of importance for the purpose of this survey. For, in the nature of things, the most important components of the inner attitude of a section of the population to their condition comprise, on the one hand, what is so obvious to them that it is not made particularly explicit for that very reason, and on the other, what they remain unaware of because it is founded on countless imperceptible influences in their specific environment. Finally, let it be expressed in the words of the 'plan of work', that *extra*-occupational 'style of living', as well as 'occupational career', is to be the object of the inquiry; not, of course, the gamut of totally disconnected details which has been tackled, sometimes in a very valuable way, by biographical and other attempts to portray typical workers' lives, but rather simply that which is demonstrably due to the nature of large-scale self-contained industry, is to be brought out in every case. The researcher will first have to put to himself the question: what kind of extra-occupational interests *can* a normal worker still pursue after being tied—not absolutely, but in *this way*, peculiar to the work involved? Next, the question will, naturally, always have to be asked: are there marked *differences*, in general first of all, of family life, upbringing of children, forms of relaxation and enjoyment, forms and customs of social life, eating and drinking habits, direction and manifestation of intellectual and aesthetic interests in terms of type and extent (reading), relationship to school, to the official forms of church life, to religious and other philosophical questions, etc., among the workers of large-scale self-contained industry as opposed to the corresponding behaviour of other sections of the population of similar *income* and *schooling*? In particular can the upper section of the best-placed workers be differentiated in these terms from junior civil servants, officials of private concerns, and the petite bourgeoisie of similar levels of income and schooling? Furthermore, however, can the individual categories of the labour force of major industries, formed by their degree of skill, position in the production process, age, family circumstances or background, be distinguished *amongst themselves* in this respect? Do differences in type of occupation, degree of skill, or position, establish purely 'social' communal intercourse and relationships, apart from groups united purely by common economic interests? And if this proves to be the case, where is the dividing line, and according to what criteria do the workers differentiate themselves socially? That such a differentiation often occurs is well known. In the lands of the Anglo-Saxons there is often not the slightest social contact between skilled trade-unionists and lower classes of worker—it is well-known that they sometimes find it hard to sit at the same table. It would be of considerable interest to investigate how far, and why, these differentiations exist in Germany, or are coming into being, or conversely are in the process of disappearing; likewise naturally, for marriage, and general social relations with junior office workers and the petite bourgeoisie.

F

Lastly, the often very far-reaching influence of membership of various types of workers' organisations on style of conduct should be described also, in so far as it belongs in the inquiry of this investigation, that is, in so far as it is due to the *nature* of the individual industries. Here firms should be examined separately according to size as well as remuneration system, since the feeling of solidarity of self-interest, 'class consciousness' or concern that one's children should get on, and conception of the organisation as an economic restraint or as the germ of an ideal organisation of the future, will predominate according to the prospects of promotion and financial betterment.

For the calculations to be made in pieces of work of the *second* type (chiefly trade-union statistics) either the personal training of the researcher in statistical technique or the constant advice of trained statisticians will be indispensable. It will probably be necessary, in counting, in any event (1) to present the figure for change of locality and firm, according to the individual categories of workers and, further, according to their background, *in tabular form*, arranged in age groups. Then (2) the 'occupational careers' of the workers should be established, likewise according to categories and divided within these into age groups. Only the evidence of the information collected is likely to show whether this is possible in tabular form or not. Let it be again explicitly pointed out that this question *is among those of central interest* to the survey. (3) For the individual categories of workers, their geographical origin and that of both parents, then the occupation of the father, grandfather, brothers, sisters, and any grown-up children, and then the type of schooling and apprenticeship, all this should be presented as far as possible *in tabular form*. A comparative description of just these factors for the individual large groups of workers' organisations (trade associations, free-trade unions, Christian organisations, etc.) would also be of interest here, as, on the other hand, would the determination of the distribution of these types of trade unions over the individual categories of workers (positions) and over the classes of *size* of firm. Then (4) the individual categories of workers would have to be counted as regards their secondary business or that of their family, house-ownership or other domicile. (5) As far as military fitness is concerned, it would be of greater interest to ascertain the relationship between military fitness and qualification (career prospects, as they become apparent in the course of the career), than to work out comparative figures for the fitness of various generations as against one another, as far as information permits. (6) The division of confessional allegiance in the individual categories of workers could offer sufficient statistical interest in the present situation, where confession appears to be significant as regards career preference, in the case of industries displaying a high degree of confessional mixture which does *not* (as with the Poles) coincide with ethnic mixture.

In almost all these cases, as with all surveys of professions and modes of occupation, the difficulty lies in the manner of *classification* of the workers, by virtue of their jobs, which must ultimately be taken as a basis. In every case, this classification can scarcely be considered carefully enough or carried out in too great detail. To what extent the conventional factory terms for the individual categories of workers would be adequate should be investigated first of all, and they should, as far as possible, be taken as a starting-point. Incidentally, in the assessment of the results of the statistical counts, it would have to take two different forms. (1) It would have to link up with the inquiry discussed earlier: what qualities are pre-eminently *crucial* in the respective jobs, according to one's own findings or in a well-founded expert view, that is to say, which qualities, in individual cases, are most strongly exposed to the influence of 'fatigue' and 'practice'; then the workers should be divided into categories according to the degree of demands made upon them in terms of essentially muscular performance or the diverse performances of a nervous and mental nature (these should be carefully differentiated); however (2) the degree and nature of 'skill', i.e. the *average duration* of training before normal and maximum output for their job, should also form the basis for classification. Then the workers should be divided from as many points of view as possible into categories, which would have to be counted in the inquiries in hand, in order that their background and the other circumstances under investigation might be examined.

All the explanations and exhortations set out here, which seemed desirable in order to make the *spirit* of the survey unequivocally apparent, are incidentally by no means intended to 'schoolmaster', as it were, my respected colleagues in their freedom to elaborate their own work. For them the most important and rewarding task will perhaps rather lie in trying out suitable inquiries and methods for *themselves;* and since it will only become apparent where the real difficulties lie when the work is actually begun, there will be ample opportunity for this. The Society for Social Policy as such requires (for work wishing to sail under its flag) simply that the questions laid down in the *official* pamphlets (plan of work and questionnaires) should be investigated. By what means this is to be achieved is left entirely to private initiative. One thing may be said straight away to those gentlemen who are of a mind to devote their knowledge and their efforts to the service of this survey: the most indispensable quality, if *any* (new!) results are to be gained, in this case more than in any of the Society's previous surveys, will be an extraordinary degree of tenacity in the pursuit of the goal, once this has been set. Let anyone who does not possess this quality refrain from participating. It is absolutely *impossible* to get results worth printing in this sphere in a matter of a few months.

Far-reaching as the inquiries of the surveys now are, they still represent, of course, only a *fraction* (admittedly an important one) of a sociological analysis of modern large-scale industry. In addition to the discussion of organisational ('morphological') questions of a technical and commercial nature, which were talked about at the beginning, the selection and career of the *administrative staff*, especially technical staff, should be investigated separately (1) for individual industries and (2) for individual clerical classes, divided according to their field of training. Finally, the by no means uninteresting question of the employers' background, the qualifications required today as opposed to those required earlier, and their capabilities, should be thoroughly investigated in individual industries.

Only all these investigations combined could furnish a picture of the *cultural significance* of the process of evolution being undergone by major industry before our eyes. The cultural problems which it ultimately brings are of enormous extent. In a memorandum for the subcommittee A. Weber stressed—in agreement with the view of many of us—that the structure of that peculiar 'system' which has been thrust upon the population by the organisation of large-scale industrial production transcends even the scope of the question of 'capitalist' or 'socialist' organisation of production in its significance for their fate, because the existence of this 'equipment' *as such is independent* of this alternative. Indeed, the modern workshop with its official hierarchy, its discipline, its chaining of worker to machine, its agglommeration and yet at the same time (compared, say, with the spinning-rooms of the past) its isolation of workers',[1] its huge calculating machinery, stretching right down to the simplest manipulation of the worker, *is*—conceptually—independent of it. It has far-reaching specific effects, entirely peculiar to itself, on men and their 'style of living'. Certainly, however—and here, again, would lie the limitation of that point of view—the substitution of *any* form of common economic 'solidarity' for today's selection on the principle of private economic viability, chaining as it does the whole existence of those confined within the factory, whether directing or obeying, to the outcome of the employer's *private* cost and profit calculations, would radically change the spirit found today in this great edifice, and no one can even surmise with what consequences. These prospects do not enter into consideration for the present survey; it may content itself, for its vindication, with the fact that the 'system' as it is today, with the effects it has (the examination of which is to be undertaken here), has changed, and will go on changing, the spiritual face of mankind almost to the point of unrecognisability.

[1] The question of how far conversation is or is not possible at work, and why, the question of what qualities (professional and otherwise) achieve respect among fellow-workers, the direction of ethical value judgements among the workers—all these and similar questions need to be studied in the way in which they are determined by the workshop—'community' (which, basically, is not a community) and by the predominance (to be examined in terms of its degree) of purely pecuniary involvement with work.

Part Two
Ideologies and Thought Forms

INTRODUCTION

Of the three passages which are taken as representative of Weber's treatment of ideologies and thought forms, the first, taken as it is from *The Protestant Ethic and the Spirit of Capitalism*, is by far the best known. The impact of an ideology in moulding the character structure of the Puritan business man, with implications for his social, sexual and cultural life, is depicted in essay form. Weber speaks of the 'chilling weight' on the life of the man who holds fast to an idea of duty to his possessions 'to which he subordinates himself as an obedient steward, or even as an acquisitive machine'. One is strongly reminded of Marx's comment on the alienating effect of the acquisitive pursuit of money on the whole man: 'The less you eat, drink and read books; the less you go to the theatre, the dance hall, the public house; the less you think, love, theorise, sing, paint, fence, etc., the more you *save*—the *greater* becomes your treasure which neither moth nor rust will devour—your *capital*. The less you *are*, the more you *have*; the less you express your own life, the greater is your *externalised* life—the greater is the store of your alienated being. . . .'[1]

Weber depicts Puritanism as a middle-class ideology. We ought properly to note, however, that he does not see the relationship between class position (economic circumstances) and ideology in any crudely deterministic manner, least of all in respect of 'the middle class'. This is brought out particularly well in *The Sociology of Religion* where he argues:

> If certain fairly uniform tendencies are normally apparent in spite of all differences in the religious attitude of the nobility and bureaucracy, the classes with the maximum social pri-

---

[1] K. Marx. *Economic and Philosophical Manuscripts of 1844*. (Lawrence and Wishart, 1970), p. 150.

vilege . . . the real 'middle' classes evince striking contrasts. Moreover this is something quite apart from the rather sharp differences of status which these classes manifest within them- selves.[1]

Further:

> Within the lower middle class, and particularly among the artisans, the greatest contrasts have existed side by side. These have included caste taboos and magical or mystagogic religions of both the sacramental and orgiastic types in India, animism in China, dervish religion in Islam, and the pneumatic-en- thusiastic congregational religion of early Christianity, practised particularly in the eastern half of the Roman Empire. Still other modes of religious expression among the lower middle class and artisan groups are the *deisidaemonie* and the orgiastic worship of Dionysos in ancient Greece, Pharisaic fidelity to the law in ancient urban Judaism, an essentially idolatrous Christianity, as well as all sorts of sectarian faiths in the Middle Ages, and various types of Protestantism in early modern times. These diverse phenomena obviously present the greatest possible contrasts to one another.[2]

Taking the case of Christianity in particular, Weber points to the existence of 'a highly chequered diversification, which at least proves that a uniform determinism of religion by economic forces never existed among the artisan class'.[3] At the same time, Weber is convinced that religious ideologies are not random affairs entirely divorced from an individual's socio-economic position:

> Yet it is still true in theory that the middle class, by virtue of its distinct pattern of economic life, inclines in the direction of a rational ethical religion, wherever conditions are present for the emergence of a rational ethical religion . . . the economic foundation of urban man's life has a far more rational essential character, viz., calculability and capacity for purposive mani- pulation . . . small traders and artisans are disposed to accept a rational world view incorporating an ethic of compensation.[4]

[1] S. R. pp. 90–1.   [2] ibid., p. 95.   [3] ibid., p. 96.
[4] ibid., p. 97.

Weber's discussion of natural law as a thought form, the second theme in this chapter, contains much that is typical of his mode of analysis. Natural law is treated as 'a collective term for those norms which owe their legitimacy not to their origin from a legitimate lawgiver, but to their immanent and teleological qualities'. One of the significant points about such a normative system is that while natural law can and has been used to buttress an existing social order, it can also be utilised by those who wish to legitimate revolutionary aspirations. Weber applies his discussion to the economic order. He makes a characteristic distinction between formal and substantive natural law, while noting that a completely formal natural law cannot exist because it would imply that general legal concepts without content could be enunciated. But at the formal level he has in mind a conception of natural law derived from an individualistic social contract theory with its concern for individual freedoms including, in the economic context, freedom of contract. For Weber 'the decisive turn towards substantive natural law is connected primarily with socialist theories of the exclusive legitimacy of the acquisition of wealth by one's own labour'. This is because the ideological basis of natural law presuppositions and applications is sharply revealed. If notions of freedom of contract justify existing property relations, beliefs about the right to the product of one's labour challenge them. Different social classes are then likely to hold different natural law ideologies, a point which Weber develops with reference to landowners and peasantries, industrial capitalists and proletariats.

The development of conflicts between formal and substantive natural law, which Weber regards as insoluble in principle, has had, in his judgement, the effect of creating widespread scepticism about the adequacy of natural law as a basis for legal systems. The metaphysical dignity of natural law conceptions has gone for ever since 'in the great majority of its most important provisions it has been unmasked all too visibly . . . as the product or the technical means of a compromise between conflicting interests.'

While Weber correctly points to a widespread disbelief in natural law among lawyers because its ideological character has been revealed, we should nevertheless recognise, as Lloyd has observed, that the natural law idea 'seems to possess almost inextinguishable powers of survival'.[1] Particularly in the field of international law,

[1] *The Idea of Law* (Penguin, 1964), p. 86.

in the aftermath of Fascism, natural law was felt by some legal commentators to have continued relevance. 'Crimes against humanity', which imply, for example, that those who carried out concentration camp massacres even if they did not abrogate the laws of their own state are punishable by a 'higher law', have strong natural law connotations. Lloyd himself does not see such judgements as necessarily standing upon natural law foundations, but in this context the point need not be pursued.

The discussion on natural law is taken from *On Law in Economy and Society*. Not all of the detailed footnotes are retained.

The third theme in this chapter takes us into the realm of political ideologies. Weber's discussion of socialism reproduced here, was originally delivered to a meeting of Austrian army officers in 1918. This explains the explicit military references which are made from time to time. Sometimes this is done in a way which might have surprised the audience. For example, in discussing the controversial question of the strike he draws a distinction (which has many applications in his work) between material and ideal interests. Both, he says, are commonly found to motivate strikers: they are fighting for wages, but they also have a conception of honour which binds them together. Not only is the distinction itself salutary for members of a class group to consider when many of them, one may suppose, would have labelled the behaviour of strikers as selfish, irresponsible and unpatriotic, but a certain irony is introduced when Weber comments that the conception of honour which such workers have is 'in the last analysis . . . a feeling upon which, only in another direction, rests the solidarity of military units'. The discussion is also a 'popular' one in the sense that the audience is non-academic. Hence there is a fair sprinkling of anecdotal comment and he approaches the heart of his subject by stealth.

Weber locates the origins of 'modern socialism' in the system of industrial production which utilises factory-based machines. The system, with its accompanying industrial discipline and the enslavement of the worker to the machine, entails the separation of the worker from ownership of the means of production. But this fact is seen within the context of a wider phenomenon which includes the separation of the soldier from ownership of the instruments of war, of the university teacher from ownership of the means of study, of the official from ownership of the means of administration. The significance of this perspective is that whatever modern socialism may mean (and allowing that it means different things to different protagonists) it has to come to terms with one inescapable fact in Weber's judgement: 'In large states everywhere modern democracy is becoming a bureaucratised democracy. And it must be so. . . . It is the same everywhere . . . it is the same within the parties too. That is inevitable, and this is the first fact which socialism has to reckon with. . . . The modern economy cannot be run in any other way.'

In the ensuing discussion Weber first sets the concept of collective economy over and against private enterprise capitalism. But a collective economy can still be guided by the profit motive and in this respect he is sceptical of those who describe nationalisation as 'true' socialism. 'The life of a worker in the Saar is just the same as in a private mining company: if the pit is badly run, i.e. not very profitable, then things are bad for the men too.' Indeed, he sees in principle that the state could more easily be identified as an instrument of working-class oppression. The possibility of what we have now learned to term the corporate state is envisaged, in which industrial and political power are so fused that 'the two administrations would then be one body with common interests and could no longer be checked'.

It is very interesting to contrast Weber's position in this respect with that of R. H. Tawney whose Labour Party pamphlet, *The Nationalisation of the Coal Industry*, was published in 1919.[1] Tawney argued that:

> Provided . . . that the obvious pitfalls of bureaucracy and over-centralisation, which are as familiar to the advocates of nationalisation as to its critics, are avoided, the advantages of public ownership are immense. It will benefit the consumer by making possible the elimination of the various sources of waste, the cost of which is at present reflected in the price of coal. It will benefit the mineworker by removing the downward pressure of capitalism upon his standard of life, by making room for considerations of social well-being which are at present subordinated to the pursuit of dividends, and by securing him an effective voice in the policy and organisation of industry. Nor is the least of its advantages that by making the most funda-

[1] Reprinted in *The Radical Tradition* (Penguin, 1966).

mental of all industries a public service carried on in partner-
ship between the State and the workers it will call into operation
motives of public spirit and professional zeal which are at
present stifled by the subordination of the industry to the
pursuit of private gain, and which will raise the whole tone and
quality of our industrial civilisation.[1]

Tawney propounded the philosophy that nationalisation should
go hand in hand with industrial democracy so that the workers
themselves would have direct responsibility for the efficiency of
the coal mines 'and sufficient power to make that responsibility
a reality'.[2] The nationalisation scheme which formed the basis of
Weber's comment would no doubt be regarded as a very poor
specimen, worthy of condemnation, by Tawney, whose point is
essentially that more socialist connotations are consistent with the
idea of nationalisation. Possibly, too, the difference between
Weber and Tawney is reflected in their differing attitudes to the
power of the state. So in a much later essay on 'Social Democracy
in Britain' (1949), Tawney acknowledges that the state is an
important instrument and hence there is a struggle to control it:

> But it is an instrument and nothing more. . . . We in England have
> repeatedly re-made the State, and are re-making it now, and
> shall re-make it again. Why, in heaven's name, should we be
> afraid of it? The faithful animal—to vary the metaphor—will
> run our errands; fetch and carry for us; convey us on our
> journeys; attend our sick beds; mind our children; show on the
> rare occasions that we tell him a handsome mouthful of sharp
> teeth, and generally behave like a useful and well-conducted
> cur. If he does not do his tricks nicely, we are quite capable of
> beating our own dog ourselves, as—to do him justice—he is
> well aware.[3]

Weber's political experience in the Germany of 1918 did not lend
itself to such a genial, optimistic attitude.

In the main part of his discussion Weber distinguishes between
revolutionary and evolutionary socialism. It is clear that he is un-
happy with the prophetic elements of socialism which appeal to
laws of nature, and casts doubt on the empirical evidence cited in

[1] *The Radical Tradition*, pp. 126–7.   [2] *ibid.*, p. 140.   [3] *ibid.*, p. 172.

support of the thesis that socialism must necessarily triumph. The evidence available would support the notion of the dictatorship of the official rather than the proletariat, he argues. What is of particular interest, however, is the typological discussion relating to both the forms of socialism and beliefs about how the socialist society will be achieved organisationally. This may be summarised in the following chart:

| Type of Socialism | Organisational vehicle of liberation | |
	Political Party	Trade Union Organisation
Revolutionary	1	2
Evolutionary	3	4

Revisionism, as evolutionary socialism was pejoratively designated by revolutionary socialists, could be exemplified by the 'English type' trade union, whose aim was to improve the immediate conditions of employment of its members, or by the 'practical politicians' who were prepared to form coalitions with non-socialist parties and participate in government. If both were the enemies of revolutionary socialism by buttressing an existing capitalist system, then too the revolutionary socialists could be at odds with one another. Syndicalism, with its anti-bureaucratic, anti-parliamentarian approach, looks askance at political parties and their campaigns, even revolutionary groups. 'Only the real working class, which is organised in the trade union, can create the new society. Away with the professional politician who lives for—and literally *off*—politics and not for the creation of the new economic society.' This doctrinal purity, however, raises in particularly acute form the question of the role of intellectuals in the movement. Their presence and the reliance of the syndicalists on other non-workers (managers, for example) is seen by Weber as a technical necessity in the post-revolutionary stage.

Throughout his discussion Weber reveals a practical interest in what happens under socialism, assuming the revolution to be accomplished or the appropriate evolutionary stage reached. He notes the ambiguity of the Communist Manifesto in treating the question: Who will command the new economy? It is, as Daniel Bell has more recently written, 'one of the most extraordinary facts in the history of social thought that the leaders of socialism from Marx down, sought to win millions of people for the idea of a new society without the slightest thought about the shape of that future society and its problems.'[1] So Weber notes the apparent need of the Russian revolutionaries to maintain the expertise of industrialists and to utilise piece-rate systems to maintain levels of production in factories. It is clear that, while he is enormously fascinated by the experiment of proletarian dictatorship, he does not really expect the socialist vision of freedom of man's domination over man to be achieved.

Weber explicitly compares revolutionary socialism with the faith of early Christians, in its sectarianism and its apocalyptic hope. This is reminiscent of the point developed in Engels's essay 'On the History of Early Christianity'.[2] There was the feeling that one was struggling against the whole world, together with the belief that the struggle would be victorious. At the same time there was 'the formation of numerous sects which fight against one another with at least the same zeal as against the common external enemy. So it was with early Christianity, so it was with the beginning of the socialist movement, no matter how much that worried the well-meaning worthies who preached unity where no unity was possible.' So, then, the Communist Manifesto announced the imminent coming of a new order; it did not provide the first five-year plan. It is, to maintain the parallel, the difference between the kerygma and a papal encyclical.

(A) The Puritan Idea of the 'Calling'[3]

To analyse the effects on the character of peoples of the penetration of life with Old Testament norms—a tempting task which,

[1] 'Two Roads from Marx', in *The End of Ideology* (Free Press, 1960), p. 367.
[2] Reprinted in L. Feuer, *Marx and Engels. Basic Writings on Politics and Philosophy*, Fontana, 1969, p. 221.
[3] Source: *The Protestant Ethic and the Spirit of Capitalism*, pp. 166–74, 272–80. (The footnotes to this section have been slightly shortened by the editor.)

however, has not yet satisfactorily been done even for Judaism—
would be impossible within the limits of this sketch. In addition
to the relationships already pointed out, it is important for the
general inner attitude of the Puritans, above all, that the belief
that they were God's chosen people saw in them a great renaissance. Even the kindly Baxter thanked God that he was born in
England, and thus in the true Church, and nowhere else. This
thankfulness for one's own perfection by the grace of God penetrated the attitude toward life of the Puritan middle class, and
played its part in developing that formalistic, hard, correct
character which was peculiar to the men of that heroic age of
capitalism.

Let us now try to clarify the ways in which the Puritan idea of
the calling and the premium it placed upon ascetic conduct were
bound directly to influence the development of a capitalistic way
of life. As we have seen, this asceticism turned with all its force
against one thing: the spontaneous enjoyment of life and all it had
to offer. This is perhaps most characteristically brought out in the
struggle over the *Book of Sports*[1] which James I and Charles I
made into law expressly as a means of counteracting Puritanism,
and which the latter ordered to be read from all the pulpits. The
fanatical opposition of the Puritans to the ordinances of the King,
permitting by law certain popular amusements on Sunday outside of church hours, was not only explained by the disturbance
of the Sabbath rest, but also by resentment against the intentional
diversion from the ordered life of the saint, which it caused. And,
on his side, the King's threats of severe punishment for every
attack on the legality of those sports were motivated by his purpose of breaking the anti-authoritarian ascetic tendency of Puritanism, which was so dangerous to the state. The feudal and
monarchical forces protected the pleasure seekers against the
rising middle-class morality and the anti-authoritarian ascetic
conventicles, just as to-day capitalistic society tends to protect
those willing to work against the class morality of the proletariat
and the anti-authoritarian trade union.

As against this the Puritans upheld their decisive characteristic, the principle of ascetic conduct. For otherwise the Puritan

[1] Printed in Gardiner's *Constitutional Documents*. One may compare this
struggle against anti-authoritarian asceticism with Louis XIV's persecution of
Port Royal and the Jansenists.

aversion to sport, even for the Quakers, was by no means simply one of principle. Sport was accepted if it served a rational purpose, that of recreation necessary for physical efficiency. But as a means for the spontaneous expression of undisciplined impulses, it was under suspicion; and in so far as it became purely a means of enjoyment, or awakened pride, raw instincts or the irrational gambling instinct, it was of course strictly condemned. Impulsive enjoyment of life, which leads away both from work in a calling and from religion, was as such the enemy of rational asceticism, whether in the form of seigneurial sports, or the enjoyment of the dance-hall or the public house of the common man.[1]

Its attitude was thus suspicious and often hostile to the aspects of culture without any immediate religious value. It is not, however, true that the ideals of Puritanism implied a solemn, narrow-minded contempt of culture. Quite the contrary is the case at least for science, with the exception of the hatred of Scholasticism. Moreover, the great men of the Puritan movement were thoroughly steeped in the culture of the Renaissance. The sermons of the Presbyterian divines abound with classical allusions, and even the Radicals, although they objected to it, were not ashamed to display that kind of learning in theological polemics. Perhaps no country was ever so full of graduates as New England in the first generation of its existence. The satire of their opponents, such as, for instance, Butler's *Hudibras*, also attacks primarily the pedantry and highly trained dialectics of the Puritans. This is partially due to the religious valuation of knowledge which followed from their attitude to the Catholic *fides implicita*.

But the situation is quite different when one looks at non-scientific literature,[2] and especially the fine arts. Here asceticism

---

[1] Calvin's own standpoint was in this respect distinctly less drastic, at least in so far as the finer aristocratic forms of the enjoyment of life were concerned. The only limitation is the Bible. Whoever adheres to it and has a good conscience, need not observe his every impulse to enjoy life with anxiety. Along with increasing anxiety over the *certitudo salutis* the most important circumstance for the later disciples was, however, that in the era of the *ecclesia militans* it was the small bourgeoisie who were the principal representatives of Calvinistic ethics.

[2] Novels and the like should not be read; they are 'wastetimes' (Baxter, *Christian Directory*, I, p. 51). The decline of lyric poetry and folk-music, as well as the drama, after the Elizabethan age in England is well known. In the pictorial arts Puritanism perhaps did not find very much to suppress. But very striking is the decline from what seemed to be a promising musical beginning (England's part in the history of music was by no means unimportant) to that absolute

descended like a frost on the life of 'Merrie old England'. And not only wordly merriment felt its effect. The Puritan's ferocious hatred of everything which smacked of superstition, of all survivals of magical or sacramental salvation, applied to the Christmas festivities and the May Pole[1] and all spontaneous religious art. That there was room in Holland for a great, often uncouthly realistic art proves only how far from completely the authoritarian moral discipline of that country was able to counteract the influence of the court and the regents (a class of *rentiers*), and also the joy in life of the parvenu bourgeoisie, after the short supremacy of the Calvinistic theocracy had been transformed into a moderate national Church, and with it Calvinism had perceptibly lost in its power of ascetic influence.[2]

musical vacuum which we find typical of the Anglo-Saxon peoples later, and even today. Except for the Negro churches, and the professional singers whom the churches now engage as attractions (Trinity church in Boston in 1904 for $8,000 annually), in America one also hears as community singing in general only a noise which is intolerable to German ears (partly analogous things in Holland also).

[1] Just the same in Holland, as the reports of the Synods show. (See the resolutions on the Maypole in the Reitmaas Collection, VI, 78, 139.)

[2] The most complex causes, into which we cannot go here, were responsible for the relatively smaller extent to which the Calvinistic ethic penetrated practical life there. The ascetic spirit began to weaken in Holland as early as the beginning of the seventeenth century (the English Congregationalists who fled to Holland in 1608 were disturbed by the lack of respect for the Sabbath there), but especially under the Stadtholder Frederick Henry. Moreover, Dutch Puritanism had in general much less expansive power than English. The reasons for it lay in part in the political constitution (particularistic confederation of towns and provinces) and in the far smaller degree of military force (the War of Independence was soon fought principally with the money of Amsterdam and mercenary armies. English preachers illustrated the Babylonian confusion of tongues by reference to the Dutch army). Thus the burden of the war of religion was to a large extent passed on to others, but at the same time a part of their political power was lost. On the other hand, Cromwell's army, even though it was partly conscripted, felt that it was an army of citizens. It was, to be sure, all the more characteristic that just this army adopted the abolition of conscription in its programme, because one could fight justly only for the glory of God in a cause hallowed by conscience, but not at the whim of a sovereign. The constitution of the British army, so immoral to traditional German ideas, had its historical origin in very moral motives, and was an attainment of soldiers who had never been beaten. Only after the Restoration was it placed in the service of the interests of the Crown.

The Dutch *schutterijen*, the champions of Calvinism in the period of the Great War, only half a generation after the Synod of Dordrecht, do not look in the least ascetic in the pictures of Hals. Protests of the Synods against their conduct occur frequently. The Dutch concept of *Deftigkeit* is a mixture of bourgeois-rational honesty and patrician consciousness of status. The division

The theatre was obnoxious to the Puritans,[1] and with the strict exclusion of the erotic and of nudity from the realm of toleration, a radical view of literature or of art could not exist. The conceptions of idle talk, of superfluities[2] and of vain ostentation, all designations of an irrational attitude without objective purpose, thus not ascetic, and especially not serving the glory of God but of man, were always at hand to serve in deciding in favour of sober utility as against any artistic tendencies. This was especially true in the case of decoration of the person, for instance clothing.[3] That powerful tendency toward uniformity of life, which to-day so immensely aids the capitalistic interest in the standardisation of production,[4] had its ideal foundations in the repudiation of all idolatry of the flesh.[5]

of church pews according to classes in the Dutch churches shows the aristocratic character of this religion even today. The continuance of the town economy hampered industry. It prospered almost alone through refugees, and hence only sporadically. Nevertheless, the worldly asceticism of Calvinism and Pietism was an important influence in Holland in the same direction as elsewhere. Also in the sense to be referred to presently of ascetic compulsion to save, as Groen van Prinsterer shows. The significance of Dutch religion as ascetic compulsion to save appears clearly even in the eighteenth century in the writings of Albertus Haller.

[1] We may recall that the Puritan town government closed the theatre at Stratford-on-Avon while Shakespeare was still alive and residing there in his last years. Shakespeare's hatred and contempt of the Puritans appear on every occasion. As late as 1777 the City of Birmingham refused to license a theatre because it was conducive to slothfulness, and hence unfavourable to trade (Ashley, *Birmingham Trade and Commerce*, 1913).

[2] Here also it was of decisive importance that for the Puritan there was only the alternative of divine will or earthly vanity. Hence for him there could be no *adiaphora*. As we have already pointed out, Calvin's own view was different in this respect. What one eats, wears, etc., as long as there is no enslavement of the soul to earthly desire as a result, is indifferent. Freedom from the world should be expressed, as for the Jesuits, in indifference, which for Calvin meant an indifferent, uncovetous use of whatever goods the earth offered (pp. 409 ff. of the original edition of the *Instit. Christ*).

[3] The Quaker attitude in this respect is well known. But as early as the beginning of the seventeenth century the heaviest storms shook the pious congregation of exiles in Amsterdam for a decade over the fashionable hats and dresses of a preacher's wife (charmingly described in Dexter's *Congregationalism of the Last Three Hundred Years*). Sanford has pointed out that the present-day male hair-cut is that of the ridiculous Roundheads, and the equally ridiculous (for the time) male clothing of the Puritans is at least in principle fundamentally the same as that of today.

[4] On this point, see Veblen's *Theory of Business Enterprise*.

[5] Again and again we come back to this attitude. It explains statements like the following: 'Every penny which is paid upon yourselves and children and friends must be done as by God's own appointment and to serve and please

Of course we must not forget that Puritanism included a world of contradictions, and that the instinctive sense of eternal greatness in art was certainly stronger among its leaders than in the atmosphere of the Cavaliers.[1] Moreover, a unique genius like Rembrandt, however little his conduct may have been acceptable to God in the eyes of the Puritans, was very strongly influenced in the character of his work by his religious environment.[2] But that does not alter the picture as a whole. In so far as the development of the Puritan tradition could, and in part did, lead to a powerful spiritualisation of personality, it was a decided benefit to literature. But for the most part that benefit only accrued to later generations.

Although we cannot here enter upon a discussion of the influence of Puritanism in all these directions, we should call attention to the fact that the toleration of pleasure in cultural goods, which contributed to purely aesthetic or athletic enjoyment, certainly always ran up against one characteristic limitation: they must not cost anything. Man is only a trustee of the goods which have come to him through God's grace. He must, like the servant in the parable, give an account of every penny entrusted to him, and it is at least hazardous to spend any of it for a purpose which

Him. Watch narrowly, or else that thievish, carnal self will leave God nothing' (Baxter, op. cit., I, p. 108). This is decisive; what is expended for personal ends is withdrawn from the service of God's glory.

[1] Quite rightly it is customary to recall that Cromwell saved Raphael's drawings and Mantegna's *Triumph of Caesar* from destruction, while Charles II tried to sell them. Moreover, the society of the Restoration was distinctly cool or even hostile to English national literature. In fact the influence of Versailles was all-powerful at courts everywhere. A detailed analysis of the influence of the unfavourable atmosphere for the spontaneous enjoyment of everyday life on the spirit of the higher types of Puritan, and the men who went through the schooling of Puritanism, is a task which cannot be undertaken within the limits of this sketch. Washington Irving (*Bracebridge Hall*) formulates it in the usual English terms thus: 'It [he says political freedom, we should say Puritanism] evinces less play of the fancy, but more power of the imagination.' It is only necessary to think of the place of the Scots in science, literature, and technical invention, as well as in the business life of Great Britain, to be convinced that this remark approaches the truth, even though put somewhat too narrowly. We cannot speak here of its significance for the development of technique and the empirical sciences. The relation itself is always appearing in everyday life. For the Quakers, for instance, the recreations which are permissible (according to Barclay) are: visiting of friends, reading of historical works, mathematical and physical experiments, gardening, discussion of business and other occurrences in the world, etc. The reason is that pointed out above.

[2] Already very finely analysed in Carl Neumann's *Rembrandt*, which should be compared with the above remarks in general.

does not serve the glory of God but only one's own enjoyment.[1] What person, who keeps his eyes open, has not met representatives of this view-point even in the present?[2] The idea of a man's duty to his possessions, to which he subordinates himself as an obedient steward, or even as an acquisitive machine, bears with chilling weight on his life. The greater the possessions the heavier—if the ascetic attitude toward life stands the test—the feeling of responsibility for them, for holding them undiminished for the glory of God and increasing them by restless effort. The origin of this type of life also extends in certain roots, like so many aspects of the spirit of capitalism, back into the Middle Ages.[3] But it was in the ethic of ascetic Protestantism that it first found a consistent ethical foundation. Its significance for the development of capitalism is obvious.[4]

[1] Compare the well-known description of Colonel Hutchinson.

[2] I think, among many other examples, especially of a manufacturer unusually successful in his business ventures, and in his later years very wealthy, who, when for the treatment of a troublesome digestive disorder the doctor prescribed a few oysters a day, could only be brought to comply with difficulty. Very considerable gifts for philanthropic purposes which he made during his lifetime and a certain openhandedness showed, on the other hand, that it was simply a survival of that ascetic feeling which looks upon enjoyment of wealth for oneself as morally reprehensible, but has nothing whatever to do with avarice.

[3] The separation of workshop, office, of business in general and the private dwelling, of firm and name, of business capital and private wealth, the tendency to make of the business a *corpus mysticum* (at least in the case of corporate property) all lay in this direction. On this, see my *Handelsgesellschaften im Mittelalter* (*Gesammelte Aufsätze zur Sozial- und Wirtschaftsgeschichte*, pp. 312 ff.)

[4] Sombart in his *Kapitalismus* (first edition) has already well pointed out this characteristic phenomenon. It must, however, be noted that the accumulation of wealth springs from two quite distinct psychological sources. One reaches into the dimmest antiquity and is expressed in foundations, family fortunes, and trusts, as well as much more purely and clearly in the desire to die weighted down with a great burden of material goods; above all to insure the continuation of a business even at the cost of the personal interests of the majority of one's children. In such cases it is, besides the desire to give one's own creation an ideal life beyond one's death, and thus to maintain the *splendour familiæ* and extend the personality of the founder, a question of, so to speak, fundamentally egocentric motives. That is not the case with that bourgeois motive with which we are here dealing. There the motto of asceticism is 'Entsagen sollst du, sollst entsagen' in the positive capitalistic sense of 'Erwerben sollst du, sollst erwerben'. In its pure and simple non-rationality it is a sort of categorical imperative. Only the glory of God and one's own duty, not human vanity, is the motive for the Puritans; and today only the duty to one's calling. If it pleases anyone to illustrate an idea by its extreme consequences, we may recall the theory of certain American millionaires, that their millions should not be left to their children, so that they will not be deprived of the good moral

This worldly Protestant asceticism, as we may recapitulate up to this point, acted powerfully against the spontaneous enjoyment of possessions; it restricted consumption, especially of luxuries. On the other hand, it had the psychological effect of freeing the acquisition of goods from the inhibitions of traditionalistic ethics. It broke the bonds of the impulse of acquisition in that it not only legalised it, but (in the sense discussed) looked upon it as directly willed by God. The campaign against the temptations of the flesh and the dependence on external things, was, as the great Quaker apologist Barclay as well as the Puritans, expressly says, not a struggle against the rational acquisition, but against the irrational use of wealth.

But this irrational use was exemplified in the outward forms of luxury which their code condemned as idolatry of the flesh,[1] however natural they had appeared to the feudal mind. On the other hand, they approved the rational and utilitarian uses of wealth which were willed by God for the needs of the individual and the community. They did not wish to impose mortification[2] on the man of wealth, but the use of his means for necessary and practical things. The idea of comfort characteristically limits the extent of ethically permissible expenditures. It is naturally no accident that the development of a manner of living consistent with that idea may be observed earliest and most clearly among the most consistent representatives of this whole attitude toward life. Over against the glitter and ostentation of feudal magnificence which, resting on an unsound economic basis, prefers a sordid elegance to a sober simplicity, they set the clean and solid comfort of the middle-class home as an ideal.[3]

On the side of the production of private wealth, asceticism condemned both dishonesty and impulsive avarice. What was

effects of the necessity of working and earning for themselves. Today that idea is certainly no more than a theoretical soap-bubble.

[1] This is, as must continually be emphasised, the final decisive religious motive (along with the purely ascetic desire to mortify the flesh). It is especially clear in the Quakers.

[2] Baxter (*Saints' Everlasting Rest*, p. 12) repudiates this with precisely the same reasoning as the Jesuits: the body must have what it needs, otherwise one becomes a slave to it.

[3] This ideal is clearly present, especially for Quakerism, in the first period of its development. The Quaker was, so to speak, a living law of marginal utility. 'Moderate use of the creature' is definitely permissible, but in particular one might pay attention to the quality and durability of materials so long as it did not lead to vanity.

condemned as covetousness, mammonism, etc., was the pursuit of riches for their own sake. For wealth in itself was a temptation. But here asceticism was the power 'which ever seeks the good but ever creates evil'; what was evil in its sense was possession and its temptations. For, in conformity with the Old Testament and in analogy with the ethical valuation of good works, asceticism looked upon the pursuit of wealth as an end in itself as highly reprehensible; but the attainment of it as a fruit of labour in a calling was a sign of God's blessing. And even more important: the religious valuation of restless, continuous, systematic work in a wordly calling, as the highest means to asceticism, and at the same time the surest and most evident proof of rebirth and genuine faith, must have been the most powerful conceivable lever for the expansion of that attitude toward life which we have here called the spirit of capitalism.[1]

When the limitation of consumption is combined with this release of acquisitive activity, the inevitable practical result is obvious: accumulation of capital through ascetic compulsion to save.[2] The restraints which were imposed upon the consumption of wealth naturally served to increase it by making possible the productive investment of capital. How strong this influence was is not, unfortunately, susceptible of exact statistical demonstration. In New England the connection is so evident that it did not escape

---

[1] For those to whom no causal explanation is adequate without an economic (or materialistic as it is unfortunately still called) interpretation, it may be remarked that I consider the influence of economic development on the fate of religious ideas to be very important and shall later attempt to show how in our case the process of mutual adaptation of the two took place. On the other hand, those religious ideas themselves simply cannot be deduced from economic circumstances. They are in themselves, that is beyond doubt, the most powerful plastic elements of national character, and contain a law of development and a compelling force entirely their own. Moreover, the most important differences, so far as non-religious factors play a part, are, as with Lutheranism and Calvinism, the result of political circumstances, not economic.

[2] That is what Eduard Bernstein means to express when he says, in the essay referred to above (pp. 625, 681), 'Asceticism is a bourgeois virtue.' His discussion is the first which has suggested these important relationships. But the connection is a much wider one than he suspected. For not only the accumulation of capital, but the ascetic rationalisation of the whole of economic life was involved.

For the American Colonies, the difference between the Puritan North, where, on account of the ascetic compulsion to save, capital in search of investment was always available, from the conditions in the South has already been clearly brought out by Doyle.

the eye of so discerning a historian as Doyle.[1] But in Holland also, which was really only dominated by strict Calvinism for seven years, the greater simplicity of life in the more seriously religious circles, in combination with great wealth, led to an excessive propensity to accumulation.

It is evident, furthermore, that the tendency which has existed everywhere and at all times, and is quite strong in Germany today for middle-class fortunes to be absorbed into the nobility, was necessarily checked by the Puritan antipathy to the feudal way of life. English mercantilist writers of the seventeenth century attributed the superiority of Dutch capital to English to the circumstance that newly acquired wealth there did not regularly seek investment in land. Also, since it is not simply a question of the purchase of land, it did not there seek to transfer itself to feudal habits of life, and thereby to remove itself from the possibility of capitalistic investment.[2] The high esteem for agriculture as a peculiarly important branch of activity, and one especially consistent with piety, which the Puritans shared, applied (for instance in Baxter) not to the landlord but to the yeoman and

[1] Doyle, *The English in America*, II, chap. i. The existence of iron-works (1643), weaving for the market (1659), and also the high development of the handicrafts in New England in the first generation after the foundation of the colonies are, from a purely economic view-point, astounding. They are in striking contrast to the conditions in the South, as well as the non-Calvinistic Rhode Island with its complete freedom of conscience. There, in spite of the excellent harbour, the report of the Governor and Council of 1686 said: 'The great obstruction concerning trade is the want of merchants and men of considerable estates amongst us' (Arnold, *History of the State of Rhode Island*, p. 490). It can in fact hardly be doubted that the compulsion continually to reinvest savings, which the Puritan curtailment of consumption exercised, played a part. In addition there was the part of Church discipline which cannot be discussed here.

[2] For England, for instance, a petition of an aristocratic Royalist (quoted in Ranke, *Engl. Geschichte*, IV, p. 197) presented after the entry of Charles II into London, advocated a legal prohibition of the acquisition of landed estates by bourgeois capital, which should thereby be forced to find employment in trade. The class of Dutch regents was distinguished as an estate from the bourgeois patricians of the cities by the purchase of landed estates. See the complaints, cited by Fruin, *Tien jaren uit den tachtigjarigen oorlog*, of the year 1652, that the regents have become landlords and are no longer merchants. To be sure these circles had never been at bottom strictly Calvinistic. And the notorious scramble for membership of the nobility and titles in large parts of the Dutch middle class in the second half of the seventeenth century in itself shows that at least for this period the contrast between English and Dutch conditions must be accepted with caution. In this case the power of hereditary moneyed property broke through the ascetic spirit.

farmer, in the eighteenth century, not to the squire but to the rational cultivator.[1] Through the whole of English society in the time since the seventeenth century runs the conflict between the squirearchy, the representatives of 'merrie old England', and the Puritan circles of widely varying social influence.[2] Both elements, that of an unspoiled naïve joy of life, and that of a strictly regulated, reserved self-control and conventional ethical conduct are even today combined to form the English national character.[3] Similarly, the early history of the North American colonies is dominated by the sharp contrast of the adventurers, who wanted to set up plantations with the labour of indentured servants and live as feudal lords, and the specifically middle-class outlook of the Puritans.[4]

As far as the influence of the Puritan outlook extended, under all circumstances—and this is, of course, much more important than the mere encouragement of capital accumulation—it favoured the development of a rational bourgeois economic life; it was the most important, and above all the only consistent influence in the development of that life. It stood at the cradle of modern economic man.

To be sure, these Puritanical ideals tended to give way under excessive pressure from the temptations of wealth, as the Puritans themselves knew very well. With great regularity we find the most genuine adherents of Puritanism among the classes which were rising from a lowly status,[5] the small bourgeois and farmers,

---

[1] Upon the strong movement for bourgeois capital to buy English landed estates followed the great period of prosperity of English agriculture.

[2] Even down into this century Anglican landlords have often refused to accept Nonconformists as tenants. At the present time the two parties of the Church are of approximately equal numbers, while in earlier times the Nonconformists were always in the minority.

[3] H. Levy (article in *Archiv für Sozialwissenschaft und Sozialpolitik*, XLVI, p. 605) rightly notes that according to the native character of the English people, as seen from numerous of its traits, they were, if anything, less disposed to welcome an ascetic ethic and the middle-class virtues than other peoples. A hearty and unrestrained enjoyment of life was, and is, one of their fundamental traits. The power of Puritan asceticism at the time of its predominance is shown most strikingly in the astonishing degree to which this trait of character was brought under discipline among its adherents.

[4] This contrast recurs continually in Doyle's presentation. In the attitude of the Puritan to everything the religious motive always played an important part (not always, of course, the sole important one).

[5] This is noted by Petty (*Pol. Arith.*), and all the contemporary sources without exception speak in particular of the Puritan sectarians, Baptists, Quakers, Mennonites, etc., as belonging partly to a propertyless class, partly to one of

while the *beati possidentes*, even among Quakers, are often found tending to repudiate the old ideals.[1] It was the same fate which again and again befell the predecessor of this wordly asceticism, the monastic asceticism of the Middle Ages. In the latter case, when rational economic activity had worked out its full effects by strict regulation of conduct and limitation of consumption, the wealth accumulated either succumbed directly to the nobility, as in the time before the Reformation, or monastic discipline threatened to break down, and one of the numerous reformations became necessary.

(B) *Natural Law*[2]

NATURAL LAW AS THE NORMATIVE STANDARD OF POSITIVE LAW

Conceptions of the 'rightness of the law' are sociologically relevant within a rational positive legal order only in so far as the particular answer to the problem gives rise to practical consequences for the behaviour of law makers, legal practitioners, and social groups interested in the law. In other words, they become sociologically relevant only when practical legal life is materially affected by the conviction of the particular 'legitimacy' of certain legal maxims, and of the directly binding force of certain principles which are

---

small capitalists, and contrast them both to the great merchant aristocracy and the financial adventurers. But it was from just this small capitalist class, and not from the great financial magnates, monopolists, government contractors, lenders to the King, colonial entrepreneurs, promoters, etc., that there originated what was characteristic of Occidental capitalism: the middle-class organisation of industrial labour on the basis of private property (see Unwin, *Industrial Organisation in the Sixteenth and Seventeenth Centuries* (London, 1914), pp. 196 ff.). To see that this difference was fully known even to contemporaries, compare Parker's *Discourse Concerning Puritans* of 1641, where the contrast to promoters and courtiers is also emphasised.

[1] On the way in which this was expressed in the politics of Pennsylvania in the eighteenth century, especially during the War of Independence, see Sharpless, *A Quaker Experiment in Government* (Philadelphia, 1902).

[2] Source: *On Law in Economy and Society*, pp. 287–300.
The footnotes to this section have been slightly shortened by the editor.

not to be disrupted by any concessions to positive law imposed by
mere power. Such a situation has repeatedly existed in the course
of history, but quite particularly at the beginning of modern times
and during the Revolutionary period, and in America it still exists.
The substantive content of such maxims is usually designated as
'Natural Law'.

We encountered the *lex naturae* earlier[1] as an essentially Stoic
creation which was taken over by *Christianity* for the purpose of
constructing a bridge between its own ethics and the norms of the
world.[2] It was the law legitimated by God's will for all men of this
world of sin and violence, and thus stood in contrast to those of
God's commands which were revealed directly to the faithful and
are evident only to the elect. But here we must look at the lex
naturae from another angle. Natural law is the sum-total of all
those norms which are valid independently of, and superior to,
any positive law and which owe their dignity not to arbitrary
enactment but, on the contrary, provide the very legitimation for
the binding force of positive law. Natural law has thus been the
collective term for those norms which owe their legitimacy not to
their origin from a legitimate lawgiver, but to their immanent and
teleological qualities. It is the specific and only consistent type of
legitimacy of a legal order which can remain, once religious
revelation and the authoritarian sacredness of a tradition and its
bearers have lost their force. Natural law has thus been the specific
form of legitimacy of a revolutionarily created order. The in-
vocation of natural law has repeatedly been the method by which
classes in revolt against the existing order have legitimated their
aspirations, in so far as they did not, or could not, base their claims
upon positive religious norms or revelation. Not every natural law,
however, has been 'revolutionary' in its intentions, in the sense that
it would provide the justification for the realisation of certain
norms by violence or by passive disobedience against an existing
order. Indeed, natural law has also served to legitimate authoritarian powers of the most diverse types. A 'natural law of the
historically real' has been quite influential in opposition to the

---

[1] No such passage can be found. [Rheinstein's footnote.]

[2] See E. Troeltsch, *The Social Teachings of the Christian Churches* (2 vols.,
tr. by O. Wyon, London, 1931) and Weber's remarks on Troeltsch's paper on
'The Stoic-Christian Natural Law' in *Verhandlungen des Deutschen Soziologen-
tags* (1910), I, pp. 196, 210, repr. in *Ges. Aufs. zur Soziologie und Sozialpolitik*
(1924), p. 462. [Rheinstein's footnote.]

type of natural law which is based upon or produces abstract norms. A natural law axiom of this provenience can be found, for instance, as the basis of the theory of the historical school concerning the pre-eminence of 'customary law', a concept clearly formulated by this school for the first time. It became quite explicit in the assertion that a legislator 'could' not in any legally effective way restrict the sphere of validity of customary law by any enactment or exclude the derogation of the enacted law by custom. It was said to be impossible to forbid historical development to take its course. The same assumption by which enacted law is reduced to the rank of 'mere' positive law is contained also in all those half-historical and half-naturalistic theories of Romanticism which regard the *Volksgeist*[1] as the only natural, and thus the only legitimate, source from which law and culture can emanate, and according to which all 'genuine' law must have grown up 'organically' and must be based directly upon the sense of justice, in contrast to 'artificial', i.e., purposefully enacted, law. The irrationalism of such axioms stands in sharp contrast to the natural law axioms of legal rationalism which alone were able to create norms of a formal type and to which the term 'natural law' has *a potiori* been reserved for that reason.

THE ORIGINS OF MODERN NATURAL LAW

The elaboration of natural law in modern times was in part based on the religious motivation provided by the rationalistic sects;[2] it was also partly derived from the concept of nature of the Renaissance, which everywhere strove to grasp the canon of the ends of 'Nature's' will. To some extent, it is derived, too, from the idea, particularly indigenous to England, that every member of the

---

[1] Folk spirit.

[2] The role of the 'rationalist' Protestant 'sects', i.e. the Puritans, Baptists, Quakers, Methodists, etc., in the rise of the spirit of modern capitalism and, in this connection, in the development of formally rational modern law, constitutes one of the central themes in Weber's thought. The problem is treated extensively in the first volume of his *Ges. Aufsätze zur Religionssoziologie* (Parsons' tr. 1930), where the role of the sects is discussed on pp. 207–36 (= Essays 302 *et seq.* and 450–9 [Weber's footnotes contain extensive references to literature]). In *W.u.G.*, sociology of religion is treated in Part II, c. IV (pp. 227–356 and, as to the sects in particular, at pp. 812–17); see, furthermore, *History* (1950 ed.), 365. [Rheinstein's footnote.]

community has certain inherent natural rights. This specifically English concept of 'birthright' arose essentially under the influence of the popular conception that certain rights, which had been confirmed in Magna Charta as the special status rights of the barons, were national liberties of all Englishmen as such and that they were thus immune against any interference by the King or any other political authority. But the transition to the conception that every human being as such has certain rights was mainly completed through the rationalistic enlightenment of the seventeenth and eighteenth centuries with the aid, for a time, of powerful religious, particularly Anabaptist, influences.

TRANSFORMATION OF FORMAL INTO SUBSTANTIVE NATURAL LAW

The axioms of natural law fall into very different groups, of which we shall consider only those which bear some especially close relation to the economic order. The natural law legitimacy of positive law can be connected either with formal or with substantive conditions. The distinction is not a clear-cut one, because there simply cannot exist a completely formal natural law; the reason is that such a natural law would consist entirely of general legal concepts devoid of any content. Nonetheless, the distinction has great significance. The purest type of the first category is that 'natural law' concept which arose in the seventeenth and eighteenth centuries as a result of the already mentioned influences, especially in the form of the 'contract theory', and more particularly the individualistic aspects of that theory. All legitimate law rests upon enactment, and all enactment, in turn, rests upon rational agreement. This agreement is either, first, real, i.e., derived from an actual original contract of free individuals, which also regulates the form in which new law is to be enacted in the future; or, second, ideal, in the sense that only that law is legitimate whose content does not contradict the conception of a reasonable order enacted by free agreement. The essential elements in such a natural law are the 'freedoms', and above all, 'freedom of contract'. The voluntary rational contract became one of the universal formal principles of natural law construction, either as the assumed real historical basis of all rational consociations including the state, or, at least, as the regulative standard of evaluation. Like every formal natural law, this type is conceived as a system of rights legitimately acquired by purposive contract, and, as far as economic goods are concerned, it rests upon the basis of a community of economic agreement created by the full development of property. Its essential components are property and the freedom to dispose of property, i.e., property legitimately acquired by free contractual transaction made either as 'primeval contract' with the whole world, or with certain persons. Freedom of competition is implied as a constituent element. Freedom of contract has formal limits only to the extent that contracts, and associational conduct in general, must neither infringe upon the natural law by which they are legitimated nor impair inalienable freedoms. This basic principle applies to both private arrangements of individuals and the official actions of the organs of society meant to be obeyed by its members. Nobody may validly surrender himself into political or private slavery. For the rest, no enactment *can* validly limit the free disposition of the individual over his property and his working power. Thus, for example, every act of social welfare legislation prohibiting certain contents of the free labour contract is, on that account, an infringement of freedom of contract. Until quite recently the Supreme Court of the United States has held that any such legislation is invalid on the purely formal ground that it is incompatible with the natural law preambles to the constitutions.[1]

'Nature' and 'Reason' are the substantive criteria of what is legitimate from the standpoint of natural law. Both are regarded as the same, and so are the rules that are derived from them, so that general propositions about regularities of factual occurrences and general norms of conduct are held to coincide. The knowledge gained by human 'reason' is regarded as identical with the 'nature of things' or, as one would say nowadays, the 'logic of things'. The 'ought' is identical with the 'is', i.e., that which exists in the universal average. Those norms, which are arrived at by the logical analysis of the concepts of the law and ethics, belong, just as the 'laws of nature', to those generally binding rules which 'not even God Himself could change', and with which a legal order must not come into conflict. Thus, for instance, the only kind of money

---

[1] *Sic.* What is meant is obviously the due process clause of the Fourteenth Amendment of the Constitution of the United States. [Rheinstein's footnote.]

which meets the requirements of the 'nature of things' and the principle of the legitimacy of vested rights is that which has achieved the position of money through the free exchange of goods, in other words, metallic money. Some fifteenth-century fanatics therefore argued that, according to natural law, the state should rather go to pieces than that the legitimate stability of the law be sullied by the illegitimacy of 'artificially' created paper money.[1] The very 'concept' of the state is said to be abused by an infringement upon the legitimate law.

This formalism of natural law, however, was softened in several ways. First of all, in order to establish relations with the existing order, natural law had to accept legitimate grounds for the

---

[1] The source for this statement could not be located. It is difficult to visualise how anyone could have argued against paper money in the fifteenth century. While paper money had been used repeatedly in China at earlier times (cf. Lexis, 'Papiergeld', 6 *Handwörterbuch der Staatswissenschaften*, 3rd ed. 1911, p. 997; Weber, *Ges. Aufs. zur Religionssoziologie*, 286), it was practically unknown in the West before the late seventeenth century. Both Lexis (loc. cit.) and W. Lotz (*Finanzwissenschaft* [2nd ed. 1931], 885) mention the occasional use of leather and similar emergency means of payment; however, 'the systematic use for the procurement of public revenue of redeemable promises of payment circulating as currency' is said to be connected with the establishment of the Bank of England in 1694. Before that time manipulations of the currency were carried on by alteration of the coinage, as it was widely practised by princes (cf. Palyi, 'Coinage', 3 *Encyc. Soc. Sci.*, 622). In France, for instance, the coinage was altered no less than seventy-one times between 1351 and 1360, resulting in serious unrest and an uprising in Paris under Etienne Marcel (cf. A. Landry, *Essay Economique sur les Mutations des Monnaies dans l'ancienne France* [1910].)

The problem of the permissibility of such manipulation was widely discussed in the literature. The legists generally supported the princes, the canonists were more reluctant, and the Aristotelians were critical, occasionally basing their position on natural law arguments. Nicolas Oresmes (c. 1320–1382) denied that the prince had any power of his own to change the coinage but conceded that he might do so with the consent of the Estates General for urgent reasons of the common weal (E. Bridrey, *Nicole Oresme* [1906]; P. Harsin, 'Oresme', 11 *Encyc. Soc. Sci.*, 479; A. E. Monroe, *Early Economic Thought* [1924] 79). Strong criticism was also voiced by Gabriel Biel (d. in 1495; cf. W. Roscher, *Geschichte der Nationalökonomik in Deutschland* [1874] 26), Cyriakus Spangenberg (1528–1604; cf. Roscher, op. cit., 169), and, particularly, in an anonymous pamphlet, published about 1530, on the occasion of a change in the monetary system of Saxony (W. Lotz, *Die drei Flugschriften über den Münzstreit der sächsischen Albertiner und Ernestiner* [1893], esp. at p. 10). No author could be found, however, who would have radically condemned any currency change under any circumstances. Nor could there be found any writer of the eighteenth or nineteenth century taking the position stated in Weber's text (cf. A. E. Monroe, op. cit.; and, by the same author, *Monetary Theory before Adam Smith* [1923]; Roscher, op. cit.). [Rheinstein's footnote.]

acquisition of rights which could not be derived from freedom of contract, especially acquisition through inheritance. There were numerous attempts to base the law of inheritance on natural law. They were mainly of philosophical rather than positively juristic origin, and so we shall disregard them here. In the last analysis, of course, substantive motives almost always enter the picture, and highly artificial constructions are thus frequent. Many other institutions of the prevailing system, too, could not be legitimated except on practical utilitarian grounds. By 'justifying' them, natural law 'reason' easily slipped into utilitarian thinking, and this shift expresses itself in the change of meaning of the concept of 'reasonableness'. In purely formal natural law, the reasonable is that which is derivable from the eternal order of nature and logic, both being readily blended with one another. But from the very beginning, the English concept of 'reasonable' contained by implication the meaning of 'rational' in the sense of 'practically appropriate'. From this it could be concluded that what would lead in practice to absurd consequences cannot constitute the law desired by nature and reason. This signified the express introduction of substantive presuppositions into the concept of reason which had in fact always been implicit in it.[1] As a matter of fact, it was with the aid of this shift in the meaning of the term that the Supreme Court of the United States was able to free itself from formal natural law so as to be able to recognise the validity of certain acts of social legislation.

In principle, however, the formal natural law was transformed into a substantive natural law as soon as the legitimacy of an acquired right came to be tied up with the substantive economic rather than with the formal modes of its acquisition. Lasalle, in his 'System of Vested Rights', still sought to solve a particular problem in natural law fashion by formal means, in his case by those derived from Hegel's theory of evolution. The inviolability of a right formally and legitimately acquired on the basis of a positive enactment is presupposed, but the natural law limitation of this type of legal positivism becomes evident in connection with the problem of the so-called retroactivity of laws and the related question of the state's duty to pay compensation where a privilege

[1] What Weber has in mind is the shift from natural law thinking to utilitarianism, as expressed by Bentham, John Stuart Mill, and Spencer. [Rheinstein's footnote.]

G

is abolished. The attempted solution, which is of no interest to us here, is of a thoroughly formal and natural law character.

The decisive turn towards substantive natural law is connected primarily with socialist theories of the exclusive legitimacy of the acquisition of wealth by one's own labour. For this view rejects not only all unearned income acquired through the channels of inheritance or by means of a guaranteed monopoly, but also the formal principle of freedom of contract and general recognition of the legitimacy of all rights acquired through the instrumentality of contracting. According to these theories, all appropriations of goods must be tested substantively by the extent to which they rest on labour as their ground of acquisition.

CLASS RELATIONS IN NATURAL LAW IDEOLOGY

Naturally, both the formal rationalistic natural law of freedom of contract and the substantive natural law of the exclusive legitimacy of the product of labour have definite class implications. Freedom of contract and all the propositions regarding as legitimate the property derived therefrom obviously belong to the natural law of the groups interested in market transactions, i.e., those interested in the ultimate appropriation of the means of production. Conversely, the doctrine that land is not produced by anybody's labour, and that it is thus incapable of being appropriated at all, constitutes a protest against the closedness of the circle of land-owners, and thus corresponds with the class situation of a pro-letarianised peasantry whose restricted opportunities for self-maintenance force them under the yoke of the land monopolists.[1] It is equally clear that such slogans must acquire a particularly dramatic power where the product of agricultural exploitation still depends primarily upon the natural condition of the soil and where the appropriation of the land is not, at least internally, completed; where, furthermore, agriculture is not carried on in rationally organised large-scale enterprises, and where the income

[1] On this and the following, see Weber's discussion of the Russian Revolution of 1905 in *Archiv f. Sozialwissenschaft* (1906), XXII, 234 and XXIII, 165; see also his article on 'Russlands Übergang zur Scheindemokratie' (1917), 23 *Die Hilfe* 272, repr. *Gesammelte Politische Schriften* (1921), 107. [Rheinstein's footnote.]

of the landlord is either derived entirely from the tenants' rent or is produced through the use of peasant equipment and peasant labour. All these conditions exist in large measure in the area of the 'black earth'.[1] As regards its positive meaning, this natural law of the small peasantry is ambiguous. It can mean in the first place the right to a share in the land to the extent of one's own labour power (*trudovaya norma*); or, secondly, a right to the ownership of land to the extent of the traditional standard of living (*potrebityelnaya norma*). In conventional terminology the postulate thus means either the 'right to work' or the 'right to a minimum standard of living'; thirdly, however, the two may be combined with the demand for the right to the full product of one's labour.

As far as one can judge today, the Russian Revolution of the last decade will in all probability have been the last of the world's natural law-oriented agrarian revolutions.[2] It has been bled to death by its own intrinsic contradictions, including those between its ideological postulates. Those two natural law positions are not only incompatible with one another, but they are also contradictory to the historical, realistically political and practically economical programmes of the peasantry, all of which are again incongruous with the evolutionist-Marxist agrarian programmes. The result has been hopeless confusion among the Revolution's own basic dogmas.

Those three 'socialist' rights of the individual have also played a role in the ideologies of the industrial proletariat. The first and the second are theoretically possible under handicraft as well as under capitalistic conditions of the working class; the third, however, is possible only under handicraft conditions. Under capitalism the third right of natural law is possible not at all or only where cost prices are strictly and universally maintained in all exchange transactions. In agriculture, it can be applied only where production is not capitalistic, since capitalism shifts the attribution of the agricultural produce of the soil from the direct place of agricultural production to the shop, where the agricultural implements, artificial fertilisers, etc., are produced; and the same holds true for

---

[1] Black earth—the fertile regions of the Ukraine and South Russia.
[2] In the second of the two articles mentioned in n.[1] *supra*, Weber, at p. 314, predicted the coming of a new revolution in Russia, which would be oriented toward communism rather than natural law and which would create a state of affairs different from anything that had ever existed before (*etwas wirklich noch nicht Dagewesenes*). [Rheinstein's footnote.]

industry. Quite generally, where the return is determined by the sale of the product in a freely competitive market, the content of the right of the individual to the full value of his product inevitably loses its meaning. There simply is no longer an individual 'labour yield', and if the claim is to make any sense it can be only as the collective claim of all those who find themselves in a common class situation. In practice, this comes down to the demand for a 'living wage', i.e., to a special variant of the 'right to the standard of living as determined by traditional needs'. It thus resembles the medieval 'just price' as demanded by ecclesiastical ethics, which, in case of doubt, was determined by the test (and occasionally experimentally) of whether or not at the given price the craftsmen in question could maintain the standard of living appropriate to their social status.

The 'just price' itself, which was the most important natural law element in canonist economic doctrine, fell prey to the same fate. In the canonistic discussions of the determinants of the 'just price' one can observe how this labour value price corresponding to the 'subsistence principle' is gradually replaced by the competitive price which becomes the new 'natural' price in the same measure as the market community progresses. In the writings of Antonin of Florence the latter had already come to prevail. In the outlook of the Puritans it was, of course, completely dominant. The price which was to be rejected as 'unnatural' was now one which did not rest on the competition of the free market, i.e., the price which was influenced by monopolies or other arbitrary human intervention. Throughout the whole puritanically influenced Anglo-Saxon world this principle has had a great influence up to the very present. Because of the fact that the principle derived its dignity from natural law, it remained a far stronger support for the ideal of 'free competition' than those purely utilitarian economic theories which were produced on the Continent in the manner of Bastiat.

PRACTICAL SIGNIFICANCE AND DISINTEGRATION OF NATURAL LAW

All natural law dogmas have influenced more or less considerably both law-making and law-finding. Some of them survived the economic conditions of the time of their origin and have come to constitute an independent factor in legal development. Formally, they have strengthened the tendency towards logically abstract law, especially the power of logic in legal thinking. Substantively, their influence has varied, but it has been significant everywhere. This is not the place to trace in detail these influences and the changes and compromises of the various natural law axioms. The codifications of the pre-revolutionary rationalistic modern state, as well as the revolutionary codifications, were influenced by the dogmas of natural law, and they ultimately derived the legitimacy of the law which they created from its reasonableness. We have already seen how easily, on the basis of such a concept, the shift from the ethical and juristically formal to the utilitarian and technically substantive could, and did, take place. This transformation, for reasons which we have already discussed, was very favourable to the pre-revolutionary patriarchal powers, while the codifications of the Revolution, which took place under the influence of the bourgeoisie, stressed and strengthened the formal natural law, which guaranteed to the individual his rights vis-à-vis the political authorities.

The rise of Socialism at first meant the growing dominance of substantive natural law doctrines in the minds of the masses and even more in the minds of their theorists from among the intelligentsia. These substantive natural law doctrines could not, however, achieve practical influence over the administration of justice, simply because, before they had achieved a position to do so, they were already being disintegrated by the rapidly growing positivistic and relativistic-evolutionistic scepticism of the very same intellectual strata. Under the influence of this anti-metaphysical radicalism, the eschatological expectations of the masses sought support in prophecies rather than in postulates. Hence in the domain of the revolutionary theories of law, natural law doctrine was destroyed by the evolutionary dogmatism of Marxism, while from the side of 'official' learning it was annihilated partly by the Comtean evolutionary scheme and partly by the historicist theories of organic growth. A final contribution in the same direction was made by Realpolitik which, under the impact of modern power politics, had come to affect the treatment of public law.

The method of the public law theorists has been, and still is to a great extent, to point to certain apparent practical-political absurdities as the consequence of the juristic theory which they happen to oppose; and then to treat the theory as effectively disposed of forever after. This method is not only directly opposed to that of formal law, but it also contains nothing of substantive natural law. In the main, continental jurisprudence, even up to the most recent times, proceeds on the basis of the largely unchallenged axiom of the logical 'closedness' of the positive law. It seems for the first time to have been expressly stated by Bentham as a protest against the case law rut and the irrationality of the common law. It is indirectly supported by all those tendencies which reject all transcendental law, especially natural law, including, to this extent, the historical school. While it would hardly seem possible to eradicate completely from legal practice all the latent influence of unacknowledged axioms of natural law, for a variety of reasons the axioms of natural law have been deeply discredited. The conflict between the axioms of substantive and formal natural law is insoluble. Evolutionist theories have been at work in various forms. All metajuristic axioms in general have been subject to ever continuing disintegration and relativisation. In consequence of both juridical rationalism and modern intellectual scepticism in general, the axioms of natural law have lost all capacity to provide the fundamental bases of a legal system. Compared with firm beliefs in the positive religiously revealed character of a legal norm or in the inviolable sacredness of an age-old tradition, even the most convincing norms arrived at by abstraction seem to be too subtle to serve as the bases of a legal system. Consequently, legal positivism has, at least for the time being, advanced irresistibly. The disappearance of the old natural law conceptions has destroyed all possibility of providing the law with a metaphysical dignity by virtue of its immanent qualities. Indeed, in the great majority of its most important provisions, it has been unmasked all too visibly as the product or the technical means of a compromise between conflicting interests.

But this extinction of the metajuristic implications of the law is one of those ideological developments which, while they have increased scepticism towards the dignity of the particular rules of a concrete legal order, have also effectively promoted the actual obedience to the power, now viewed solely from an instrumentalist standpoint, of the authorities who claim legitimacy at the moment.

Among the practitioners of the law this attitude has been particularly pronounced.

LEGAL POSITIVISM AND THE LEGAL PROFESSION

The vocational responsibility of maintaining the existing legal system seems to place the practitioners of the law in general among the 'conservative' forces. This is true in the twofold sense that legal practitioners are inclined to remain cool, not only toward the pressure of substantive postulates put forward from 'below' in the name of 'social' ideals, but also towards those from 'above' which are put forward in the name of patriarchal power, or the welfare-interests of the sovereign. Of course, this statement should not be taken as representing the whole truth without qualifications. The role of the representative of the underprivileged, and of the advocate of formal equality before the law is particularly suited to the attorney by reason of his direct relationship with his clients, as well as by reason of his character as a private person working for a living and his fluctuating social status. This is why attorneys, and lawyers in general, have played such a leading role in the movements of the popolani of the Italian communes and, later, in all the bourgeois revolutions of modern times as well as in the socialist parties. It also explains why in purely democratic countries, such as in France, Italy, or the United States, the lawyers, as the professionally expert technicians of the legal crafts, as honoratiores, and as the fiduciaries of their clients, are the natural aspirants to political careers.

Under certain circumstances, judges, too, have maintained strong opposition to patriarchal powers, either for ideological reasons or because of considerations of status group solidarity or, occasionally, for economic reasons. To them, the fixed and regular determinateness of all external rights and duties is apt to appear as a worthwhile value to be pursued for its own sake; this specifically 'bourgeois' element in their thought has determined their attitudes in the political conflicts which were fought for the purpose of limiting authoritarian patrimonial arbitrariness and favouritism.

Whether the legal profession would take the side either of the authoritarian or of the anti-authoritarian powers, once the 'rule-boundedness' of the social order had been achieved, depended upon whether the emphasis was more upon mere 'order', or upon 'liberty', in the sense of guaranty and security of the individual. The choice depended, in the terminology of Radbruch, on whether law was viewed more as 'regulation' or as the source of 'rights'.[1] But quite apart from this antinomy, it was also the previously mentioned alternative between the formal and substantive legal ideals and the vigorous, economically conditioned revival of the latter, both in the upper and lower strata of the social hierarchy, that weakened the oppositionist tendencies of the lawyers as such. We shall discuss later just what technical devices authoritative powers have used to overcome resistance from within the judiciary.[2] Among the general ideological factors which account for the change in the lawyers' attitude, the disappearance of the belief in natural law has played a major role. If the legal profession of the present day manifests at all typical ideological affinities to various power groups, its members are inclined to stand on the side of 'order', which in practice means that they will take the side of the 'legitimate' authoritarian political power that happens to predominate at the given moment. In this respect, they differ from the lawyers of the English and French revolutionary periods and of the period of enlightenment in general. They differ also from those who had to act within the framework of patrimonial despotism or had been sitting in [German ninteenth-century] parliamentary bodies and municipal councils down to Prussia's 'circuit judges' parliament' of the 1860's.

[1] Cf. *Rechtsphilosophie* (1914 ed.); the terminology is no longer used, however, in the versions of 1932 and 1950. [Rheinstein's footnote.]
[2] This intended investigation was not carried out by Weber. [Rheinstein's footnote.]

(C) Socialism[1]

SPEECH FOR THE GENERAL INFORMATION OF AUSTRIAN OFFICERS IN VIENNA, 1918
[Translated by D. Hÿtch]

As it is the first time that I have had the honour of addressing the Officer Corps of the Royal Imperial Army, you will understand that this is a somewhat embarrassing situation for me, principally because I am completely ignorant of the conditions, of the internal relations in the operation of the R.I.A., the conditions which are crucial for the exertion of influence by the officer corps on the troops also. It is obvious that the officer of the Reserve or the Civil Defence is always a dilettante, not only through his lack of scientific training at military school, but also through not being in constant touch with the whole internal nervous system of the organisation. Nevertheless, when one has spent periods of time within the German Army, as I have, in very different areas of Germany, repeatedly and over a number of years, I believe myself to have a sufficient notion of the relations between officers, N.C.O.'s and men to be able to see at least that this or that method of wielding influence is *possible*, or that this or that way is difficult or impossible. As far as the R.I.A. is concerned, of course, I have not the slightest idea of all this. If I have any idea whatsoever of the internal relations of the R.I.A., it is only one of colossal real difficulties which for me follow simply from the linguistic circumstances. Officers of the R.I.A. Reserve have tried on several occasions to explain to me how they manage to maintain contact with the men without any real knowledge of their language—that contact which is indispensable in order to exert any influence of any kind over the service. For myself, I can only speak from German conceptions, and I should like first to make some introductory observations about the way in which this exercising of influence proceeded in Germany.

These observations are made from a 'worm's-eye view'; that is, on my sometimes frequent journeys in Germany I had made it a rule, when the distances were not very great and when the work

[1] Source: *Gesammelte Aufsätze zur Soziologie und Sozialpolitik* (Tübingen: J. C. B. Mohr, 1924).

before me was not too arduous, always to travel third class, and thus in the course of time I came across many hundreds of people returning from or travelling to the front, just at the period when what was known as the task of education by the officers was introduced. So, without having had any motive for interrogating the men or inducing them to speak, I heard extraordinarily numerous opinions about the matter from the men's side. Moreover, these were invariably reliable men, for whom the officer's authority stood firm as a rock; only rarely were there also some who mentally adopted a somewhat different attitude. The point was always this, that the great difficulty of any education work had to be recognised very soon. There was one thing in particular: as soon as the suspicion arose among the men that it was in some way a matter of *party* politics being directly or indirectly promoted, irrespective of their nature, mistrust was always there among a great proportion of them. When they went on leave, they came into contact with men from their party, and then, naturally, it became difficult to maintain a real relationship of confidence in them. Moreover there was also this great difficulty: admittedly the men acknowledged the military expertise of the officer completely without reservation—I have never encountered anything else, although of course even in Germany there was abuse on occasion, sometimes to do with the staff, sometimes with something else, but military authority has never been fundamentally called into question—on the other hand one came across the feeling: 'Hm, when we receive instruction from the officers about the conditions of our private life and their consequences, the plain fact emerges that the officer still belongs to a different class from ours, and with the best will in the world it is impossible for him to put himself in our situation, at the machine or behind the plough, as completely as we do ourselves.' That was repeatedly expressed in a series of sometimes naive remarks, and I had the feeling that due to enlightenment being carried out in the wrong way the authority of the officer could perhaps suffer, even in the military sphere where it remains steadfast, because the men do not entirely accept authority where they claim they are on their own ground.

Now a further mistake which was often made, not now, but in earlier altercations with socialism. It has long been the practice, and with good reason, to start, as the party-political opponents of social democracy used to do, by reproaching the workers as follows, with reference to trade union and party officials: 'They, in fact, are the people who live off the workers' pennies in the literal sense of the phrase, far more than the employers do.' To which every worker, of course, replies: 'Certainly these people live off my pennies. I pay them. But for that very reason I can rely on them, they are dependent on me, I know that they must represent my interests. I shan't change my mind on that. That's worth a few coppers.' Now people have rightly started by seeking in that way to discredit that class of intellectuals who are coining all over the place the watchwords, slogans and—you may say in solace—phrases which are being employed by all parties without exception, including, then, the parties of the left and the social democratic party. It is in my opinion especially to be welcomed that such a good position vis-à-vis the trade unions was adopted in Germany. You can, however, take any attitude you please towards the trade unions. They make their blunders too. Nevertheless this attitude towards the trade unions was intelligent from a military point of view; for they still represent something which is also characteristic of military units. Think what you like about strikes. They are usually a fight for interests, for wages; yet very often not only for wages, but also for ideals: for honour, as the workers understand it—and each man claims for himself that he knows what is to be understood by that. The feeling of honour, of fellowship, among comrades in one factory or in one and the same departments binds them together, and in the last analysis this is a feeling upon which, in another way, the solidarity of military units rests. And as there is absolutely no means of abolishing strikes—one can merely choose between openly recognised and secret organisations of this kind—I consider it well-advised also from the military point of view to take up a position on the basis of this fact: such is the situation, and as long as one can get on with the men and they do not endanger *military* interests, one comes to terms with them, as in fact has been the case in Germany. Those are my personal impressions.

Now I should like to turn to the subject upon which you have done me the honour of asking me to speak, and which is indeed one which it would take six months to deal with adequately—for it is customary to lecture at that length on such subjects to educated academic audiences—the position of socialism and attitudes towards it. Firstly I draw attention to the fact that there are 'socialists' of the most diverse kinds. There are people who call themselves socialists whom no socialist party member of whatever brand would ever recognise as such. All *parties* of purely socialistic character are *democratic* parties nowadays.

I should like first, briefly, to examine this democratic character. What, then, is democracy at the present time? The point is very relevant to our subject. Today I can, indeed, only touch upon it briefly. Democracy can mean an infinite variety of things. *Per se* it means simply that no formal inequality of political rights exists between the individual classes of the population. Yet what different consequences that has! Under the old type of democracy, in the Swiss cantons of Uri, Schwyz, Unterwalden, Appenzell and Glarus, the entire population—in Appenzell the electorate is 12,000, in the others between 3,000 and 5,000—still assembles in a big square and there they vote, when discussion is over, by a show of hands, on everything from the election of the cantonal president to the passing of a new tax law or upon any question of administration. However, if you study the lists of the presidents who were elected under such an old-style Swiss democracy over fifty or sixty years, you will find that remarkably often they were the same men, or at least that certain families had control of these offices from time immemorial; that is, that although there was a democracy in law, this democracy was in fact run aristocratically, for the simple reason that not every artisan could take on an office like that of cantonal president without ruining himself professionally. He had to be 'superfluous' in the economic sense, and only a man of some wealth is that as a rule. Or he must be highly paid and given a pension. Democracy has only these alternatives: being run cheaply by the rich in titular office, or expensively by paid professional administrators. This latter, the evolution of a professional administration, has become the fate of all modern democracies in which titular office was inadequate, that is, in the great states. That is America's current position. In theory the situation there is similar to that in Switzerland. The president of the whole Union and a good proportion of state officials are elected, if not by state assemblies, then nevertheless by direct or indirect equal franchise. The president nominates the other officials of the Union. It has been found that the officials nominated by the president are on the whole far superior to those chosen by popular election, in terms of capability and above all of incorruptibility, because the

president and the party he leads are naturally held responsible by the
electorate for seeing that the officials they nominate have at least
in some degree the qualities the voter expects.

This American democracy—which rests on the principle that
every four years, when the president changes, the 300,000 odd
officials he has to nominate will change too, and that every four
years all the governors of the individual states will change, and
with them again many thousands of civil servants—this democracy
is drawing to its end. It has been administration by dilettantes;
for these civil servants appointed by the party were nominated
according to the principle that they had rendered services to the
party and were given their posts on that account. Few questions
were asked about their qualifications; examinations and that sort
of thing were until a short while ago formally unknown to American
democracy. On the contrary, the point of view was often taken that
the office had to go round from one to the other in rotation to some
extent, so that everyone could get a slice of the cake.

I have talked to American workers about this on several
occasions. The genuine American Yankee worker stands at a
high level of wages and education. The pay of an American worker
is higher than that of many an American university lecturer. These
have all the trappings of bourgeois society, they appear in their
top hats with their wives, who behave perhaps with somewhat less
savoir faire and elegance but otherwise just like any other ladies,
while the immigrants from Europe flood into the lower classes.
When I sat, then, in company with such a worker and said to
him: 'How can you let yourselves be ruled by these people who are
put in office over you and who naturally make every bit as much
money out of their position as possible, since they owe their post
to the party and since they pay so much of the salary they draw in
taxes to the party and then have to relinquish their office after
four years without qualifying for a pension; how can you let yourselves be governed by this corrupt society which is notorious for
robbing you of hundreds of millions?' I would from time to time
receive the characteristic reply which I will repeat word for word
in all its poignancy: 'That doesn't matter, there's enough money
for stealing and still enough left for the rest to earn—for us too.
We keep an eye on these "professionals", these public servants,
we're suspicious of them. But when a trained, qualified class takes
office like they do in your country—they keep an eye on us.'

That was the decisive point for these people. The fear that such a bureaucracy as actually exists in Europe might come into being, a class of university educated, specially trained civil servants.

Now the time has, of course, long since come when even in America administration can no longer be carried on by dilettantes. Specialist civil services are growing at an enormous rate. The specialist examination was introduced; in theory it was at first obligatory only for certain more technical officials, but it quickly snowballed. There are already about 100,000 officials to be nominated by the president who can only be appointed when they have passed certain examinations. With that the first and most important step towards the reforming of the old democracy has been taken. And with that, too, the university in America has begun to play an entirely different role and the ethos of the universities has fundamentally changed also. For, and this is not always appreciated outside America, the American universities and the strata produced by them, not the war-mongers who exist in every country, were the originators of the war. When I was over there in 1904 the question American students put to me more than any other was, how are duels arranged in Germany and how do people go about getting scars. They thought it a chivalrous institution: they had to have this sport too. The serious aspect of it was that, particularly in my subject, literature was tailored to this mood: it was actually in the best works of the day that I came upon the following conclusion: 'It is fortunate that world economy is moving to a point at which it will be worth while ("a sound business view") to deprive one another of world trade by means of *warfare*; for then at last an end will come to the age in which we Americans have been undignified dollar-earners, then a warlike spirit and chivalry will rule the world once more.' They probably thought of modern warfare as being similar to the battle of Fontenoy, when the herald of the French cried to the enemy: 'Gentlemen of England, shoot first!' They thought of war as a kind of knightly sport which would re-establish class sensibility and refined feelings in place of this sordid money-grabbing. You see it: this caste judges America in just the same way as America is, in my experience, repeatedly judged in Germany, and—draws its own conclusions. The vital statesmen sprang from this caste. For America, this war will result in its emergence as a state with a large army, a corps of officers and a bureaucracy. At the time, I spoke to American

officers who were in very scant agreement with what was expected
of them by American democracy. For instance, it happened that
one day I was at the home of a colleague's daughter and the maid
was away—maids could give two hours' notice over there. The
two sons, who were naval cadets, happened to come in and their
mother said: 'You must go out now and sweep snow, otherwise it
will cost me a fine of 100 dollars a day.' The sons—they had
just been with German naval officers—thought it no fit work for
them, whereupon the mother said: 'If you won't do it, then I
must.'

This war will mean for America the evolution of a bureaucracy
and with it opportunities of advancement for university circles
(that is, of course, at the root of it as well), in short, it will result
in the Europeanisation of America in at least the same measure as
people have been talking about the Americanisation of Europe. In
large states everywhere modern democracy is becoming a bureaucratised democracy. And it must be so; for it is replacing the
aristocratic or other titular officials by a paid civil service. It is the
same everywhere, it is the same within the parties too. This is
inevitable, and is the first fact which socialism has to reckon with:
the necessity for years of specialist training, for increasingly
extensive specialisation and for administration by a specialist
civil service trained in this manner. The modern economy cannot
be run in any other way.

However, this inescapable universal bureaucratisation is, in
particular, that which is concealed behind one of the most frequently quoted socialist slogans—the slogan of the 'separation of
the worker from the tools of his trade'. What does that mean? The
worker is, so we are told 'separated' from the material resources
with which he produces, and on this separation rests the wage
slavery in which he finds himself. In this they have in mind the fact
that in the Middle Ages the worker was the owner of the technical
tools with which he produced, while the modern worker, of course,
neither does nor can own his tools whether the mine or factory in
question is run by an employer or the state. They have in mind,
further, that the artisan himself bought the raw materials which
he processed, while that is not the case, and cannot be, with the
paid worker of today; and that accordingly the product was in the
Middle Ages, and is still, in places where crafts survive, at the
disposal of the individual craftsman, who can sell it on the market

and turn it to his own profit; while in a large concern it is at the disposal not of the worker but of the owner of these tools of the trade, who again may be the state or a private employer. That is true, but the fact is by no means peculiar to the process of economic production. We encounter the same thing, for example, within the university. The old-time lecturer and university professor worked with the books and the technical resources which they procured or made for themselves; chemists, for instance, produced the things which were required by scientific industry. The mass of today's manpower within the modern university set-up, particularly the assistants in the big faculties, are on the contrary in precisely the same situation as any worker in this respect. They can be given notice at any time. Their rights in the domain of the faculty are no different from those of the worker in the domain of the factory. They must conduct themselves, just like the latter, in accordance with the regulations in force. They have no ownership of the materials or apparatus, machines, etc. which are used in a chemical, physical or biological faculty or a clinic; these are rather the property of the state, but are managed by the director of the department who levies charges for the purpose, while the assistant receives an income which does not fundamentally differ in amount from that of a trained worker.

We find just the same situation in the military sphere. The knight of olden days was the owner of his horse and his armour. He had to equip and provide for himself. The army constitution of the time was based on the principle of self-equipment. In both the cities of antiquity and the armies of the Middle Ages a man had to supply his own armour, lance and horse, and bring provisions. The modern army came into being with the establishment of the princely household, that is, when the soldier and the officer (who is indeed something other than another official, but who corresponds exactly to the official in this sense) ceased to own the tools of war-fare. It is on this, indeed, that the solidarity of the modern army rests. This, too, is why it was for so long impossible for the Russian soldiers to get away from the trenches, because of the existence of this machinery of the officer corps, the quarter-master general and other officials, and everyone in the army knew that his whole existence, including his food, depended on the functioning of this machinery. They were all 'separated' from the tools of war, just as the worker is from the tools of his trade. In a similar position to that of the knight stood the official of the feudal era, that is, a vassal invested with high administrative and judicial rank. He bore the expense of administration and jurisdiction out of his own pocket and made levies accordingly. He was therefore in possession of the tools of administration. The modern state emerges when the prince takes it into his own control, appoints salaried officials and thereby brings about the 'separation' of the officials from the tools of their trade. Everywhere we find the same thing: the tools within the factory, the state administration, the army and the university faculties are concentrated by means of a bureaucratically constructed human machine in the hands of him who controls this machine. This is due partly to purely technical considerations, to the nature of modern tools—machines, guns, etc.—but partly simply to the greater efficiency of this kind of co-operation: to the development of 'discipline', army, office, shop-floor and factory discipline. In any event it is a serious mistake to think that this separation of the worker from the tools of his trade is something peculiar to industry and, moreover, to *private* industry. The basic state of affairs is unaltered when the person of the head of this machine changes, when, say, a state president or minister controls it instead of a private industralist. The 'separation' from the means continues in any case. As long as there are mines, furnaces, railways, factories and machines, they will never be the property of an individual or of several individual workers in the sense in which the materials of a medieval craft were the property of one guildmaster or of a local trade association or guild. That is out of the question because of the nature of present-day technology.

What, then, is *socialism* in relation to this fact? The word has, as I have said, various meanings. However, what one usually thinks of as the opposite of socialism is a private economic system, a state of affairs in which provision for economic need is in the hands of private employers and is so arranged that these employers procure for themselves the material resources, administrative staff and labour force by means of bills of sale and wage contracts, and that they then have the goods made and sell them on the market at their own economic risk and in the expectation of personal gain.

This system of private economy has furnished socialist theory with the slogan of the 'anarchy of production', because it leaves open the question of whether the personal interest of the individual employers in the turnover of their products (the profit interest) functions in such a way that provision for those who need these goods is guaranteed.

It is historical fact that a change has come over the question of which of a society's needs are taken care of by business (i.e. privately) and which not privately, but socialistically, in the broadest sense of the word (i.e. by systematic organisation).

In the Middle Ages, for instance, republics such as Genoa had their great colonial wars in Cyprus conducted by limited share companies, the so-called 'Maonen'. They clubbed together to raise the necessary funds, hired mercenaries as appropriate, conquered all resistance, received the protection of the republic and naturally exploited the country, as plantation land or as an object of taxation, for their own purposes. Similarly the East India Company conquered India for England and exploited it for itself. The condottiere of the late Italian Renaissance period belonged in the same category. Like the last of them, Wallenstein, he recruited his army in his own name and out of his own capital, a proportion of the army's spoils went into his pocket, and of course he would stipulate that a certain sum be paid to him by the prince or king or emperor as a reward for his success and to cover his expenses. In a somewhat less autonomous fashion, the eighteenth-century colonel was still an employer who had to recruit and clothe troops for himself; sometimes, admittedly, he could draw on the prince's stores, but he always ran his unit largely at his own risk and for his own profit. The private management of warfare was, therefore, considered quite normal, which would seem monstrous to us today.

On the other hand, no medieval town or guild would ever have thought it conceivable that the town's corn supply or the guild's indispensable raw materials, which had to be imported for the craftsmen's work, could simply be left to free trade. On the contrary, from the days of antiquity, on a large scale in Rome, and throughout the Middle Ages it was the business of the town, not of free trade which was only supplementary. Roughly as now, in the days of wartime economy, co-operation—'nationalisation' as it is popularly called today—exists between broad branches of the economy.

What characterises our current situation is this, that private economy, bound up with private bureaucratic organisation and hence with the separation of the worker from the tools of his trade, dominates the sphere of *industrial* production which has never before in history borne these two characteristics together on such a scale; and this process coincides with the establishment of mechanical production within the factory, thus with a local accumulation of labour on the same premises, enslavement to the machine and common working discipline within the machine-shop or pit. It is the discipline which lends the contemporary mode of 'separation' of worker from materials its particular stamp.

This situation, this factory *discipline*, gave birth to modern socialism. Socialism of the most diverse types has existed everywhere, at every period and in every country of the earth. Modern socialism in its uniqueness is only possible on this basis.

This subjection to working discipline is so extraordinarily marked for the industrial worker because, in contrast to, say, a slave plantation or a socage-farm, modern industry functions on the basis of an extraordinarily keen process of *selection*. A modern factory proprietor does not employ just any worker, just because he might work for a low wage. Rather he puts the man at the machine on piece-wages and says: 'All right, now work, I shall see how much you earn'; and if the man does not prove himself capable of earning a certain minimum wage he is told: 'We are sorry, you are not suited to this occupation, we cannot use you'. He is dismissed because the machine is not working to capacity unless the man in front of it knows how to utilise it fully. Everywhere it is the same, or similar. Every modern concern, in contrast to those of antiquity which employed slave labour, where the lord was bound to the slaves he owned—if one of them died, it was a capital loss for him—rests on the principle of selection, and this selection on the other hand is intensified to the extreme by competition between employers, which constrains the individual employer to certain maximum wages: the inherent necessity of the worker's earnings corresponds to the inherent necessity of the discipline.

If the worker goes to the employer today and says: 'We cannot live on these wages and you could pay us more', in nine out of ten cases—I mean in peacetime and in those branches where there is really fierce competition—the employer is in a position to show the workers from his books that it is impossible; my competitor pays such and such wages; if I pay you even only so much more, all the profit I could pay to the shareholders disappears from my books, I could not carry on the business, for I would get no credit from the bank. Thereby he is very often just stating the naked truth. There is the additional point that under the pressure of competition profitability depends on as much human labour as possible being eliminated by labour-saving machines, and especially the highest-paid variety who cost the business most. Hence skilled workers must be replaced by unskilled workers or workers trained directly at the machine. This process is inevitable and is continually occurring.

Socialism terms all this the 'domination of men by matter', which means the domination of the end (supply meeting demand) by the means. It recognises that, while in the past there were individuals who could be held responsible for the fate of the client, bondsman or slave, this is impossible today. Therefore it attacks not individuals but the organisation of production as such. Any educated socialist will absolutely decline to hold an individual employer responsible for the worker's destined fate, but he will say it is inherent in the system, in the plight into which all parties, employer and employed, find themselves driven.

What, then, in positive terms, is socialism relative to this system? In the broadest sense of the phrase, it is what is also frequently termed 'collective economy': an economy which is, firstly, without profit, and without a situation in which private businessmen direct production at their own risk. Instead, the economy would be in the hands of officials of a people's combine which would assume control along lines which I shall discuss presently. Secondly, there would be in consequence no so-called anarchy of production, i.e. competition among employers. There is at this time, especially in Germany, much talk about our being, as a result of the war, already actually in the middle of the evolution of such a 'collective economy'. In view of this let it be briefly pointed out that the organised economy of a particular people could be based, in the manner of its organisation, on two essentially different principles: firstly, what is nowadays called nationalisation, with which all those gentlemen who work in the war industries are doubtless acquainted. It rests on the collaboration of the amalgamated firms in a particular field with state officials, be they civil or military. Supplies of raw materials, procurement of credit, prices, and the market can thus to a large extent be systematically regulated, and there can be state participation in the profits and in the policy

decisions of these syndicates. It is thought that the employer
would then be inspected by these officials, and production governed
by the state. We should then have 'true', 'real' socialism, or be
heading towards it. In Germany there is widespread scepticism
about this theory. I do not propose to discuss how it works in
wartime. However, anyone who can do sums knows that the
economy could not be carried on in peacetime as it is now if we
are not to go to our ruin, and that in peacetime this kind of
nationalisation, i.e. the compulsory syndication of the firms of
each branch of industry and the participation of the state in these
syndicates with a share in the profits in exchange for the concession
of extensive rights of control, would mean in reality not the control
of industry by the state but the control of the state by industry;
and that in a most disagreeable manner. Within the syndicates the
representatives of the state would sit at a table with the industrialists whose knowledge of the trade, commercial training,
and degree of self-interest would be far in excess of their own. In
parliament, however, would sit the representatives of the workers
who would demand that those state representatives must ensure
high wages on the one hand and low prices on the other; for, they
would say, they had the power to do it. Then again, in order not
to ruin its finances, the state, which would be sharing in the profit
and loss of such a syndicate, would naturally have an interest in
high prices and low wages. And finally the private members of the
syndicates would expect the state to guarantee the profitability of
their concerns. In the eyes of the workers, therefore, such a state
would appear to be a class state in the most literal sense of the
phrase, and I doubt whether that is politically desirable; I am
even more dubious whether it would be sensible to represent this
state of affairs now to the workers as really 'true' socialism, which
certainly seems a temptingly obvious suggestion. For the workers
would very soon find out that the lot of a miner is not affected in
the slightest by whether the pit is privately or state-owned. The
life of a worker in the coal-mines of the Saar is just the same as in
a private mining company: if the pit is badly run, i.e. is not very
profitable, then things are bad for the men too. The difference,
however, is that to strike against the state is impossible, hence that
under this kind of state socialism the dependence of the worker is
quite substantially increased. That is one of the reasons why social
democracy generally rejects this nationalisation of the economy,

this form of socialism. It is a consortium of syndicates. The decisive factor is, as before, profit; the question of what is earned by the individual industrialists who have joined forces in the syndicate and of whom one is now the treasurer continues to determine the lines along which the economy is run. And the distressing thing would be that, while at present the political and private industrial administrations (of syndicates, banks, and giant concerns) stand side by side as separate bodies, and therefore industrial power can still be curbed by political power, the two administrations would then be one body with common interests and could no longer be checked. In any event, profit would not be done away with as the guiding light of production. The state as such, however, would then have to bear in addition the hatred of workers, which is at present directed at the employers.

The contrary principle to this, in the last-named respect, could only be embodied by something like a consumer organisation, which would ask: which *needs* are to be catered for within this area of state economy? You are probably aware that numerous consumer associations, especially in Belgium, have gone over to founding their own factories. If this were extended and put in the hands of a state organisation, it would be a totally and fundamentally different kind of socialism—a consumer socialism. However, no one as yet has the slightest notion of where its leaders are to come from, nor where the interested parties might be found to bring it into being in the first place; for experience has shown that consumers as such are only to a very limited extent capable of organisation. People with a definite commercial interest can be very easily united when they are shown that by this union they obtain a profit or guaranteed profitability; this is what makes possible the creation of a socialism of industrialists such as is represented by nationalisation. On the other hand it is extraordinarily difficult to unite people who have nothing more in common with one another than their desire to purchase, or to maintain themselves, because the whole situation of the purchaser stands in the way of socialisation; even the present starvation, in Germany at least, has not, or only with great difficulty, brought the housewives of the mass of the population to accept war canteen meals, which everyone found tasty and excellently prepared, instead of their own amateurish home cooking, although they were far cheaper.

Having said this, I come finally to the kind of socialism to which the major socialist parties as they are today, i.e. the social-democratic parties, are committed in their programmes. The document which lays the foundation of this socialism is the Communist Manifesto of the year 1847, published and distributed in January 1848 by Karl Marx and Friedrich Engels. This document, however strongly we may reject it in its critical theses (at least *I* do), is in its way a work of scholarship of the highest order. That cannot be denied, neither may one deny it, because nobody believes one and it is impossible to deny it with a clear conscience. Even in the theses we nowadays reject, it is an imaginative error which politically has had very far-reaching and perhaps not always pleasant consequences, but which has brought very stimulating results for scholarship, more so than many a work of dull correctness. One thing must be said at the outset about the Communist Manifesto: it refrains, in intention if not always in practice, from moralising. It simply does not occur to the authors of the Communist Manifesto, at least according to their contention (in reality they were men of very strong feelings who by no means always adhered to it) to raise a hue and cry about the baseness and wickedness of the world. Neither do they think it their task to say: such and such institutions in the world should be arranged differently, namely in such and such a way. Rather the Communist Manifesto is a prophetic document; it *prophesies* the fall of the private industrial, or capitalistic, as they say, organisation of society and the replacement of this society first, as a transitional stage, by a proletarian dictatorship. However, beyond this transitional stage lies the actual ultimate hope: the proletariat *cannot* free itself from servitude without putting an end to all dominion of man over man. That is the real prophecy, the core of the manifesto, without which it would never have been written: the proletariat, the working masses will first, through their leaders, seize political power; but this is a transitional stage which will lead to an 'association of individuals', as it is known: this is, then, the final situation.

What this association will look like the Communist Manifesto omits to say, as do all the programmes of all the socialist parties. We are informed that we cannot know that. It can only be stated that our present society is doomed, it will fall by the laws of nature, it will be relieved in the first place by a proletarian dictatorship.

But of what comes after that, nothing can yet be foretold, except the absence of man's dominion over man.

What reasons are advanced to show that the fall of the present society is in the nature of things inevitable? For strictly according to the laws of nature it is drawing to a close: that was the second cardinal sentence of this solemn prophecy, which attracted to it the jubilant faith of the masses. Engels once uses the image that, just as in due time the planet earth will collide with the sun, so this capitalist society is doomed to destruction. What reasons are advanced for this?

The first is as follows: a social class like the bourgeoisie—by which are always understood ,in the first instance, the industrialists and all those who directly or indirectly share the same interests—such a ruling class can only maintain its control if it can guarantee at least bare subsistence to the governed class, the wage-earners. That, say the authors, was the case with slavery, it was so with the socage-farm system, etc. Here the people were assured of at least bare subsistence and therefore control could be maintained. The modern bourgeoisie cannot do this, however. It is unable to do so because competition between employers compels them to undercut each other further and further and, with the advent of new machines, repeatedly to throw workers breadless on the streets. They must have at their disposal a broad stratum of unemployed, the so-called 'industrial reserve', from whom they can at any time select any number of suitable workers for their factories, and this stratum is being created by increasing mechanical automation. The result is, however, or so the Communist Manifesto thought, that an ever-increasing class of permanently unemployed, of 'paupers', appears, and undercuts the minimum subsistence level, so that the proletarian class does not even get its bare means of livelihood guaranteed by this social order. Where this is the case the society becomes untenable, i.e. at some point it collapses via a revolution.

This so-called pauperisation theory, in *this* form, has nowadays been abandoned as incorrect, explicitly and without exception by all levels of social democracy. In the jubilee edition of the Communist Manifesto it was expressly conceded by its publisher, Karl Kautsky, that evolution had followed another path and not this one. The thesis is maintained in a different form with a new interpretation, which, incidentally, is likewise not undisputed, but which in any case has divested itself of its former solemn character.

Be that as it may, on what are based the chances of a revolution's success? Could it not be doomed to eternal failure?

This brings us to the second argument: competition between employers means victory for him who is stronger by virtue of his capital and his business capabilities, but above all his capital. This means an ever-diminishing number of employers, as the weaker ones are eliminated. The smaller this number of employers becomes, the bigger, in relative and absolute terms, becomes the number of the proletariat. At some point, however, the number of employers will have shrunk so much that it will be impossible for them to maintain their overlordship, and then it will be possible, perhaps peaceably and politely—let us say, in return for an annuity—to dispossess these 'expropriators', for they will see that the ground will have become so hot under their feet, and that they will have become so few, that they cannot maintain their supremacy.

This thesis, if in modified form, is still upheld today. However, it has become clear that, nowadays at least, it is not *generally* valid in any form. In the first place it is not valid for agriculture, where on the contrary there has been in very many cases a fairly marked increase in the peasantry. Furthermore, it has proved to be not incorrect, but different in its consequences from what was expected, for broad areas of industry, where it has been demonstrated that the mere numerical diminution of employers does not exhaust the process. The elimination of the financially weak occurs in the form of their subjugation by capital, by syndicates or by trust organisations. Parallel to these very complex processes, however, there appears a rapid rise in the number of clerks, i.e. in private *bureaucracy*—its growth rate is statistically much greater than that of the workers—and their interests certainly do not lie with one accord in the direction of a proletarian dictatorship. Then again, the advent of highly diverse and complicated ways of sharing interests means that at the present time it is quite impossible to maintain that the power and number of those directly or indirectly interested in the bourgeois order are on the wane. For the time being, at any rate, the situation does not permit a definite assertion that in the future only half a dozen, a few hundred or a few thousand magnates will stand alone in the face of millions upon millions of proletarians.

The third argument, finally, was the calculation of the effects of crises. Because employers compete with one another (and here comes an important but very involved discussion in the classic socialist texts, which I must spare you) it is inevitable that periods of overproduction will recur which are dispelled by bankruptcies, collapses and so-called 'depressions'. By the law of economics— Marx only hinted at it in the Communist Manifesto; however, it has since become a minutely elaborated theory—these periods follow one another at fixed intervals. There has, in fact, been approximate regularity of occurrence of such crises for nearly a century. Even the leading scholars of our subject are not yet completely in agreement on the reasons for this, therefore it would be quite out of the question to discuss it here at the moment.

Now classic socialism pinned its hopes on these crises. It hoped above all that they, by their very nature, would increase in destructive power and intensity, producing a terrifying mood of revolution, that they would accumulate and increase and eventually create such a climate that the preservation of the existing economic system would no longer be attempted even in nonproletarian circles.

This hope has been essentially given up today. For while the danger of a crisis admittedly has not entirely disappeared, its relative importance has diminished now that businessmen have progressed from ruthless competition to syndication, i.e. since they began to eliminate competition to a large extent by the regulation of prices and turnover, and, furthermore, now that the great banks, e.g. the German Reichsbank, have advanced to a point where, by the regulation of credit concessions, they see to it that periods of overspeculation also occur in more sparse measure than before. Thus, while we cannot say it 'has not been fulfilled', this third hope of the Communist Manifesto and its successors has somewhat radically shifted in its presuppositions.

The very high hopes which were placed in the collapse of bourgeois society in the Communist Manifesto have therefore been replaced by very much more sober expectations. Firstly, there is the theory that socialism will come of its own accord by evolution, because economic production is becoming increasingly 'socialised'. What is meant by this is that share companies with salaried managers will take the place of the actual individual employers, and that national, communal and trust firms will be set up which will no longer be founded, as before, on the risk and profit of a single, or indeed any, private employer. This is to the point, though it must be added that a share company very often conceals one or several finance magnates who control the general meeting: every shareholder knows that shortly before the annual general meeting he will receive a communication from his bank asking him to make over his voting right to them, if he does not wish to go and vote himself, which is pointless for him in the face of a capital of millions of crowns. Above all, however, this kind of socialisation means on the one hand the spread of officialdom, of specialist, commercially or technically trained clerks, but on the other, the propagation of men of *private means*, i.e. a class who just draw dividends and interest, without doing mental work for it, as the employer does, but who, with all their financial interests, are committed to the capitalist system. Public and trust concerns, however, are strongly and quite exclusively dominated by the *official*, not the worker, who has more difficulty in achieving anything by strike action here than against private employers. It is the dictatorship of the official, not that of the worker, which, for the present at any rate, is on the advance.

Secondly, there is the hope that the machine, as it causes the old specialists, the skilled craftsman and those highly skilled workers who filled the old English trade unions, to be replaced by unskilled workers and makes anyone capable of working at a machine, will bring about such unity in the working class that the old division into discrete professions will come to an end, and the consciousness of this unity will become overwhelming and benefit the struggle against the propertied classes. The answer to that is not quite straightforward. It is correct that the machine endeavours to replace to a very extensive degree the highly paid and skilled workers, for naturally every industry is seeking to introduce precisely such machines as will replace those workers who are hardest to come by. The most prodigiously increasing group in industry today are the so-called 'trained' workers, i.e. not the skilled workers who under the old scheme followed a particular course of instruction, but those who are put directly at the machine and there trained in the use of it. Even so they are often still specialists to a considerable extent. Several years go by, for example, before a trained weaver reaches the highest degree of learning, i.e. makes the fullest use of the machine for the employer and earns the highest wage for himself. Admittedly, the typical normal training period for some categories of workers is substantially less than for that cited here. Nevertheless, while this increase in trained workers means a noticeable decline in professional specialisation, it does not mean the end of it. And on the other side professional specialisation and the need for specialist education is growing at all levels in industry *above* that of the workers, down to the foreman and the overseer, and the relative number of persons belonging to this class is growing at the same time. It is true to say that they, too, are 'wage slaves', but mostly not on piece-wages or weekly wages, but a fixed salary. And above all, the worker naturally hates the foreman, who is perpetually breathing down his neck, far more than the industrialist, and the industrialist in turn more than the shareholder, although the shareholder is the one who really draws his income without working, while the industrialist has to do very arduous intellectual work, and the foreman stands far closer still to the worker. That is something which occurs in the army too: in general it is the corporal who attracts the strongest resentment, or at least is likely to do so, as far as I have been able to observe. In any case the evolution of the whole class system is far from being unequivocally proletarian.

And finally there is the argument based on the increasing standardisation of production. Everything everywhere seems to be striving—and war in particular requires it supremely—towards increasing uniformity and interchangeability of products, and more and more extensive schematisation of businesses. The old, free, pioneer spirit of the bourgeois businessman of the past now holds sway, they say, only in the highest circle of employers, and even here it is permanently on the decline. Consequently, so the argument runs, there is a constantly growing possibility of managing this production even without having the specific business qualities which bourgeois society maintains are indispensable for management. This would be especially true of syndicates and trusts, which have a huge administrative staff instead of individual employers. This is again very true; but again only with the same reservation, that the importance of a class is also enhanced by this standardisation, namely that of the administrative class, whom I have frequently mentioned, who have to be *educated* in a quite definite way, and who, therefore (this by way of being complementary) have a definite *class* character. It is no coincidence that everywhere we see commercial high schools, trade schools and technical schools springing up like mushrooms out of the earth. At least in Germany, this is due in part to the desire to join a students' association at these schools, get scars on the face, become capable of giving satisfaction and therefore of being an officer in the reserves, and later on in the office have a preferential chance of the hand of the boss's daughter: i.e. a desire to be assimilated into the classes of so-called 'society'. Nothing is further from this class than solidarity with the proletariat, from whom, indeed, they endeavour rather to differentiate themselves increasingly. In varying degrees, but noticeably, the same is true of many sub-classes among these clerks. They all strive at least for similar *class* qualities, be it for themselves or for their children. A *uniform* trend to proletarianisation is not in evidence today.

Be that as it may, these arguments show at any rate that the old revolutionary hope of catastrophe, which gave the Communist Manifesto its compelling power, has given way to an evolutionistic view, i.e. a view of the gradual growth of the old economy with its enormous competitive concerns into a controlled economy, whether it is controlled by civil servants or by syndicates with the participation of civil servants. This, and no longer the fusion of individual employers by competition and crises, now emerges as the preliminary to the real socialist, rulerless society. This evolutionistic mood, which expects from this slow transformation a development to the socialist society of the future, was in fact in the thought of the trade unions before the war and had for many socialist intellectuals taken the place of the old catastrophe theory. From there the familiar conclusions have been drawn. The so-called 'revisionism' arose. At least some of its own leaders were aware what a grave step it was to take from the masses the faith in the sudden arrival of a blissful future which was given them by a gospel which told them, like the early Christians: Salvation may come tonight. A creed such as the Communist Manifesto and the later theory of catastrophe can be dethroned, but it is then very difficult to replace it with another. Meanwhile, development has long since left this discussion behind in the struggle with the old orthodoxy which arose out of moral doubts about the orthodox faith. The struggle became mixed up with the question of whether, and how far, social democracy as a party should indulge in 'practical politics' in the sense that they would form coalitions with bourgeois parties, have a share in politically responsible government by taking over ministerial posts, and thereby endeavour to improve the present lot of the workers; or whether that would be 'treachery to the class' and political heresy, as the confirmed politician of catastrophe naturally would have to view it. Meanwhile, however, other questions of principle have arisen, and on these opinions are divided. Let us suppose that via a gradual evolution, i.e. a general syndication, standardisation and bureaucratisation, the economy were to take on such a form that at some point it would be technically possible for a means of control to be introduced which would take the place of the private industrial economy of today and hence of private onwership of the means of production, and completely eliminate the employer. *Who* would then be the one to take over the command of this new economy? On this point the Communist Manifesto remained resolutely silent, or rather it expressed itself very ambiguously.

What will that 'association' it speaks of look like? What, in particular, can socialism show in the way of germ cells of such organisations, in case the opportunity should ever come its way of seizing power and governing as it pleases? In the German Reich, and probably everywhere, it has two categories of organisations. Firstly, the political party of social democracy with its members of parliament, the editors, party officials and shop stewards it employs, and the local and central groups, by whom these people are elected or employed. Secondly, the trade unions. Each of these two organisations can assume a revolutionary as well as an evolutionistic character. And opinions are divided about which character they have and which is destined and desired for them for the future.

Taking the hope of revolution as our starting point, we find two mutually opposed views. The first was that of ordinary Marxism, based on the old tradition of the Communist Manifesto. It placed all its expectations in the *political* dictatorship of the proletariat and thought it necessary to look chiefly to the political *party* organisation, inevitably tailored to the *election* campaign, as the vehicle of it. The party, or a political dictator with its support, was to seize political power and by this means the new organisation of society was to come about.

The opponents, against whom this revolutionary line turned, were firstly those trade unions which were nothing more than trade unions in the old English sense, that is, which had no interest in these plans for the future because they seemed a long way off, but which wanted chiefly to struggle about the working conditions which made life possible for them and their children: high wages, short working hours, protection of the workers etc. This radical political Marxism turned against this kind of trade unionism on the one hand. On the other it opposed that which has been called 'Millerandism' since Millerand became a minister in France, and which is the exclusively parliamentary form of socialism's policy of compromise. That, they say, is a policy which ends in the leaders being more interested in their ministerial portfolios and the lower leaders being more interested in getting an official position than in revolution; revolutionary spirit would thus be killed. Beside the 'radical', 'orthodox' line, in the old sense, a new one has appeared in the course of the last decade which is known as 'syndicalism', from syndicat, the French term for the trade union. Just as the old radicalism wants the revolutionary interpretation of the aim of the political party organisation, so syndicalism wants the revolutionary interpretation of the trade unions. Its starting-point is this: it is to be not political dicatorship, not the political leaders, and not the officials who are appointed by these political leaders, but the trade unions and their federation who, when the great moment has come, will take the control of the economy into their own hands via so-called 'action directe'. Syndicalism originates in a somewhat strict view of the class character of the movement. The working *class* is to be the vehicle of the final liberation. However, all the politicians who hang about the capital cities and merely inquire how this and that ministry is doing or what chance this and that parliamentary trend has, are people with political interests and not comrades. Behind their interest in the constituency there are always the interests of editors and private officials who wish to profit from the number of votes gained. Syndicalism rejects all these interests which are bound up with the modern parliamentary electoral system. Only the real working class, which is organised in the trade unions, can create the new society. Away with the professional politicians who live for and, literally, *off* politics and not for the creation of a new economic society. The typical measures of the syndicalists are the general strike and terror. The general strike: of which they hope that (by the sudden paralysation of all production) those involved, in particular the employers, will be driven to renounce their management of the factories and place it in the hands of committees to be formed by the trade unions. Terror: which some preach openly, some secretly, and some reject—opinions diverge here—and which this organisation is to strike into the ranks of the crucial ruling classes in order to paralyse them politically as well. This syndicalism is, of course, a brand of socialism which is a quite ruthless opponent of any kind of army organisation, for every kind gives rise to interested parties, right down to the N.C.O.; even the soldier, who at the moment at least is dependent for his food on the functioning of the military and state machines, is therefore partially interested in the actual failure of the general strike, and is an obstacle to it at the least. Its opponents are, firstly, all political socialist parties which are active in parliament. Parliament could be used by the syndicalists at the most as a platform from which they could continue to announce, under the protection of parliamentary immunity, that the general strike will come and must come, in order to incite the masses to revolutionary fervour. Even this distracts syndicalism from its real task and is therefore dubious. However, seriously to practise politics in parliament is not merely nonsense but from this point of view simply objectionable. Also among their opponents are, of course, all the evolutionists of every variety. Even if they are trade unionists who just want to lead campaigns to improve working conditions: on the contrary, the syndicalists must argue, the poorer the wages, the longer the working hours, the worse the circumstances in general, the greater is the chance of a general strike. Or if they are the evolutionists of party politics, who say the state today is growing into socialism because of increasing democratisation (for which the syndicalists have the greatest abhorrence) they prefer tsarism. To the syndicalists this is, at the least, gross self-deception. The critical question is this: where do the syndicalists hope to get the manpower to take charge of production? For it would of course be a grave error to think that even a highly trained worker, even if he has been at his job for years and knows the *working* conditions perfectly, therefore understands the workings of the *factory* as such, since the management of all modern factories is based entirely on calculation, market research, knowledge of demand and technical schooling: all things which need increasingly to be practised by specialists, and with which the trade unionists, the real workers, have absolutely no opportunity to become acquainted. Therefore, whether they like it or not, they too will have to fall back on *non-*workers, on ideologists from the intellectual classes. And, indeed, it is remarkable that—in flat contradiction of the dictum that salvation can only come from the real workers uniting in the trade union federation and not from politicians or any outsiders—within the syndicalist movement, whose principal flock before the war was in France and Italy, there is a vast number of learned intellectuals. What are they looking for in it? It is the *romance* of the general strike and the *romance* of the hope of revolution as such which fascinates them. One can tell by looking at them that they are romantics who have not matured emotionally or have taken a dislike to everyday life and its demands and who therefore languish for the great revolutionary miracle—and the opportunity to feel powerful. Naturally there are men of organisational ability amongst them. Only the question is whether the workers would subject themselves to *their* dictatorship. Certainly, in wartime, with the incredible upheavals it brings with it, taking into account what the workers go through, especially under the effect of hunger, the mass of the workers may be stirred by syndicalist ideas and, if they have weapons to hand, they may seize power under the leadership of such intellectuals, if the political and military collapse of a state affords them the opportunity. However, I cannot see the manpower for the running of production in peacetime either in the trade union members themselves or among the syndicalist intellectuals. The great experiment now is—Russia. The difficulty is this: that today we cannot look in over the border there to find out how the management of production is being carried on in reality. From what one hears, it happens this way: the Bolshevik government, which is known to consist of intellectuals, some of whom studied here in Vienna and in Germany and among whom there are very few Russians, has now gone over to the reintroduction in those factories which are working at all—10 per cent of peacetime production, according to social-democratic reports—of a piece-wage system, for the reason that output would suffer otherwise. They leave the industrialists at the head of the concerns, because they alone have the expert knowledge, and pay them very considerable subventions. Furthermore, they have reverted to paying officers' salaries to officers of the old regime, because they need an army and have realised that is impossible without trained officers. Whether these officers, when they once

H

again have the troops in hand, will continue to put up with government by these intellectuals, seems doubtful to me. For the moment, of course, they have had to do so. And finally, by the withdrawal of the bread card, they have forced part of the bureaucracy to work for them. However, in the long term the state machinery and economy cannot be run in this way and the experiment is as yet not very encouraging.

The astonishing thing is that this organisation has functioned as long as it has. It has been able to do so because it is a military dictatorship, not, it is true, of generals, but of corporals, and because the war-weary soldiers returning from the front saw eye to eye with the land-hungry farmers, used to agrarian communism; or the soldiers with their weapons took possession of the villages by force and there made levies, and shot down anyone who came too near them. It is the only large-scale experiment with a 'proletarian dictatorship' that has been made to date, and we can give an assurance in all sincerity that on the German side the discussions in Brest-Litovsk were carried on in the most loyal manner, in the hope of achieving real peace with these people. This happened for different reasons: those who stood as interested parties on the basis of bourgeois society were in favour because they said, for Heaven's sake, let's let them carry out their experiment, it's bound to flop and then it will be a warning; and the rest of us were in favour because we said, if this experiment were to succeed and we were to see that culture is possible on this basis, then we would be converted.

The one who prevented that was Mr Trotsky, who would not be content to carry out this experiment in his own house and to put his hopes in the fact that it would mean, if it succeeded, propaganda for socialism unparalleled in the whole world. With the typical vanity of the Russian man of letters he wanted more, and hoped by means of verbal action and the misuse of such words as 'peace' and 'self-determination' to unleash civil war in Germany. He was, however, so ill-informed as not to know that at least two-thirds of the German army is recruited from the country and a further one-sixth from the petit bourgeoisie, for whom it would be a real pleasure to bash the workers, or anyone else who wanted to start such revolutions, on the jaw. There is no making peace with fanatics, one can only make them harmless, and that was the import of the ultimatum and the forced peace at Brest. Every socialist must realise this, and I do not know any, of whatever line, who does not, inwardly at least, realise it.

When one gets into discussion with socialists of today and wishes to proceed objectively—and that is intelligent on its own—there are, in the contemporary situation, two questions to put to them: what is their attitude towards evolutionism? i.e. to the idea which is a fundamental tenet of what is nowadays regarded as orthodox Marxism, that society and its economic system is evolving strictly according to the laws of nature, in degrees of age as it were, and that therefore a socialist society can never come about anywhere until bourgeois society has reached full maturity; this, even in socialist opinion, is not yet the case anywhere, for there are still small farmers and craftsmen; what, then, is the attitude of the socialists concerned to this basic evolutionistic tenet? And then it will emerge that, outside Russia at least, they *all* take the same position, i.e. they all, even the most radical of them, expect a *bourgeois* social order, *not* one run by the proletariat, to come about as the only possible result of a revolution, because as yet there is nowhere where the times are ripe for the latter. It is hoped simply that the social order will be in some particulars a few steps nearer to that final stage from which, it is expected, the transition to the socialist order of the future will one day result.

If he is guided by his conscience, every honest socialist intellectual will have to reply thus. As a result there is indeed a broad class of social democrats within Russia, the so-called Menscheviks, who take the point of view that this Bolshevik experiment of grafting a socialist order on to the current state of bourgeois society from above is not only folly, it is a violation of the Marxist dogma. The terrible mutual hatred between the two factions is due to this charge of heresy against the dogma.

Now if the overwhelming majority of the leaders, at least all the ones I have ever known, take this evolutionistic position, this of course justifies the question: what, in these circumstances, particularly in wartime, is a revolution supposed to achieve, from their own point of view? It may bring civil war and with it perhaps victory for the Entente, but not a socialist society; moreover it can and will, produce in the ruins of the state a regiment of interested parties from the peasantry and the petit bourgeoisie, that is, the most radical opponents of *any* kind of socialism; and, above all, it would bring immense destruction of capital and disorganisation, i.e. retrogression of the social development demanded by Marxism, which presupposes the increasing saturation of the economy with capital. It should, however, be borne in mind that the West European *farmer* thinks differently from the Russian farmer living in his agrarian communism. There the crucial point is the land question, which does not come into it here. The German farmer at least is an individualist nowadays and clings to his inheritance and his soil. He will hardly let himself be driven from it. He will sooner ally himself with the landed proprietor than with the radical-socialist worker, if he believes himself threatened.

From the point of view of socialist hopes for the future, then, the prospects of a wartime revolution are now the worst imaginable, even if it were to succeed. The most it could possibly bring would be for the *political* constitution to approach the form desired by democracy, which would remove it from socialism by the *economically* reactionary consequences which would necessarily attend it. No socialist can in all honesty deny that either.

The second question is the attitude towards *peace*. We are all aware that radical socialism today has among the masses become fused with pacifist leanings, with the desire that peace be reached as soon as possible. Now it is established, and every leader of radical, i.e. really revolutionary social democracy, will have, if asked, to concede it honestly: for him, the *leader*, peace is *not* the crucial factor on which all depends. If we have the choice—he will have to say, if he is unreservedly open—between another three years' war and then revolution on the one hand and immediate peace *without* revolution on the other, then of course we are in favour of the three years' war. Let him reconcile his fanaticism and his conscience. The question is, however, whether the majority of the troops who have to stand out in the field, including the socialists, are of the same opinion as these leaders who dictate this sort of thing to them. And of course it is only right and completely in good faith if they are compelled to show their colours. It is established and conceded that Trotsky did *not* want peace. No socialist I know disputes that any longer today. But the same applies to the radical leaders of every country as well. Given the choice, they would *not* want peace above all either but, if it would benefit revolution, i.e. civil war, they would choose war. War in the interest of revolution, *although* in their own opinion (I repeat this revolution *cannot* lead to a socialist society, but at the most—this is the only hope—to a 'higher form of development', from a socialist standpoint, of bourgeois society, which would be somewhat nearer (how much, it is impossible to say) than that of today to the socialist society that will arrive sometime in the future. Precisely this hope is indeed, for the reason I have given, extremely dubious.

A discussion with convinced socialists and revolutionaries is always an awkward affair. In my experience one can never convince them. One can only coerce them into showing their colours to their own adherents, on the one hand on the question of peace, and on the other on the question of what revolution is actually supposed to bring, i.e. on the question of evolution by stages, which is to the present day a tenet of true Marxism and has only been rejected in Russia by a firmly established sect there who thought Russia could omit these West European stages of development. This is a totally upright way to proceed, and the only effective or possible one as well. For it is my opinion that there is no means of getting rid of socialist conviction and socialist hopes. Any working class will recurrently be socialist in some sense or other. The only question is whether this socialism will be such that it can be tolerated, from the point of view of the national interest and at present in particular from the point of view of military interests. No regime, not even a proletarian one, like that of the commune in Paris or now that of the Bolsheviks, has ever got by without martial law in cases where the foundations of its discipline were endangered. This Trotsky conceded with laudable honesty. But the surer the feeling among the troops that only the *objective* interests in the maintenance of discipline, and *not* party or class interests, determine the behaviour of the military courts, i.e. that only the *objectively* inevitable in war occurs, the more steadfast military authority will remain.

Part Three
Social Structures and Social Change

INTRODUCTION

We begin the chapter on Social Structure and Social Change with some comments by Weber on the role of ideal types in the analysis of social change. He is particularly concerned to warn against the danger of confusing analytical concepts (which for him are fictional in character) with historical reality. The orderliness of ideal type constructions could be transformed in an unwarranted way into 'laws' of social development. As a particular example Weber says that Marxist interpretations of social change have immense heuristic value in enabling one to appraise actual historical events, so long as the ideal typical concepts used are not identified with historical reality. To do so is to give the concepts a 'truly metaphysical' status in Weber's judgement. It should be added that how far Marx himself is guilty of what in Weber's view is a methodological misdemeanour is a matter of some dispute. Taking the important case of capitalism, for example, Avineri has recently argued that Marx's position was more complicated and sophisticated than that attributed to him by Weber:

> Historically, Marx is fully aware that British factory legislation infringes on the capitalist model and changes capitalism from within. . . . England, the country of the realised model, has already moved beyond the model. The model cannot ultimately exist as a historical reality. Since all historical reality is always in a process of becoming, the model is either a criterion for a reality developing towards it—or, if adequacy between model and reality is maximised, internal circumstances have given rise to a reality that has overtaken the model and moved farther and farther away from it.[1]

This point, of course, has precise application back to Weber's own

[1] A. Avineri, *The Social and Political Thought of Karl Marx* (C.U.P., 1968), p. 160.

treatment of the sociology of capitalism, which we have discussed above.

In the section dealing explicitly with innovation we have included a discussion of the by now familiar concept of charisma. Again the ideal typical character of the concept needs to be clearly recognised. So, in commenting on the three types of authority (including charismatic) which he has delineated, Weber later writes:

> . . . the kind of terminology and classification set forth above has in no sense the aim—indeed it could not have it—to be exhaustive or to confine the whole of historical reality in a rigid scheme. Its usefulness is derived from the fact that, in a given case, it is possible to distinguish what aspects of a given organised group can legitimately be identified as falling under or approximating to one or another of these categories. For certain purposes this is unquestionably an advantage.[1]

Possibly our familiarity with the concept of charisma in Weber's sociology has tended to make us over-emphasise the importance of charismatic personages in explaining innovations in social life. The two passages which follow in this section certainly do not deny the significance of charisma in promoting social change, but other factors are seen as significant in their own right. So, for example, the development of the modern piano as the musical instrument of the middle classes can indeed be understood with reference to virtuoso composers and performers, but not exclusively. There are purely technical factors affecting its development and market factors affecting its diffusion. These factors Weber describes and draws together the 'international virtuousity of Mozart and the increasing need of music publishers and of concert manufacturers to satisfy the large music consumption of the mass market' as bringing about 'the final victory of the hammer piano'.

How do particular legal rules arise in communities and how do they change? These questions form the heart of Weber's discussion of the emergence of legal norms. One answer is that there may be explicit imposition of legal rules from above and derived originally from charismatic revelation (either enunciating general principles of law or expressing judgement on particular cases). But there

[1] *Theory*, p. 383.

could also be changes in legal rules because of a more generalised demand to 'solve' problems created by socio-economic changes. Weber cites particularly the effect of 'war and war-like expansion [which] have at all stages of historical development been connected with a systematic fixation of the law both old and new'. Another important non-charismatic factor upon which Weber lays emphasis is the role of interest groups purposively seeking new legal arrangements and, in addition, he stresses the significance of judicial precedent, as in the case of English common law, in accounting for the emergence of legal norms.

Not all the detailed footnotes have been retained in the passage from *Law in Economy and Society*, from which the reading has been extracted.

Two macro studies of social change complete the chapter. The first is a little known translation of a lecture first given in 1897 on the social causes of the decay of ancient civilization. In his methodological writings Weber always insisted on the utility of economic interpretations of history and here the conviction is acted upon. The key to his analysis is that since slave labour formed the basis of Roman society, what one has to study is the reasons both for the existence of a slave economy and its subsequent decline. To do this is to move away from psychological explanations: 'much more powerful factors than the guilt of individuals destroyed ancient civilisation'. Rather the emphasis is upon the unforeseen consequences of the acute shortage of slave labour already apparent by the time of Tiberius: both directly for the social structure of the agricultural estates and indirectly for the exchange economy of the cities. Weber also regarded as crucial the effects of incorporating large inland areas (Spain, Gaul, Illyria and the Danubian countries) into the Empire:

> . . . ancient civilization made an attempt to change its scene of action, to turn from a coastal into an inland civilization. It expanded over an immense economic area which even in the course of centuries could not have been converted into an exchange and market economy similar to that existing along the coasts of the Mediterranean. . . . In these inland regions, progress of civilization in the way of a free division of labour through the development of an *intensive* exchange of commodities was virtually *impossible*.

The social process which Weber depicts is the undermining of
the material foundations of the ancient city economy and the returning of economic life to predominantly rural forms. It is, in
short, a commentary on the origins of feudalism in Europe.

The discussion of the evolution of the capitalist spirit, taken
from his *General Economic History*, provides us with perhaps the
most concise formulation of his view. Some of the main issues have
already been raised in our introductory essay[1] and we will not add
to this. It should, however, be remembered that this extract forms
only part of Weber's treatment of the origins of modern capitalism,
which comprises the whole of Part 4 in the *General Economic
History*.

(A) Ideal Types and the Study of Social Change[2]

The fact that ideal types, even classificatory ones, can be and are
applied, first acquires methodological significance in connection
with another fact.

Thus far we have been dealing with ideal types only as abstract
concepts of relationships which are conceived by us as stable in the
flux of events, as historically individual complexes in which
developments are realised. There emerges, however, a complication,
which reintroduces with the aid of the concept of 'type' the naturalistic prejudice that the goal of the social sciences must be the reduction of reality to '*laws*'. *Developmental* sequences too can be
constructed into ideal types and these constructs can have quite
considerable heuristic value. But this quite particularly gives rise to
the danger that the ideal type and reality will be confused with one
another. One can, for example, arrive at the theoretical conclusion
that in a society which is organised on *strict* 'handicraft' principles,
the only source of capital accumulation can be ground rent. From
this, perhaps, one can—for the correctness of the construct is not

---

[1] See above, pp. 33–53.
[2] Source: " 'Objectivity' in Social Science and Social Policy" in *The Methodology of the Social Sciences*, pp. 101–3.

in question here—construct a pure ideal picture of the shift, conditional by certain specific factors—e.g., limited land, increasing population, influx of precious metals, rationalisation of the conduct of life—from a handicraft to a capitalistic economic organisation. Whether the empirical-historical course of development was actually identical with the constructed one, can be investigated only by using this construct as a heuristic device for the comparison of the ideal type and the 'facts'. If the ideal type were 'correctly' constructed and the actual course of events did *not* correspond to that predicted by the ideal type, the hypothesis that medieval society was *not* in certain respects a *strictly* 'handicraft' type of society would be proved. And if the ideal type were constructed in a heuristically '*ideal*' way—whether and in what way this could occur in our example will be entirely disregarded here—it will guide the investigation into a path leading to a more precise understanding of the non-handicraft components of medieval society in their peculiar characteristics and their historical significance. *If* it leads to this result, it fulfils its logical purpose, even though, in doing so, it demonstrates its divergence from reality. It was, in this case, the test of an hypothesis. This procedure gives rise to no methodological doubts so long as we clearly keep in mind that ideal-typical developmental *constructs* and *history* are to be sharply distinguished from each other, and that the construct here is no more than the means for explicitly and validly imputing an historical event to its real causes while eliminating those which on the basis of our present knowledge seem possible.

The maintenance of this distinction in all its rigour often becomes uncommonly difficult in practice due to a certain circumstance. In the interest of the concrete demonstration of an ideal type or of an ideal-typical developmental sequence, one seeks to *make it clear* by the use of concrete illustrative material drawn from empirical-historical reality. The danger of this procedure, which in itself is entirely legitimate, lies in the fact that historical knowledge here appears as a *servant* of theory instead of the opposite role. It is a great temptation for the theorist to regard this relationship either as the normal one or, far worse, to mix theory with history and indeed to confuse them with each other. This occurs in an extreme way when an ideal construct of a developmental sequence and a conceptual classification of the ideal types of certain cultural structures (e.g., the forms of industrial production deriving from the 'closed domestic economy' or the religious concepts beginning with the 'gods of the moment') are integrated into a *genetic* classification. The series of types which results from the selected conceptual criteria appears, then, as an historical sequence unrolling with the necessity of a law. The logical classification of analytical concepts on the one hand and the empirical arrangements of the events thus conceptualised in space, time, and causal relationship, on the other, appear to be so bound up together that there is an almost irresistible temptation to do violence to reality in order to prove the real validity of the construct.

We have intentionally avoided a demonstration with respect to that ideal-typical construct which is the most important one from our point of view: namely, the Marxian theory. This was done in order not to complicate the exposition any further through the introduction of an interpretation of Marx and in order not to anticipate the discussions in our journal which will make a regular practice of presenting critical analyses of the literature concerning and following the great thinker. We will only point out here that naturally all specifically Marxian 'laws' and developmental constructs, in so far as they are theoretically sound, are ideal types. The eminent, indeed unique, *heuristic* significance of these ideal types when they are used for the *assessment* of reality is known to everyone who has ever employed Marxian concepts and hypotheses. Similarly, their perniciousness, as soon as they are thought of as empirically valid or as real (i.e., truly metaphysical) 'effective forces,' 'tendencies', etc, is likewise known to those who have used them.

Class or generic concepts (*Gattungsbegriffe*)—ideal types— ideal-typical generic concepts—ideas in the sense of thought-patterns which actually exist in the minds of human beings—ideal types of such ideas—ideals which govern human beings—ideal types of such ideals—ideals with which the historian approaches historical facts—*theoretical* constructs using empirical data illustratively—*historical* investigations which utilise theoretical concepts as ideal limiting cases—the various possible combinations of these which could only be hinted at here; they are pure mental constructs, the relationships of which to the empirical reality of the immediately given is problematical in every individual case. This list of possibilities only reveals the infinite ramifications of the conceptual-methodological problems which face us in the sphere of the cultural sciences.

(B) Innovation
(1) Charismatic Authority[1]

THE PRINCIPAL CHARACTERISTICS OF CHARISMATIC AUTHORITY AND ITS RELATION TO FORMS OF COMMUNAL ORGANISATION

The term 'charisma' will be applied to a certain quality of an individual personality by virtue of which he is set apart from ordinary men and treated as endowed with supernatural, superhuman, or at least specifically exceptional powers or qualities. These are such as are not accessible to the ordinary person, but are regarded as of divine origin or as exemplary, and on the basis of them the individual concerned is treated as a leader. In primitive circumstances this peculiar kind of deference is paid to prophets, to people with a reputation for therapeutic or legal wisdom, to leaders in the hunt and heroes in war. It is very often thought of as resting on magical powers. How the quality in question would ultimately be judged from any ethical, aesthetic or other such point of view is naturally entirely indifferent for purposes of definition. What is alone important is how the individual is actually regarded by those subject to charismatic authority, by his 'followers' or 'disciples'.

For present purposes it will be necessary to treat a variety of different types as being endowed with charisma in this sense. It includes the state of a 'berserker' whose spells of maniac passion have, apparently wrongly, sometimes been attributed to the use of drugs. In medieval Byzantium a group of people endowed with this type of charismatic war-like passion were maintained as a kind of weapon. It includes the 'shaman', the kind of magician who in the pure type is subject to epileptoid seizures as a means of falling into trances. Another type is that of Joseph Smith, the founder of Mormonism, who, however, cannot be classified in this way with absolute certainty since there is a possibility that he was a very sophisticated type of deliberate swindler. Finally it includes the type of intellectual, such as Kurt Eisner,[2] who is carried away with his own

[1] Source: *Theory of Social and Economic Organisation*, pp. 358–73, 386–92.
[2] The leader of the communistic experiment in Bavaria in 1919. [Parsons' footnote.]

demagogic success. Sociological analysis, which must abstain from value judgements, will treat all these on the same level as the men who, according to conventional judgements, are the 'greatest' heroes, prophets and saviours.

1. It is recognition on the part of those subject to authority which is decisive for the validity of charisma. This is freely given and guaranteed by what is held to be a 'sign' or proof,[1] originally always a miracle, and consists in devotion to the corresponding revelation, hero worship, or absolute trust in the leader. But where charisma is genuine, it is not this which is the basis of the claim to legitimacy. This basis lies rather in the conception that it is the *duty* of those who have been called to a charismatic mission to recognise its quality and to act accordingly. Psychologically this 'recognition' is a matter of complete personal devotion to the possessor of the quality, arising out of enthusiasm, or of despair and hope.

No prophet has ever regarded his quality as dependent on the attitudes of the masses toward him. No elective king or military leader has ever treated those who have resisted him or tried to ignore him otherwise than as delinquent in duty. Failure to take part in a military expedition under such leader, even though re-cruitment is formally voluntary, has universally been met with disdain.

2. If proof of his charismatic qualification fails him for long, the leader endowed with charisma tends to think his god or his magical or heroic powers have deserted him. If he is for long unsuccessful, above all if his leadership fails to benefit his followers, it is likely that his charismatic authority will disappear. This is the genuine charismatic meaning of the 'gift of grace'.[2]

Even the old Germanic kings were sometimes rejected with scorn. Similar phenomena are very common among so-called 'primitive' peoples. In China the charismatic quality of the mon-arch, which was transmitted unchanged by heredity, was upheld so rigidly that any misfortune whatever, not only defeats in war, but drought, floods or astronomical phenomena which were con-sidered unlucky, forced him to do public penance and might even force his abdication. If such things occurred, it was a sign that he did not possess the requisite charismatic virtue, he was thus not a legitimate 'Son of Heaven'.

[1] *Bewährung*. [Parsons' footnote.]
[2] *Gottesgnadentum*. [Parsons' footnote.]

3. The corporate group which is subject to charismatic authority is based on an emotional form of communal relationship.[1] The administrative staff of a charismatic leader does not consist of 'officials'; at least its members are not technically trained. It is not chosen on the basis of social privilege not from the point of view of domestic or personal dependency. It is rather chosen in terms of the charismatic qualities of its members. The prophet has his disciples; the war lord his selected henchmen; the leader, generally, his followers. There is no such thing as 'appointment' or 'dismissal', no career, no promotion. There is only a 'call' at the instance of the leader on the basis of the charismatic qualification of those he summons. There is no hierarchy; the leader merely intervenes in general or in individual cases when he considers the members of his staff inadequate to a task with which they have been entrusted. There is no such thing as a definite sphere of authority and of competence, and no appropriation of official powers on the basis of social privileges. There may, however, be territorial or functional limits to charismatic powers and to the individual's 'mission'. There is no such thing as a salary or a benefice. Disciples or followers tend to live primarily in a communistic relationship with their leader on means which have been provided by voluntary gift. There are no established administrative organs. In their place are agents who have been provided with charismatic authority by their chief or who possess charisma of their own. There is no system of formal rules, of abstract legal principles, and hence no process of judicial decision oriented to them. But equally there is no legal wisdom oriented to judicial precedent. Formally concrete judgements are newly created from case to case and are originally regarded as divine judgements and revelations. From a substantive point of view, every charismatic authority would have to subscribe to the proposition, 'It is written . . ., but I say unto you. . .'[2] The genuine prophet, like the genuine military leader and every true leader in this sense, preaches, creates or demands *new* obligations. In the pure type of charisma, these are imposed on the authority of revolution by oracles, or of the leader's own will, and are recognised by the members of the reli-

---

[1] Weber uses the term *Gemeinde*, which is not directly translatable. [Parsons' footnote.]
[2] Something contrary to what was written, as Jesus said in opposition to the Scribes and Pharisees. [Parsons' footnote.]

gious, military, or party group, because they come from such a source. Recognition is a duty. When such an authority comes into conflict with the competing authority of another who also claims charismatic sanction, the only recourse is to some kind of a contest, by magical means or even an actual physical battle of the leaders. In principle, only one side can be in the right in such a conflict; the other must be guilty of a wrong which has to be expiated.

Charismatic authority is thus specifically outside the realm of everyday routine and the profane sphere.[1] In this respect, it is sharply opposed both to rational, and particularly bureaucratic, authority, and to traditional authority, whether in its patriarchal, patrimonial, or any other form. Both rational and traditional authority are specifically forms of everyday routine control of action; while the charismatic type is the direct antithesis of this. Bureaucratic authority is specifically rational in the sense of being bound to intellectually analysable rules; while charismatic authority is specifically irrational in the sense of being foreign to all rules. Traditional authority is bound to the precedents handed down from the past and to this extent is also oriented to rules. Within the sphere of its claims, charismatic authority repudiates the past, and is in this sense a specifically revolutionary force. It recognises no appropriation of positions of power by virtue of the possession of property, either on the part of a chief or of socially privileged groups. The only basis of legitimacy for it is personal charisma, so long as it is proved; that is, as long as it receives recognition and is able to satisfy the followers or disciples. But this lasts only so long as the belief in its charismatic inspiration remains.

The above is scarcely in need of further discussion. What has been said applies to the position of authority of such elected monarchs as Napoleon, with his use of the plebiscite. It applies to the 'rule of genius,' which has elevated people of humble origin to thrones and high military commands, just as much as it applies to religious prophets or war heroes.

4. Pure charisma is specifically foreign to economic considerations. Whenever it appears, it constitutes a 'call' in the most emphatic sense of the word, a 'mission' or a 'spiritual duty'. In the

---

[1] Weber used the antithesis of *Charisma* and *Alltag* in two senses. On the one hand, of the extraordinary and temporary as opposed to the everyday and routine; on the other hand, the sacred as opposed to the profane. See Parsons' *Structure of Social Action*, ch. xvii. [Parsons' footnote.]

pure type, it disdains and repudiates economic exploitation of the gifts of grace as a source of income, though, to be sure, this often remains more an ideal than a fact. It is not that charisma always means the renunciation of property or even of acquisition, as under certain circumstances prophets and their disciples do. The heroic warrior and his followers actively seek 'booty'; the elective ruler or the charismatic party leader requires the material means of power. The former in addition requires a brilliant display of his authority to bolster his prestige. What is despised, so long as the genuinely charismatic type is adhered to, is traditional or rational everyday economising, the attainment of a regular income by continuous economic activity devoted to this end. Support by gifts, sometimes on a grand scale involving foundations, even by bribery and grand-scale honoraria, or by begging, constitute the strictly voluntary type of support. On the other hand, 'booty', or coercion, whether by force or by other means, is the other typical form of charismatic provision for needs. From the point of view of rational economic activity, charisma is a typical anti-economic force. It repudiates any sort of involvement in the everyday routine world. It can only tolerate, with an attitude of complete emotional indifference, irregular, unsystematic, acquisitive acts. In that it relieves the recipient of economic concerns, dependence on property income can be the economic basis of a charismatic model of life for some groups; but that is not usually acceptable for the normal charismatic 'revolutionary'.

The fact that incumbency of church office has been forbidden to the Jesuits is a rationalised application of this principle of discipleship. The fact that all the 'virtuosi' of asceticism, the mendicant orders, and fighters for a faith belong in this category, is quite clear. Almost all prophets have been supported by voluntary gifts. The well-known saying of St Paul, 'If a man does not work, neither shall he eat', was directed against the swarm of charismatic missionaries. It obviously has nothing to do with a positive valuation of economic activity for its own sake, but only lays it down as a duty of each individual somehow to provide for his own support. This because he realised that the purely charismatic parable of the lilies of the field was not capable of literal application, but at best 'taking no thought for the morrow' could be hoped for. On the other hand, in such a case as a primarily artistic type of charismatic discipleship, it is conceivable that insulation from economic struggle should mean limitation of those who were really eligible to the 'economically independent'; that is, to persons living on income from property. This has been true of the circle of Stefan George, at least in its primary intentions.

5. In traditionally stereotyped periods, charisma is the greatest revolutionary force. The equally revolutionary force of 'reason' works from without by altering the situations of action, and hence its problems, finally in this way changing men's attitudes toward them; or it intellectualises the individual. Charisma, on the other hand, may involve a subjective or internal reorientation born out of suffering, conflicts or enthusiasm. It may then result in a radical alteration of the central system of attitudes and directions of action with a completely new orientation of all attitudes toward the different problems and structures of the 'world'.[1] In pre-rationalistic periods, tradition and charisma between them have almost exhausted the whole of the orientation of action.

THE ROUTINISATION OF CHARISMA AND ITS CONSEQUENCES

In its pure form charismatic authority has a character specifically foreign to everyday routine structures. The social relationships directly involved are strictly personal, based on the validity and practice of charismatic personal qualities. If this is not to remain a purely transitory phenomenon, but to take on the character of a permanent relationship forming a stable community of disciples or a band of followers or a party organisation or any sort of political or hierocratic organisation, it is necessary for the character of charismatic authority to become radically changed. Indeed, in its pure form charismatic authority may be said to exist only in the process of originating. It cannot remain stable, but becomes either traditionalised or rationalised, or a combination of both.

The following are the principal motives underlying this transformation: (a) the ideal and also the material interests of the followers in the continuation and the continual reactivation of the

---

[1] Weber here uses *Welt* in quotation marks, indicating that it refers to its meaning in what is primarily a religious context. It is the sphere of 'worldly' things and interests as distinguished from transcendental religious interests. [Parsons' footnote.]

community, (b) the still stronger ideal and also stronger material interests of the members of the administrative staff, the disciples or other followers of the charismatic leader in continuing their relationship. Not only this, but they have an interest in continuing it in such a way that both from an ideal and a material point of view, their own status is put on a stable everyday basis. This means, above all, making it possible to participate in normal family rela- tionships or at least to enjoy a secure social position in place of the kind of discipleship which is cut off from ordinary wordly connec- tions, notably in the family and in economic relationships.

(2) The emergence of the Piano as a Modern Keyboard Instrument[1]

The piano had two technically different historical roots. One was the clavichord, in all probability the invention of a monk.

By increasing the number of strings the clavichord originated from the early medieval monochord, an instrument with one string and a movable bridge which was the basis for the rational tone arrangement of the entire Western civilisation. Originally the clavichord had conjunct strings for several tones which, thus, could not be struck simultaneously. It had free strings for only the most important tones. The free strings were gradually increased at the expense of the conjunct strings. With the oldest clavichords, the simultaneous touching of c and e, the third, was impossible.

Its range comprised twenty-two diatonic tones in the fourteenth century (from g to e′ including b-flat next to b). By Agricola's time the instrument had been brought to a chromatic scale from a to b′. Its tones, which rapidly died away, encouraged swift, ani- mated figuration making it an instrument adaptable to art music. The instrument was struck by tangents which limited the sounding part of the string, simultaneously silencing the latter. At the peak of its perfection, the particular sonorous effects of its expressive tone oscillations permitted it to yield before the hammer piano

[1] Source: *The Rational and Social Foundations of Music*, pp. 117–24. Footnotes to this passage have not been included.

only when a small stratum of musicians and amateurs with delicate ears no longer presided over the fate of musical instruments, but when market situations prevailed and the production of instruments had become capitalistic.

The second source of the piano was the clavicembalo, clavecin, or cembalo, which was derived from the psalterium and English virginal. It differs in many ways. Its strings, one for each tone, were plucked by quills, therefore without capacity for modulation in volume or colour, but permitting great freedom and precision of touch.

The clavecin had the same disadvantages as an organ and similar technical devices were employed in the attempt to correct them. Until the eighteenth century organists were normally the builders of keyboard instruments. Also they were the first creators of piano literature. Since the free touch was favourable to the use of the instrument for the reproduction of folk tunes and dances, its specific audience was formed essentially by amateurs, particularly and quite naturally all folk circles tied to home life. In the Middle Ages it was the instrument of monks, later of women led by Queen Elizabeth. As late as 1722 as a recommendation for a new complicated keyboard type it is emphasised that even an experienced woman is able to handle the customary playing of the keyboard.

In the fifteenth and sixteenth centuries the clavecin doubtless participated in the development of music which was melodically and rhythmically transparent. It was one of the mediators for the penetration of popular simple harmonic feeling opposite the polyphonic art music. The theorists built keyboard-like instruments or themselves for experimental purposes. In the sixteenth century, the period of general experimentation with the production of purely tempered instruments for many-voiced compositions, the clavecin was still less important than the lute for vocal accompaniment. However, the cembalo gained territory and became the characteristic instrument for the accompaniment of vocal music, then for the opera. In the seventeenth and eighteenth centuries the conductor sat in the middle of the orchestra. As far as art music is concerned, the instrument remained strongly dependent on the organ in its musical technique until the end of the seventeenth century. Organists and pianists felt themselves to be separated, but solitary artists and representatives of harmonic music in contrast, above all, to the string instruments which 'could not produce any full harmony',' withdrew (with this motivation) in France from the dominance of the king of the viols.

EMANCIPATION OF THE PIANO AND ITS EMERGENCE AS THE INSTRUMENT OF THE MIDDLE CLASSES

French instrumental music showed the influence of the dance, determined by the sociological structure of France. Then, following the example of violin virtuoso performance, musical emancipation of piano music from the organ style of writing was carried out. Chambonnières may be considered the first creator of specific piano works. Domenico Scarlatti, at the beginning of the eighteenth century, is the first to exploit in virtuoso fashion the peculiar sonorous effects of the instrument. Piano virtuosity developed hand in hand with a heavy harpsichord industry which was based on the demand of orchestras and amateurs. Continued development led on to the last great technical changes of the instrument and its typification. The first great builder of harpsichords (around 1600 the family Ruckers in Belgium) operated like a manufacturer creating individual instruments commissioned by specific consumers (orchestras and patricians) and thus in very manifold adaptation to all possible special needs quite in the manner of the organ.

The development of the hammer piano occurred by stages, partly in Italy (Christoferi), partly in Germany. Inventions made in Italy remained unexploited there. Italian culture (until the threshold of the present) remained alien to the indoor culture of Nordic Europe.

Italian ideals lacked the influence of the culture of the bourgeois-like home. They retained the ideal of *a capella* singing and the opera. The arias of the opera supplied the popular demand for easily comprehensible and singable tunes.

The centre of gravity of the production and technical improvement of the piano lies in the musically most broadly organised country, Saxony. The bourgeois-like musical culture derived from the *Kantorelen* virtuosi and builders of instruments proceeded hand in hand with an intense interest in the orchestra of the count. Beyond this it underwent continuous improvement and popularisation. In the foreground of interest was the possibility of muffling and increasing the volume of the tone, the sustaining of the tone, and the beautiful perfection of the chords played in the form of arpeggios at any tone distance. In contrast to these advantages was the disadvantage (especially according to Bach) of deficient freedom, in contrast to the harpsichord and clavichord, in playing fast passages. The removal of this disadvantage was of major concern.

In place of the tapping touch of the keyboard instruments of the sixteenth century, beginning with the organ a rational fingering technique was in progress, soon extended to the harpsichord. This presented the hands working into each other, the fingers crossing over one another. To our conception this was still tortured enough. Eventually the Bachs placed fingering technique, one would like to say on a 'physiological tonal' basis, by a rational use of the thumb. In antiquity the highest virtuoso achievements occurred in the aulos. Now the violin and, above all, the piano presented the most difficult tasks.

The great artists of modern piano music, Johann Sebastian and Philipp Emanuel Bach were still neutral toward the hammer piano. J. S. Bach in particular wrote an important part of his best work for the old types of instruments, the clavichord and harpsichord. These were weaker and more intimate than the piano and with respect to sonority calculated for more delicate ears. Only the internationally famous virtuosity of Mozart and the increasing need of music publishers and of concert managers to satisfy the large music consumption of the mass market brought the final victory of the hammer piano.

In the eighteenth century the piano-builders, above all the German, were still artisans who collaborated and experimented physically (like Silbermann). Machine-made mass production of the piano occurred first in England (Broadwood) then in America (Steinway) where first-rate iron could be pressed into construction of the frame. Moreover, iron helped to overcome the numerous purely climatic difficulties that could affect adoption of the piano. Incidentally, climatic difficulties also stood in the way of adoption of the piano in the tropics. By the beginning of the nineteenth century the piano had become a standard commercial object produced for stock.

The wild competitive struggle of the factories played a role in the development of the instrument. So, too, did the virtuosi with the

special modern devices of the press, exhibitions, and finally, analogous to salesman techniques, of breweries, of the building of concert halls, of the instrument factories of their own (with us, above
all those of the Berliner). These forces brought about that technical
perfection of the instrument which alone could satisfy the ever increasing technical demands of the composers. The older instruments were already no match for Beethoven's later creations.

Meanwhile, orchestra works were made accessible for home use
only in the form of piano transcriptions. In Chopin a first-rank
composer was found who restricted himself entirely to the piano.
Finally in Liszt the intimate skill of the great virtuoso elicited
from the instrument all that had finally been concealed of expressive possibilities.

The unshakable modern position of the piano rests upon the
universality of its usefulness for domestic appropriation of almost
all treasures of music literature, upon the immeasurable fullness of
its own literature and finally on its quality as a universal accompanying and schooling instrument. In its function as a school in-
instrument, it displaced the antique kithara, the monochord, the
primitive organ, and the barrel-lyre of the monastic schools. As an
accompanying instrument it displaced the aulos of antiquity, the
organ, and the primitive string instruments of the Middle Ages
and the lute of the Renaissance. As an amateur instrument of the
upper classes it displaced the kithara of antiquity, the harp of the
North, and the lute of the sixteenth century. Our exclusive
education toward modern harmonic music is represented quite
essentially by it.

Even the negative aspects of the piano are important. Temperament takes from our ears some of the delicacy which gave the decisive flavour to the melodious refinement of ancient music culture.
Until the sixteenth century the training of singers in the Occident
took place on the monochord. According to Zarline, the singers
trained in this manner attempted to reintroduce perfect temperament. Today their training takes place almost exclusively on the
piano; and today, at least in our latitudes, tone formation and
schooling of string instruments is practised from the beginning at
the piano. It is clear that delicate hearing capacity, possible with
training by means of instruments in pure temperament, cannot be
reached. The notoriously greater imperfection in the intonation of
Nordic as compared to Italian singers must be caused by it.

The idea of building pianos with twenty-four keys in the octave, as suggested by Helmholtz, is not promising for economic reasons. The building of the piano is conditioned by the mass market. It is the peculiar nature of the piano to be a middle-class home instrument. As the organ requires a giant indoor area, the piano requires a moderately large indoor space to display its best enchantments. All the successes of the modern piano virtuosi cannot basically change the fact that the instrument in its independent appearances in the large concert hall is involuntarily compared with the orchestra and obviously found to be too light.

Therefore it is no accident that the representatives of pianistic culture are Nordic peoples, climatically housebound and home-centred in contrast to the South. In southern Europe the cultivation of middle-class home comforts was restricted by climatic and historical factors. The piano was invented there but did not diffuse quickly as in the North. Nor did it rise to an equivalent position as a significant piece of middle-class furniture.

(3) The Emergence and Creation of Legal Norms[1]

THE EMERGENCE OF NEW LEGAL NORMS— THEORIES OF CUSTOMARY LAW INSUFFICIENT AS EXPLANATIONS

How do new legal rules arise? At the present time, they usually arise by way of legislation, i.e., conscious human lawmaking in conformity with the formal constitutional requirements, be they customary or 'made', of a given political society. Obviously, this kind of lawmaking is not aboriginal; it is not the normal one even in economically or socially complex and advanced societies. In England, the 'common law' is regarded as the very opposite of 'made' law. In Germany, non-enacted law is usually called 'customary law'. But the concept of 'customary law' is relatively

---

[1] Source: *Law in Economy and Society*, pp. 65–77 *passim*, 91–7 *passim*.
Most of the footnotes to this passage have been omitted.

modern; in Rome it did not emerge before the very late period; in Germany it resulted from civilian doctrine. That theory which was developed in Germany and according to which a custom, in order to be law, must be actually observed, must be commonly believed to be binding, and must be rational, was particularly of such academic origin. Also the other definitions which are current today are but theoretical constructs. For purposes of legal dogmatics, the concept of customary law is still indispensable, however, provided it is used in such refined ways as those formulated by Zitelmann or Gierke. Otherwise we would have to confine our concept of law to statute law on the one side and judge-made law on the other. The violent struggle against the concept of customary law which the legal sociologists have carried on, especially Lambert and Ehrlich, is not only devoid of any foundation but also represents a confusion between the legal and sociological methods of analysis.

But we are concerned with a different problem, namely that of discovering the empirical processes in which non-statutory norms arise as valid customary law. On that problem the traditional doctrines tell us little if anything. As a matter of fact, they are even incorrect where they purport to explain the actual development of law in the past, particularly in periods in which there was little or no enacted law. It is, of course, true that these doctrines find some support in late Roman as well as medieval conceptions, both continental and English, about the meaning and the presuppositions of *consuetudo* as a source of law. There, however, the problem was that of finding an adjustment between a body of rational law claiming universal validity and a multitude of actually prevailing systems of laws of locally or personally limited application. In the late Roman Empire the conflict was between the imperial law and the laws of the peoples of the provinces; in England, between the law of the land (*lex terrae*), i.e., the Common Law, and the local laws; on the Continent it was between the 'received' Roman law and the indigenous bodies of law. Only the various particularistic bodies of law were classified by the jurists as 'customary law', and in order to give legal recognition to customary law the jurists devised certain tests of validity which customary law had to fulfil. This was a necessary step in view of the fact that the universal law claimed an exclusive applicability. But it would not have occurred to anyone to classify as customary law the English Common Law, which certainly was not statute law. Similarly, the definition of the Islamic *Idjmâ* as the *tacitus consensus omnium*[1] is completely unconnected with 'customary law', simply because it purported to be 'sacred' law.

THE ROLE OF PARTY PRACTICES IN THE EMERGENCE AND DEVELOPMENT OF LEGAL NORMS

Theoretically, the origin of legal norms might, as we have already seen, be thought of most simply in the following way: The psychological 'set' which arises with the habituation of an action causes conduct which in the beginning constitutes plain habit later to be experienced as binding; then, with the awareness of the diffusion of such conduct among a plurality of individuals, it comes to be incorporated as 'consensus' into people's semi- or wholly conscious 'expectations' as to the meaningfully correspond-ing conduct of others. Finally these 'consensual understandings' acquire the guaranty of coercive enforcement by which they are distinguished from mere 'conventions'. Even on this purely hypothetical construction there arises the question of how any-thing could ever change in this inert mass of canonised custom which, just because it is considered as binding, seems as though it could never give birth to anything new. The Historical School of Jurisprudence tended to accept the hypothesis that evolutionary impulses of a 'folk spirit' are produced by a hypostatised supra-individual organic entity. Karl Knies also inclined toward this view. Scientifically, however, this conception leads nowhere. Of course, empirically valid rules of conduct, including legal rules, have at all times emerged, and still emerge today, unconsciously, that is, without being regarded by the participants as newly created. Such unconscious emergence has occurred primarily in the form of unperceived changes in meaning; it also takes place through the belief that a factually new situation actually presents no new elements of any relevance for legal evaluation. Another form of 'unconscious' emergence is represented by the application of

---

[1] *Idjmâ*—in Mohammedan law that consent of the scholars which has been held necessary to establish law supplementary to the word of the Prophet as expressed in the Koran and his other alleged sayings (*hadith*).

what actually is new law to old or somewhat different new situations, with the conviction that the law so applied has always obtained and has always been applied in that manner. Nonetheless, there also exists a large class of cases in which both the situation as well as the rule applied are felt to be 'new', although in different degrees and senses.

What is the source of such innovation? One may answer that it is caused by changes in the external conditions of social life which carry in their wake modifications of the empirically prevailing 'consensual understandings'. But the mere *change of external conditions* is neither sufficient nor necessary to explain the changes in the 'consensual understandings'. The really decisive element has always been *a new line of conduct*, which then results either in a change of the meaning of the existing rules of law or in the creation of new rules of law. Several kinds of persons participate in these transformations. First we should mention those individuals who are interested in some concrete communal action. Such an individual may change his behaviour, especially his communal actions, either to protect his interests under new external conditions or simply to promote them more effectively under existing conditions. As a result, there arise 'new' consensual understandings and sometimes new forms of rational association with substantively new meanings; these, in turn, generate the rise of new types of customary behaviour.

It may also be, however, that, without any such reorientation of behaviour by individuals, the total structure of communal action changes in response to changes in external conditions. Of several types of action, all may have been well suited to existing conditions; but, when the conditions change one may turn out to be better suited to serve the economic or social interests of the parties involved; in the process of selection it alone survives and ultimately becomes the one used by all so that one cannot well point out any single individual who would have 'changed' his conduct. In its pure form, such a situation may be a theoretical construct, but something of the kind does actually occur in the selective process which operates between ethnic or religious groups which cling tenaciously to their own respective usages. More frequent, however, is the injection of a new content into communal actions and rational associations as a result of individual invention and its subsequent spread through imitation and selection. Not merely in modern times has this latter situation been of significance as a source of economic reorientation, but in all systems in which the mode of life has reached at least a measure of rationalisation. The parties to the new arrangements are frequently unconcerned about the fact that their respective positions are insecure in the sense of being legally unenforceable. They regard legal enforceability by the state as either unnecessary or as self-evident; even more frequently they simply rely upon the self-interest or the loyalty of their partners combined with the weight of convention. Prior to the existence of any coercive machinery, and prior even to the regulated enforcement of norms through the sib members' duty to participate in vengeance, the function later fulfilled by the 'legal' guaranty of a norm was undoubtedly performed by the general convention that the person who was admittedly 'in the right' could find others who would help him against an offender; and, where some special guaranty appeared desirable, magical self-malediction, i.e., the oath, superseded under very diversified circumstances and to a very large extent, as far as the interested parties themselves were concerned, all other forms of guaranty, including an existing guaranty of legal coercion. In most periods, the preponderant part of the consensual order, including that of economic matters, has operated in this way and without concern for the availability of the legal coercive power of the state or of any coercive enforcement at all. Such an institution, however, as the Yugoslav Zadruga (household community), which is so often cited as evidence of the dispensability of legal coercion, actually dispensed only with the coercive legal power of the state, while during the period of its universal diffusion it undoubtedly enjoyed effective protection through the coercive power of the village authorities. Such forms of consensual action, once they have become firmly embedded in usage, may continue to exist for centuries without any recourse to the coercive power of the state. Although the Zadruga was not recognised by official Austrian law, and was even contrary to many of its rules, it still dominated the life of the peasantry. But such instances should not be regarded as normal nor used as a basis for general conclusions.

Where several religiously legitimated legal systems coexist side by side on a completely equal footing, with equal religious legitimacy and with freedom of choice between them for the individuals, the fact that one of them is supported not only by the religious sanction but also by the coercive power of the state may well decide the rivalry between them, even though state and economic life are dominated by traditionalism. Thus, in Islam, the same status is officially enjoyed by all the four orthodox schools of law. Their application to the individuals is determined by the principle of personality in much the same way as the application of the several tribal laws was determined in the Frankish empire. At the University of Cairo all four schools are represented. Nevertheless, the fact that the Hanefite system was adopted by the Osmanic sultans and that, in consequence, its rules were enjoying the sanction of coercive enforcement by the secular officialdom and the courts,[1] condemned to a slow death the Malekite system which had once enjoyed that support in the past, as well as that of the other two systems; and this development has taken its course despite the complete absence of any other negative factors. In business affairs proper, that is, in the contracts of the market, the interested parties' concern for the availability of the coercive power of the state is considerable. In this field, the development of new forms of association has taken place, and still does so through exact estimates of the probability of enforcement by the courts as organs of the political authority. The contracts to be concluded are being adapted to this estimate and the invention of new contractual forms proceeds by taking these estimates into account.

While changes in the meaning of the prevailing law are thus initiated by the parties or their professional counsellors, they are consciously and rationally adapted to the expected reaction of the judiciary. As a matter of fact, this kind of activity, the *cavere* of the Romans, constitutes the very oldest type of activity performed by 'professional', rationally working lawyers. Among the conditions for the development of a market economy, the calculability of the functioning of the coercive machinery constitutes the technical prerequisite as well as one of the incentives for the inventive genius of the cautelary jurists (*Kautelarjuristen*), whom we find as an autonomous element in legal innovation resulting from private initiative everywhere, but most highly developed and most clearly perceptible in Roman and English law.

On the other hand, the spread of consensual and rational agree-

---

[1] Weber's reference is to the old Turkey of the time before the Kemalist reforms of the 1920s; cf. Vesey-Fitzgerald, *Muhammedan Law* (1931), 36–49 [Rheinstein's note.]

ments of a certain type naturally exercises a marked influence upon the probability of their coercive enforcement by the law. While under normal circumstances only the unique case lacks the guaranty of enforcement, established custom and type agreement, once they enjoy universal diffusion, cannot be persistently ignored except under the compelling necessity of certain formal considerations or because of the intervention of authoritarian powers, or where the agencies of legal coercion have no contact with the life of business as is the case where they are imposed by an ethnically or politically alien authority, or where, in consequence of extreme vocational specialisation, the organs of legal coercion have become far removed from private business as occasionally happens under conditions of sharp social differentiation. The intended meaning of an agreement may be in dispute or its use may be an as yet unstabilised innovation. In such situations the judge, as we shall call the agency of legal coercion *a potiori*, is a second autonomous authority. But even in more normal cases the judge is doing more than merely placing his seal upon norms which would already have been binding by consensual understanding or agreement. His decision of individual cases always produces consequences which, acting beyond the scope of the case, influence the selection of those rules which are to survive as law. We shall see that the sources of 'judicial' decision are not at first constituted by general 'norms of decision' that would simply be 'applied' to concrete cases, except where the decision relates to certain formal questions preliminary to the decision of the case itself. The situation is the very opposite: in so far as the judge allows the coercive guaranty to enter in a particular case for the most concrete reasons, he creates, at least under certain circumstances, the empirical validity of a general norm as 'law', simply because his maxim acquires significance beyond the particular case. . . .

New legal norms have two primary sources: first, the standardisation of certain consensual understandings, especially purposive agreements, which are made with increasing deliberateness by individuals who, aided by professional 'counsel', thereby demarcate their respective spheres of interest; and, second, judicial precedent. In this way, for example, the English common law developed. The extensive participation in the process of juridically experienced and trained experts, who to an ever increasing degree devoted themselves 'professionally' to the tasks of 'counsel' or judge, has placed the stamp of 'lawyers' law' upon the type of law thus created.

Not excluded, of course, is the role played in the development of the law by purely 'emotional' factors, such as the so-called 'sense of justice'. Experience shows, however, that the 'sense of justice' is very unstable unless it is firmly guided by the 'pragma' of objective or subjective interests. It is, as one can still easily see today, capable of sudden fluctuations and it cannot be expressed except in a few very general and purely formal maxims. No national legal peculiarities, in particular, can be derived from any differences in the operation of the 'sense of justice', at least not as far as present knowledge goes.[1] Being mainly emotional, that 'sense' is hardly adequate for the maintenance of a body of stable norms; it rather constitutes one of the diverse sources of irrational adjudication. Only upon this basis can one ask to what extent 'popular' attitudes, i.e., attitudes widely diffused among those actually concerned in these interests, can prevail against the 'lawyers' law' of the professionals (attorneys and judges) who are continuously engaged in the invention of new contracts and in adjudication. The answer to this question depends, as we shall see, upon the type of adjudicative procedure prevailing in a given situation.

DEVELOPMENT OF NEW LAW THROUGH IMPOSITION FROM ABOVE

But apart from the influence and, mostly, the confluence of these factors, innovation in the body of legal rules may also occur through their deliberate imposition *from above*. Of course, this took place at first in ways very different from those we know in our present society. Originally there was a complete absence of the notion that rules of conduct possessing the character of 'law', i.e. rules which are guaranteed by 'legal coercion', could be intentionally created as 'norms'. As we have seen, legal decisions did

---

[1] Weber's remark is directed against those scholars of the historical school of jurisprudence who regarded all law as the emanation of every nation's peculiar 'national spirit' (*Volksgeist*); see especially Savigny, *Vom Beruf unserer Zeit für Gesetzgebung und Rechtswissenschaft* (1814), translated by Hayward (*On The Vocation of Our Age for Legislation and Jurisprudence*, 1831). The theory of the national peculiarity of the sense of justice was taken up by the National-Socialists and used by them as one of the foundations of their legal theory. [Rheinstein's footnote.]

I

not originally have any normative element at all. Today, we take it for granted that legal decisions constitute the 'application' of fixed and stable rules; but in earlier times they were not looked upon in that way at all. Even where there had emerged the conception that norms were 'valid' for behaviour and binding in the resolution of disputes, they were not conceived as the products, or as even the possible subject matter, of human enactment. Their 'legitimacy' rather rested upon the absolute sacredness of certain usages as such, deviation from which would produce either evil magical effects, such as the restlessness of the spirits, or the wrath of the gods. As 'tradition' they were, in theory at least, immutable. They had to be correctly known and interpreted in accordance with established usage, but they could not be created. Their interpretation was the task of those who had known them longest, i.e. the physically oldest persons or the elders of the kinship group, quite frequently the magicians and priests, who, as a result of their specialised knowledge of the magical forces, knew and had to know the techniques of intercourse with the supernatural powers.

Nevertheless, new norms have also emerged through explicit imposition. But this could happen in one way only: through a new charismatic revelation which could assume two forms. In the older it would indicate what was right in an individual case; in the other, the revelation might also point to a general norm for all future similar cases. Such revelation of law constitutes the primeval revolutionary element which undermines the stability of tradition and is the parent of all types of legal 'enactment'. The revelation could be, and indeed often was, revelation in the literal sense; the new norms found their source in the inspiration or impulses, either actual or apparent, of the charismatically qualified person and without being in any way required by new external conditions. But, usually, revelation was an artificial process. Various magical devices were used to obtain new rules when a change in economic or social conditions had created novel and unsolved problems. The men who normally used these primitive methods of adapting old rules to new situations were the magicians, the prophets, or the priests of an oracular deity. Of course, the line where interpretation of old tradition slides into the revelation of new norms is unprecise. But the transition must take place once the interpretative wisdom of the priests or elders proves inadequate. A similar need may also arise for the determination of disputed facts. . . .

Among the most important factors which secularised the thinking about what should be valid as a norm and especially its emancipation from magically guaranteed traditions, were war and its uprooting effects. Although the *imperium* of the conquering warrior chief was inevitably very wide, he could not exercise it in important cases without the free consent of the army. It was in the very nature of the situation that this *imperium* was in the vast majority of cases oriented towards the regulation of conditions which in times of peace could have been regulated only by revealed norms, but which in times of war required that new norms be created by agreed or imposed enactment. The war lord and the army disposed of prisoners, booty, and particularly of conquered land. They thus created new individual rights and, under certain circumstances, new law. On the other hand, the war lord, both in the interest of common security and to prevent breaches of discipline and the instigation of domestic disorder, had to have more comprehensive powers than a 'judge' possessed in times of peace. These circumstances would alone have been sufficient to increase the *imperium* at the expense of tradition. But war also disrupts the existing economic and social order, so that it becomes clear to everyone that the things one has been accustomed to are not absolutely sacred. It follows that war and warlike expansion have at all stages of historical development often been connected with a systematic fixation of the law both old and new. Again, the pressing need for security against internal and foreign enemies induces a growing rationalisation of lawmaking and lawfinding. Above all, those various social elements by whom legal procedure is guided and presided over, enter into new relationships with each other. In the same way that the political association assumes a permanently military character because of war and preparation for war, the military as such increases its decisive influence over the settlement of disputes between its members and, consequently, upon the development of the law. The prestige of age and, to a certain extent, the prestige of magic tend to decrease. But many different solutions would be found for the problem of how to adjust the various claims for a share in the making of new law between the war lord, the secular and spiritual guardians of sacred tradition, and the army, which is likely to be comparatively free from the restraints of tradition.

From this point of view, the type of military organisation is a highly important factor. The Germanic *thing* of the district and also the *gemot* (*Landsgemeinde*) of the total political community were assemblies of the men who were able to bear arms and, consequently, were owners of land. Similarly, the Roman *populus* consisted of the property-holders assembled in their tactical units. During the great upheavals of the migration of the Germanic tribes, the assemblies of the Germanic political communities seem to have assumed, as against the war lord, the right to participate in the creation of new law. Sohm's contention that all enacted law was the King's law is quite improbable. In fact, the bearer of the *imperium* does not seem to have played a predominant role in this kind of lawmaking. Among more sedentary peoples, the power of the charismatic legal sage continued unbroken; among those who were faced with new situations in the course of their warlike wanderings, especially the Franks and the Langobards, the sense of power of the warrior class increased. They claimed and exercised the right of active and decisive participation in the enactment of laws and the formation of judgements

In early medieval Europe, on the other hand, the Christian Church, by its example of episcopal power, everywhere strongly encouraged the interference of the princes in the administration and enactment of the law. Indeed, the Church often instigated this intervention for its own interests as well as in the interests of the ethics it taught. The capitularies of the Frankish kings developed in the same way as the sub-theocratic courts of the itinerant justices. In Russia, very shortly after the introduction of Christianity, the second version of the *Russkaya Pravda* is evidence of the prince's intervention in adjudication and enactment which had been lacking in the first version; the result was the development of a considerable body of new substantive law having its source in the prince.[1] In the Occident, this tendency of the *imperium* conflicted

---

[1] Weber's assumption of the existence of successive versions of the *Russkaya Pravda* seems to be based upon the writings of Goetz (*Das russische Recht* [1910], 24 Z.f. Vgl. Rw. 241; (1914) 31 Z.f. Vgl. Rw. 1) and Kohler (*Die Russkaja Prawda und das altslawische Recht* (1916) 33 Z.f. Vgl. Rw. 289). Upon these studies doubt has been thrown by the latest investigation (Academy of the U.S.S.R., *Pravda Russkaya* (1940), I, 29, 55), where it is pointed out that the oldest existing manuscript dates from 1282 and all that earlier dates ascribed to later editions have been purely conjectural. Controversy also exists with reference to the nature of the *Russkaya Pravda*. According to Kluchevsky (*History of Russia*, trans. Hogarth (1911), cc. ix and x) the book is neither a princely enactment nor a private law book but a collection of secular customs

with the firm structure of charismatic and corporative justice within the military community. On the other hand, the Roman *populus*, in accordance with the development of discipline in the hoplite army,[1] could only accept or reject what was proposed by the holder of the *imperium*, i.e. apart from legal enactments, nothing but decisions in capital cases brought before it by *provocatio*.[2] In the German *thing* a valid judgement necessarily required the acclamation of the audience (*Umstand*). The Roman *populus*, on the other hand, was not concerned with any judgement save its power to rescind, by way of grace, a death sentence rendered by a magistrate. The right of every member of the German *thing* assembly to challenge the decision proposed (*Urteilsschelte*) was due to its lesser degree of military discipline. The charismatic quality of adjudication was not the exclusive possession of a special occupational group, but every member of the *thing* community could at all times express his superior knowledge and attempt to have it prevail over the judgement proposed. Originally, a decision between them could only be arrived at by an ordeal, frequently with penal sanctions for the one whose 'false' judgement constituted blasphemy against the divine guardians of the law. In fact, of course, the murmur of approval or disapproval by the community, whose voice was, in this sense, the 'voice of God', would always carry considerable weight. The strict discipline of the Romans found expression in the magistrate's exclusive right of guiding the course of the lawsuit as well as in the exclusive right of initiative (*agere cum populo*) of the several magistrates who were competing with each other.

The Germanic dichotomy between lawfinding and law enforcement constitutes one type of separation of powers in the administration of justice; another is represented by the Roman system of concurrent powers of several magistrates entitled to 'intercede' against each other and of dividing the functions of a lawsuit between magistrate and *judex*. Separation of powers in the administration of justice was also guaranteed by the necessity of collaboration in

which was made by the Church to be applied in its courts when they had to exercise general jurisdiction over its nonclerical subjects. For an English translation of the *Russkaya Pravda*, see Vernadsky, *Mediæval Russian Laws* (1947). [Rheinstein's footnote.]

[1] Hoplite army (Greek): an army composed of heavily-armed soldiers. The term is used by Weber as a term of art. Cf. W.u.G. 568, 592, 644; *Essays* 57, 227, 256, 345. [Rheinstein's footnote.]

[2] *Provocatio*—the right of a Roman citizen convicted of a capital crime to appeal to the people assembled in the *comitia centuriata*. [Rheinstein's footnote.]

various forms among magistrates, juridical *honoratiores*, and the military or political assembly of the community. It was on this basis that the formalistic character of the law and its administration was preserved.

Where, however, 'official' authorities, that is, the *imperium* of the prince and his officials or the power of the priests as the official guardians of the law, succeeded in eliminating the independent bearers of charismatic legal knowledge on the one side, and the participation of the popular assembly or its representatives on the other, the development of law acquired quite early that theocratic-patrimonialistic character which, as we shall see, produced peculiar consequences for the formal aspects of the law. Although a different course developed where, as for instance in the Hellenic democracies, a politically omnipotent popular assembly completely displaced all magisterial and charismatic agents of adjudication and set itself up as the sole and supreme authority in the creation and the finding of the law, the effects upon the formal qualities of the law were similar. We shall speak of 'lawfinding by the folk assembly' (*dinggenossenschaftliche Rechtsfindung*) whenever the folk assembly, while it participates in adjudication, does not have supreme authority over it but can accept or reject the decision recommended by the charismatic or official possessor of legal knowledge and can influence the decision in some particular way, for instance, through the challenge of the judgement proposed. Illustrations of this situation are the Germanic military community and, although in a rationally highly modified way, the military community of Rome, The type is not characterised, however, by the mere fact of the popular assembly participating in adjudication, examples of which occur frequently, for instance, among the Negroes of Togoland or among the Russians of the period of the first pre-Christian version of the *Russkaya Pravda*. In both these situations we can find a small body of 'judgement finders'—twelve among the Russians—corresponding to the Germanic council of aldermen. Among the Negroes of Togoland the members of this body are taken from among the elders of the kinship or neighbourhood groups, and we may assume a similar basis more generally for the origin of the council of judgement finders. In the *Russkaya Pravda*, the prince did not participate at all; among the Togoland Negroes, however, he presides over the deliberations, and the judgement is arrived at by joint and secret consultation between him and the elders. In neither case, however, does the participation of the people impart any charismatic character to the process of decision finding. Cases where popular participation does have that character seem to be rare in Africa and elsewhere.

Where the folk community exists, the formal character of the law and of lawfinding is largely preserved because the lawfinding is the product of revelation of the legal sage rather than the whimsical or emotional enunciation of those for whom the law is effective, i.e. those whom it purports to dominate rather than to serve. On the other hand, the sage's charisma, like every other genuine charisma, must 'prove' itself by its own persuasive and convincing power. Indirectly, the sense of fairness and the everyday experience of the members of the legal community can thus make themselves felt strongly. But formally, the law is a 'lawyers' law', for without specific expert knowledge and skill it cannot assume the form of a rational rule. However, as far as its content is concerned, it is at the same time also 'popular law'. It is probable that the origin of 'legal proverbs' may be ascribed to the epoch of administration of justice by the folk assembly. It should be realised, however, that the folk assembly was not a universal phenomenon, if we use the term in the precise sense of a peculiar variety of several possible ways of dividing power between the authority of legal charisma and ratification by the popular and military community. The specific feature of such legal proverbs is usually a combination of the formal legal norms with a concrete and popular reason, as, for example, in such sayings as these: 'Where you have left your faith, there you must seek it again', or 'Hand must warrant hand'. They originate, on the one hand, in the popular character of the law which arises both from the participation of the community and the relatively considerable knowledge which it has of the law. On the other hand, legal proverbs also originated in certain maxims formulated by individuals, who, either as experts or as interested observers, gave thought to the common features of frequently recurring decisions. It is certain that legal prophets must have coined many a maxim in this fashion. In short, legal proverbs are fragmentary legal propositions expressed as slogans.

THE ROLE OF THE LAW SPECIALISTS

Yet formally elaborated law constituting a complex of maxims consciously applied in decisions has never come into existence without the decisive co-operation of trained specialists. We have already become acquainted with their different categories. The stratum of 'practitioners of the law' concerned with adjudication comprises, in addition to the official administrators of justice, the legal *honoratiores*, i.e. the *lag sagas*, *rachimburgi*, aldermen, and, occasionally, priests. As the administration of justice requires more and more experience and, ultimately, specialised knowledge, we find as a further category private counsellors and attorneys, whose influence in the formation of the law through 'legal invention' has often been considerable. The conditions under which this group has developed will later be discussed in detail. The increased need for specialised legal knowledge created the professional lawyer. This growing demand for experience and specialised knowledge and the consequent stimulus for increasing rationalisation of the law have almost always come from increasing significance of commerce and those participating in it. For the solution of the new problems thus created, specialised, i.e. rational, training is an ineluctable requirement. Our interest is centred upon the ways and consequences of the 'rationalisation' of the law, that is, the development of those 'juristic' qualities which are characteristic of it today. We shall see that a body of law can be 'rationalised' in various ways and by no means necessarily in the direction of the development of its 'juristic' qualities. The direction in which these formal qualities develop is, however, conditioned directly by 'intrajuristic' conditions: the particular character of the individuals who are in a position to influence 'professionally' the ways in which the law is shaped. Only indirectly is this development influenced, however, by general economic and social conditions. The prevailing type of legal education, i.e. the mode of training of the practitioners of the law, has been more important than any other factor.

(C) The Social Causes of the Decay of Ancient Civilization[1]

The Roman Empire was not destroyed from without; its destruc-

[1] From *The Journal of General Education*, Vol. V (1950), pp. 75–88. A public

tion was not caused by the numerical superiority of its opponents
nor by the inadequacy of its political leaders. In the last century of
its existence Rome had her iron chancellors: heroic figures, like
Stilicho, men who combined Teutonic boldness with the art of cun-
ning diplomacy, were at the head of the state. Why could they not
accomplish what the illiterate princes of the Merovingian, Carolingian and Saxon houses were able to achieve and to defend against
Saracens and Huns? The Empire had, long before, undergone a
change in its very essence; when it disintegrated it did not suddenly
collapse under one powerful blow. The Teutonic invaders brought
to its logical climax a development that had been long in the making.

But most important: the decay of ancient *civilisation* was not
caused by the destruction of the Roman *Empire*. The Empire as a
political structure survived by centuries the acme of Roman culture.
This culture had vanished much earlier. As early as the beginning
of the third century Roman literature had come to an end. The art
of the jurists decayed together with their schools. Greek and Roman
poetry were dead. Historiography languished and almost disappeared. The Latin language was soon in a state of full degeneration.
When, one and a half centuries later, with the extinction of the
office of the emperor in the West, the books are closed, it becomes
obvious that barbarism, long ago, has conquered the Empire from
within. The barbarian invaders, moreover, are far from establishing completely new conditions on the soil of the demolished Empire;
the Merovingian kingdom, in Gaul at least, continues for some
time the pattern of the Roman province. The problem, therefore,
arises for us: What has caused the decline of ancient civilisation?

Quite a few different explanations have been offered by different
scholars, some missing the point completely, others getting off to a
good start but making a wrong use of correct premises.

Some authors maintain that despotism necessarily strangled the
soul of the ancient Romans and so destroyed their state and their
civilisation. But the despotism of Frederick the Great was, on the
contrary, a powerful force of growth.

Others assert that the alleged luxury and the undeniable decline

lecture delivered before the Academic Society of Freiburg in 1896. The German
title is *Die sozialen Gründe des Untergangs der antiken Kultur*. Published in the
magazine *Die Wahrheit* (Stuttgart, 1896), reprinted in **Weber's** *Gesammelte
Aufsätze zur Sozial- und Wirtschaftsgeschichte* (Collected Essays on Social and
Economic History) (Tübingen, 1924), pp. 289–311. Translated by Christian
Mackauer.

of the morality in the highest social ranks called forth the revenge of History. But both phenomena are symptoms themselves. We shall see that much more powerful factors than the guilt of individuals destroyed ancient civilisation.

Still others believe that the foundations of society were dissolved by the emancipation of the Roman woman and the loosening of the ties of marriage in the ruling classes. The fables told by a biased reactionary like Tacitus about the Germanic woman, that miserable slave of a peasant-warrior, are repeated by modern reactionaries. In fact, the ubiquitous 'German woman' decided the victory of the Germanic invaders as little as the ubiquitous 'Prussian schoolmaster' decided the battle of Königgrätz. On the contrary, we shall see that the *re-establishment* of the family among the *lower* classes of society was connected with the decay of ancient civilisation.

Pliny, an eye-witness, assures us: *Latifundia perdidere Italiam* ['the large estates have ruined Italy']: 'Here you see it,' one School among the moderns says, 'it was the Junkers who ruined Rome.' 'Yes,' their opponents reply, 'but only because they were ruined themselves by grain imports from foreign countries.' If the Romans had protected their agriculture with high tariff walls, the Caesars, apparently, would still be on their throne today. But we shall see that the destruction of ancient civilisation was a first step on the way towards the *re-establishment* of a *peasant* class.

There is even what people call a 'Darwinistic' hypothesis: a quite recent author contends that the process of selection by which the strongest men were drafted into the army and so condemned to celibacy led to the degeneration of the Roman race. We shall rather see that increasing recruiting of the army from its own ranks was a symptom of the decay of the Roman Empire.

But enough of these examples. Only one more remark before we take up our proper subject:

The interest in a story is always keener when the audience has the feeling: *de te narratur fabula*, and when the story-teller can conclude his yarn with a *discite moniti*! Unfortunately, the discussion which follows does not fall into this enviable category. We can learn little or nothing for our contemporary social problems from ancient history. A modern proletarian and a Roman slave would be as unable to understand one another as a European and a Chinese. Our problems are of a completely different character. The drama we are going to study has only an *historical* interest; but it presents one of the most singular historical phenomena, indeed, the internal dissolution of an old civilisation.

Our first task will be to understand those peculiarities of the social structure of ancient society that we have just mentioned. We shall see how they determined the cycle of ancient civilisation.

The civilisation of classical antiquity is, in its essence, first of all an urban civilisation. The city is the foundation of political life as well as of art and literature. With regard to its economic system also, the ancient world, at least during its earlier period, represents what we call today a 'city economy'. The ancient city, during the Greek period, is not essentially different from the medieval city. As far as differences exist, they can be explained by the differences between the climate and race of the Mediterranean, on the one hand, and those of Central Europe, on the other, just as even today English workers are different from Italian workers and German craftsmen from Italian ones. Originally, the economic basis of the ancient, just as of the medieval city, is the exchange in the urban market of the products of urban craftsmanship for those of its immediate rural neighbourhood. Almost the whole demand is satisfied by this direct exchange between producer and consumer, without any importation from outside. Aristotle's ideal of urban autarchy had been realised in the majority of Greek cities.

To be sure, since very ancient times an international trade has been built on these local foundations; it comprises a vast area and numerous objects. Our historical reports are almost exclusively concerned with those cities whose ships are engaged in this trade; but because we hear only about them, we are prone to forget how insignificant, quantitatively, this trade was. In the first place, the civilisation of European antiquity is a *coastal* civilisation, just as European ancient history remains for a long time the history of coastal towns. Side by side with the technically highly developed urban exchange economy, and in sharp contrast to it, the 'natural economy' of the barbaric peasants of the inland regions presents itself, entrammeled in tribal communities or bent under the rule of feudal patriarchs. A steady and regular international traffic is carried on exclusively by sea or on large rivers. No inland traffic comparable to that of even the Middle Ages existed in ancient Europe. The glorified Roman highways never carried a traffic even remotely comparable to modern conditions; the same applies to the Roman postal service. There is an immense difference in revenue between estates lying inland and those located on rivers or on the sea-shore. To be close to a highway was generally considered not an advantage in Roman times but rather a nuisance because of billeting and— vermin: Roman highways are military not commercial roads.

On the ground of such a still intact 'natural economy', international exchange is unable to strike deep roots. Only a small number of high-priced articles such as precious metals, amber, valuable textiles, some iron ware and pottery, are objects of regular trade. Such a trade just cannot be compared to modern commerce. It would be the same as if today nothing but champagne and silk were exchanged, while all trade statistics show that *mass* demand alone accounts for the big figures in the balance of international trade. At some time or other, to be sure, cities like Athens and Rome become dependent on imports for their grain supply. But such conditions are highly abnormal; and in all these cases the *community* takes over the responsibility of supplying these goods. The citizens are not inclined to leave this task to uncontrolled private trade nor can they afford to do so.

Not the masses with their day-to-day needs, but a small group of well-to-do people are interested in international commerce. This has one implication: increasing differentiation of wealth is a prerequisite of the development of commerce in the ancient world. This differentiation—and here we reach a third, decisive point— takes a quite definite form and direction: ancient civilisation is a *slave* civilisation. From the very beginning, unfree labour in the countryside exists side by side with free labour in the city; unfree division of labour on the rural estate, producing for the master's own use, side by side with the free division of labour regulated by the conditions of exchange in the urban market, just as in the Middle Ages. And in the ancient world, as in the Middle Ages, these two forms of productive co-operation were naturally antagonistic. Progress is based on progressing division of labour. Under conditions of free labour, this progress is, in its beginnings, identical with a progressive growth of the market, extensively through geographical, intensively through personal extension of the area of exchange; the citizens of the towns, therefore, try to destroy the manorial estates and to include the serfs in the process of free exchange. Where unfree labour prevails, however, economic progress takes place through the progressive accumulation of human beings;

the more slaves or serfs are combined on one estate, the higher the degree of specialisation which can be attained with unfree workers. But while during the Middle Ages the development leads more and more to the victory of free labour and of free exchange, the outcome in the ancient world is exactly the opposite. What is the reason for this difference? It is the same reason which determines the limits of technological progress in antiquity: the 'cheapness' of human beings resulting from the character of the uninterrupted warfare in the ancient world. Wars in ancient times are always slave raids; they continually throw new supplies upon the slave market and so favour unfree labour and the accumulation of human beings as in no other period of history. The development of free handicraft, therefore, was arrested at the level of non-capitalistic wage-work for a narrowly defined local clientele. No competition arose between (capitalistic) free enterprises and free (non-capitalistic) wage-work for supplying the market, and so the economic premium on labour-saving devices, which has called forth such inventions in our modern epoch, was absent. In the ancient world, on the contrary, the economic importance of unfree labour in the *oikos* (the autarchic estate) is all the time on the increase. Only slave-owners are able to satisfy their economic needs by division of labour, through slave labour, and so to raise their standard of living. Only they can—in addition to satisfying their own needs—produce more and more for the market.

This determines the peculiar economic development of the ancient world and its difference from that of the Middle Ages. In medieval Europe, free division of labour first expands *intensively* within the economic area of the city, in the form of production for a clientele and for the local market. Later, increasing external trade on the basis of a geographical division of labour creates new forms of production for foreign markets; making use of free labour, it takes the form first of the putting-out system, then of manufacture. The development of a *modern* system of economy is also accompanied by the phenomenon that the masses increasingly satisfy their demand through interlocal and finally international exchange of goods. In the ancient world, as we see, development of international commerce is accompanied, on the contrary, by the conglomeration of unfree labour on the big slave-estates. Thus, under the superstructure of the exchange economy, one finds a ceaselessly expanding substructure of an economy without exchange (a 'natural economy'): the slave-combines, constantly absorbing human beings and satisfying their demand essentially not in the market but by their own production. The higher the standard of living of the slave-owning top stratum of society rises, and the more, therefore, the *extensive* development of commerce increases, the more this commerce loses in *intensity*; it is transformed into a thin net spread out over a substructure of a 'natural economy', a net whose meshes become finer while its thread becomes thinner and thinner all the time. During the Middle Ages, the transition from production for a local clientele to production for an interlocal market is prepared by the slow infiltration of (capitalistic) enterprise and the principle of competition from the circumference towards the centre of the local economic community; during the ancient period, however, international commerce leads to the growth of the *oikoi* which stifle the *local* exchange economy.

This development has reached its most gigantic dimension in the Roman Empire. Rome is first—after the victory of the *plebs*—a conquering state of peasants, or better: of townsmen cultivating their own land. Every war ends with the annexation of more land for colonisation. The younger sons of land-owning citizens, who cannot expect to inherit their father's estate, fight in the army for an estate of their own and so, at the same time, for full citizenship. This is the secret of Rome's expansive strength. This development comes to an end with the extension of Roman conquests to territories overseas. Now, the peasants' interest in acquiring new land for settlement is no longer decisive, but rather the interest of the aristocracy in exploiting the newly conquered province. The purpose of these wars consists in slave raids and in the confiscation of land to be exploited by the farmer of state land or the tax-farmer. In addition, the Second Punic War decimated the peasantry in the homeland—the consequences of its decline are partly a belated triumph for Hannibal. The reaction following the Gracchan movement finally decides the victory of slave-labour in agriculture. From this time on, the slave-owners alone are the representatives of a rising standard of living, of an increase in buying-power, of the development of production for the market. This does not mean that free labour completely disappears; but the slave-using enterprises alone represent the *progressive* element. The Roman agricultural writers presuppose slave-labour as the natural basis of the labour system.

The cultural importance of unfree labour was finally re-enforced decisively through the inclusion of large inland areas—like Spain, Gaul, Illyria, the Danubian countries—into the Roman world. The centre of gravity of the Roman Empire shifted into the inland regions. This means that ancient civilisation made an attempt to change its scene of action, to turn from a coastal into an inland civilisation. It expanded over an immense economic area which even in the course of centuries could not have been converted into an exchange and market economy similar to that existing along the coasts of the Mediterranean. Even in these coastal areas, as we have pointed out, interlocal exchange of commodities was only a superficial net, getting thinner all the time; in the inland regions, the meshes of the net of exchange were, of necessity, much looser still. In these inland regions, progress of civilisation in the way of a free division of labour through the development of an *intensive* exchange of commodities was virtually *impossible*. Only through the rise of a landed aristocracy, based on slave-ownership and unfree division of labour (the *oikos*), could these regions gradually be drawn into the orbit of Mediterranean civilisation. In the inland regions, to a higher degree still than along the coasts, the immensely more expensive commerce could serve only the luxury needs of the uppermost social stratum, the slave-owners; and, at the same time, the possibility of producing for the market was restricted to a small number of large slave-owning enterprises.

Thus the slave-owner became the economic representative of ancient civilisation; the organisation of slave-labour forms the indispensable basis of Roman society. We have to study, therefore, somewhat more closely its specific social character.

Our sources are mostly concerned with the *agricultural* enterprises of the late republican and early imperial periods. Extensive land-ownership constitutes, anyway, the main form of wealth; even wealth that is speculatively used rests on this basis: the large-scale Roman speculator is, as a rule, also a great land-owner; if for no other reason, than because security in the form of landed property was legally required for the most lucrative kinds of speculation, tax-farming and contracting.

The typical large Roman land-owner is not a gentleman-farmer, supervising his own estate, but a man who lives in town, devotes his time to political activity, and is interested above all in receiving a money rent. The supervision of his estate is entrusted to unfree bailiffs (*villici*). The methods of cultivation are influenced mainly by the following circumstances.

Production of grain for the market is, in most cases, not profitable. The market of the city of Rome, for instance, is closed to private producers because of public grain distributions; transportation of grain from inland estates to distant markets is impossible in any case because the price cannot support the costs. In addition, slave-labour is not suited to grain production, especially since the Roman agricultural technique requires scrupulous and intensive work and therefore presupposes a personal interest on the worker's part. For this reason, land for grain production is usually, at least in part, leased to *coloni*, small tenants, the descendants of the free peasantry who are deprived of their former property. But such a *colonus* is, even in earlier times, not an independent tenant and self-responsible farmer. The owner provides the inventory, the *villicus* controls the cultivation. From the very beginning, apparently, it was a frequent practice for the tenant to do a certain amount of work on the owner's estate, especially during harvest time. Leasing of land to *coloni* is considered a form of cultivation of the land by the *owner* 'by means of' the tenants (*per colonos*).

The part of the estate under direct management by the owner produces for the market high-priced products primarily, like olive-oil and wine, and secondarily garden vegetables, cattle, poultry and luxuries for the table of the highest stratum of Roman society, for the people who alone have the money to purchase them. By these products grain is pushed back to the less fertile land which is in the hands of the *coloni*. The master's own estate resembles a plantation, and the workers on it are slaves. *Coloni* and a herd of slaves (the *familia*), side by side, represent, under the Empire as well as during the late Republic, the normal population of a large estate.

We first turn to the slaves. What is their condition?

Let us look at the ideal pattern which the agricultural writers describe. The lodging of the 'talking inventory' (*instrumentum vocale*), i.e. the slave stable, is found close to that of the cattle (*instrumentum semi-vocale*). It contains the dormitories, in addition a hospital (*valetudinarium*), a lockup (*carcer*), a workshop for the craftsmen (*ergastulum*). Whoever has worn the king's colours will be reminded by this picture of a familiar experience: the barracks. And indeed, the life of a slave normally is a barracks life. The slaves sleep and eat together, under supervision of the *villicus*; their better piece of clothing is left at the store-room with the bailiff's wife (*villica*) who takes the place of the store-room sergeant; every month the clothing is inspected at a roll-call. The work is disciplined in a strictly military manner: squads (*decuriae*) are formed every morning; they march to work under supervision of the 'drivers' (*monitores*). This was absolutely necessary. It never has been possible to use unfree labour for market production on a permanent basis without resorting to the lash. For us one implication of this form of life is of special importance: the slave in his barracks is not only without property but without family as well. Only the *villicus* lives permanently with his wife in his special cell in some form of slave-marriage (*contubernium*), comparable to the married sergeant or staff-sergeant in modern barracks; according to the agricultural writers, this is even a 'standing regulation' for the *villicus*, in the interest of the master. And as the institutions of private property and private family always go hand in hand, so it is here: the slave who owns property owns a family as well. The *villicus*—and only the *villicus*, as the agricultural writers seem to indicate—has a *peculium*, originally, as the name tells, his own cattle which he grazes on the master's pasture, just as the agricultural labourer does today on the large estates of eastern Germany. As the masses of the slaves have no *peculium*, they also do not live monogamously. Sexual intercourse for them is a kind of controlled prostitution with bounties awarded to female slaves for the raising of children—some masters granted them liberty when they had raised three children. This last practice already indicates what the consequences of the absence of monogamous marriage were. Human beings thrive only in the circle of the family. The slave barracks were unable to reproduce themselves, they depended for their recruitment on the continual purchase of slaves, and the agricultural writers assume, indeed, that new slaves are bought regularly. The ancient slave estate devours human beings as the modern blast-furnace devours coal. A slave market and its regular and ample supply with human material is the indispensable presupposition of slave barracks producing for the market. The buyer looked for cheap wares: Varro recommends that one should choose criminals and similar cheap material; the reason he gives is characteristic: such rabble, he maintains, is mostly 'sharper' (*velocior est animus hominum improborum*). So this form of enterprise depends on the regular supply of the slave market with human cattle. What would

happen if this supply should collapse? The effect on the slave barracks must be the same as that of exhaustion of the coal deposits on
the blast-furnaces. And the time came when it happened. Here we
have reached the turning-point in the development of ancient
civilisation.

When we are being asked from which event we should date the—
first latent, soon manifest—decline of Roman power and civilisation, it is difficult, at least for a German, not to think of the battle in
the Forest of Teutoburg. There is, indeed, a kernel of truth in this
popular conception, although it seems to be contradicted by the
obvious facts which show the Roman Empire at the zenith of its
power at the time of Trajan. To be sure, the battle itself was not
decisive—a reverse like this occurs in every war of expansion waged
against barbarians; decisive was the aftermath: the suspension of
offensive warfare on the Rhine by Tiberius. This brought to an end
the expansive tendencies of the Roman Empire. With the internal
and in the main also external pacification of the area of ancient
civilisation, the regular supply of the slave-markets with human
cattle began to shrink. As a result of this, an immense and *acute*
scarcity of labour seems to have developed already at the time of
Tiberius. We are told that under his regime it was necessary to inspect the *ergastula* of the large estates because the big landowners
resorted to kidnapping; like the robber-barons of later times, it
seems, they were lying in ambush along the highways, on the look-
out, not for merchants' goods, but for hands to work on their
deserted land. More important was the slow but steadily spreading
long-term result: it became impossible to continue production on
the basis of slave barracks. They presupposed a continuous supply
of new slaves; they could not provide for their own needs. They
were liable to break down when this supply came to a permanent
standstill. From later agricultural writers we get the impression
that the decline in the 'cheapness' of human cattle first led to an
improvement in agricultural technique: one tried to raise the performance of the workers by careful training. But when the last
offensive wars of the second century were over (they had already
acquired the character of slave-raids), the large plantations with
their celibate and propertyless slaves were bound to dwindle away.

That this really happened and how it happened we learn from a
comparison of the conditions of the slaves on large estates as described by the Roman writers with the conditions prevailing on the

estates we know from Charlemagne's regulations for the royal demesnes (*capitulare de villis imperialibus*) and from the surveys of monasteries of this time. In either epoch we find the slaves as agricultural labourers; in either case they are equally without rights, especially equally subject to the unlimited exploitation of their labour-power by their master. No change has occurred in this regard. In addition, numerous individual traits have been taken over from the Roman estate; even in the terminology used we rediscover, for instance, the women's house (*gynaikeion*) of the Romans under the name of *genitium*. But one thing has changed fundamentally: the Roman slaves live in 'communistic' slave barracks, the *servus* of the Carolingian epoch has his own cottage (*mansus servilis*) on the land which he holds from his master; he is a small tenant, subject to service on the lord's demesne. He has a family, and with the family individual property has returned. This separation of the slave from the *oikos* occurred in late-Roman times; and it was bound to occur, indeed, as the result of the absence of self-recruitment in the slave barracks. By restoring the individual family and by making the slave his hereditary serf, the lord secured for himself the offspring and so a permanent labour supply which could not be provided any more through purchases in the shrinking slave market whose last remnants disappeared during the Carolingian epoch. The risk of the maintenance of the slave (which on the plantations the master had to carry) was now shifted to the slave himself. The impact of this slow but irreversible development was deep. We are faced here with a gigantic process of change in the lower strata of society: family and individual property were given back to them. I can only indicate with one word here how this development runs a parallel to the victory of Christianity: in the slave barracks Christian religion could hardly have taken root, but the unfree African peasants of the time of St Augustine were already supporters of a sectarian movement.

While in this way the slave advanced in his social status and became a serf, the *colonus*, on the other hand, was sliding down into serfdom. The reason for this change in his social position was that his relation to the landowner took on more and more the character of a *labour* relation. *Originally*, the lord was mainly interested in the *rent* which the tenant paid, although, as we have pointed out, there probably were some cases from the very beginning where the man had to work on the lord's own land in addition. But already early in the Empire the agricultural writers put the main emphasis on the *labour* of the *colonus*, and this interest was bound to increase as slave labour became scarcer. African inscriptions of the time of Commodus show that in that county the *colonus* had already become a kind of serf who, in return for the use of the land he held, was forced to render certain services. This *economic* change in the position of the *colonus* was followed soon by a *legal* change which expressed in legal terms his treatment as part of the *labour* force of the estate: he was tied to the soil. In order to understand how this happened we have to discuss briefly some concepts of Roman public administration.

The basis of Roman public administration, at the end of the Republic and the beginning of the Empire, was the *city*, the *municipium*, just as the city was the *economic* basis of ancient civilisation. The Romans had all the areas which they incorporated into their Empire consistently organised in the form of urban communities (in various gradations of political dependence) and so had expanded the administrative form of the *municipium* over the whole Empire. The city regularly was the lowest administrative unit. The city magistrates were responsible to the state for taxes and military recruitment. In the course of the imperial epoch, however, the development takes a new turn. The great estates successfully attempt to escape incorporation into the urban communities. The more the centre of gravity of the Empire moves inland (with the increase of population in the inland regions), the more the rural inland population supplies the recruits for the army. But these same circumstances more and more make the interests of the 'agrarians' of antiquity, of the great land-owners, the controlling factor in state politics. Whereas today we meet with strong resistance in our attempt to integrate the large estates of eastern Germany in the rural communities, the government of the Roman Empire hardly resisted the tendency of the large estates to withdraw from the urban communities of which they formed a part. In great numbers the *saltus* and *territoria* appear side by side with the cities, administrative districts in which the landowner is the local government, just like the squire of eastern Germany in the so-called 'manorial districts'. The landowner, in those districts, was responsible to the state for the taxes of the *territorium*—in some cases he advanced them for his 'vassals' and then collected from them—and he supplied the contingent of recruits imposed upon his estate. Supplying recruits, therefore, was soon considered, like any other assessment, as an impost on the estate whose labour force—the *coloni*—were decimated by it.

Those developments paved the road for the legal fettering of the *colonus* to the estate.

The right of free movements never was legally guaranteed to all inhabitants of the Roman Empire. We all remember how familiar an idea it is to the author of the Gospel of Luke that, for the purpose of taxation, everybody can be ordered to return to his home community (*origo*)—to his 'place of settlement', as we would say— as Christ's parents returned to Bethlehem. The *origo* of the *colonus*, however, is the estate of his lord.

Quite early we see it happen that a man is forced to return to his community for the performance of public duties. The senator, to be sure, who played truant all year long, was just fined. But the councillor of a provincial town, the *decurio*, who shirked his duties did not escape so lightly; he was brought back if his community required it. Such a request was often enough necessary, for the position of the councillor—who was accountable for the tax arrears of his community—was not an enviable one. Later, when, with the decay and mixture of all legal forms, these claims for return were resolved into the one concept of the claim for restitution (the old 'real action': *vindicatio*), the communities chased their run-away councillors just like a run-away parish bull.

What was good for the *decurio* was good for the *colonus*. No distinction was made between his public obligations and the statute-labour he owed to his lord, because lord and magistrate were the same person, and he was forced to return to his duties when he tried to escape. So, in the way of administrative practice, he became a real serf, permanently tied to the estate and therefore subject to the manorial rule of the landowner. In his relation to the state he was, so to speak, 'mediatised'. And above the ranks of these new serfs there arose the group of independent seigneurs (the *possessores*) which we meet, as a well-established social type, in the later Roman Empire as well as in the Ostrogothian and Merovingian kingdoms. A *caste order* had taken the place of the old simple distinction of free and unfree. This was the result of an almost imperceptible development which was forced upon society by the change in economic conditions. The signs of *feudal society* were already apparent in the later Roman Empire.

So, on the late-imperial estate, two categories of tenants existed side by side: those who were unfree (*servi*) with 'indefinite' service obligations, and those who were personally free (*coloni, tributarii*) with strictly defined money payments or payments in kind and later on, more and more frequently, payments in the form of a fixed share of the produce and, in addition (not always, but as a rule) regular labour duties. It is apparent that such an estate already represents the type of the medieval manor.

Under the economic conditions of the ancient world, production *for the market* could not be based on statute-labour of free or unfree tenants. Well-disciplined slave barracks were the precondition of any market production. Especially in the inland regions, market production disappeared as soon as the peasants' cottages took the place of the barracks; the thin threads of commerce which were spun over the substratum of a 'natural economy' were bound to become looser still and finally to break. This is quite evident already in an argument of the last important agricultural writer, Palladius, who advises the owner to see to it that as far as possible the estate provides through its own labour for all its needs in order that any buying be made superfluous. Spinning and weaving as well as the grinding and baking of the grain had always been done by the women of the estate under the estate's own management; but now, smiths, joiners, stone masons, carpenters, and other unfree craftsmen were added, and they finally produced the total supply on the estate itself. By this development, the small group of urban craftsmen who mostly worked for wages plus board, diminished still further in relative importance; the economically prominent households of the great landowners provided for their needs without any resort to exchange.

Supplying the landowner's own needs, on the basis of an internal division of labour, necessarily became the proper economic purpose of the *oikos*. The large estates dissociate themselves from the urban market. The majority of the medium-sized and small towns thereby more and more lose their economic basis, the exchange of services and commodities with the surrounding countryside, this very essence of the city economy. The resulting decay of the cities remains visible to us even through the dim and broken glass of late Roman legal sources. Again and again the emperors inveigh against the flight from the city, they especially take the *possessores* to task for giving up and tearing down their town residences and conveying wainscotting and furniture to their country seats.

This collapse of the cities is re-enforced by the financial policy of the government. As its financial needs increase, the state increasingly adopts the pattern of a 'natural economy'; the exchequer becomes an *oikos*, it purchases as little as it can in the market and covers its needs as far as possible through its own production. This prevents the accumulation of private fortunes in money form. For the subjects it was a boon that one of the main forms of speculative enterprise, tax-farming, was abolished and tax collection by state officials took its place. Transporting the public grain supply on ships whose owners were rewarded by land grants was perhaps more efficient than leaving it to private enterprise. The increasing monopolisation of numerous lucrative trades and management of the mines by the government brought certain financial advantages with it. But all these measures naturally hindered the accumulation of private capital and nipped in the bud the development of a social class comparable to our modern bourgeoisie. And such a financial system on a 'natural economy' basis was increasingly emerging the more the Empire developed from a conglomeration of cities exploiting the countryside, and having its economic point of gravity on the coast and in coastal traffic, into a political system that tried to incorporate and to organise large inland regions which had not advanced beyond the stage of a 'natural economy'. This expansion led to an enormous increase in public expenses, and the shell of exchange was much too thin to make possible the satisfaction of the growing public needs by means of a money economy. Hence, the scope of 'natural economy' within public finance was bound to expand.

The provinces had always paid their taxes largely in kind, especially in grain, which was stored in the public warehouses. During the Empire, even the manufactured products needed by the government were less and less frequently bought in the market or procured by contracts, but their supply was assured by forcing urban craftsmen to deliver them *in natura*; they were often forced, for this purpose, to form compulsory guilds. This development made of the wretched free craftsman actually a hereditary serf of his guild. This income in kind was used up by the exchequer through corresponding expenses in kind. In this way, without resort to money payments the two main expense items in the budget were taken care of: the bureaucracy and the army. But here the 'natural economy' reached its limit.

A large inland state can be ruled permanently only by means of a salaried bureaucracy, an institution unknown to the ancient city states. Since Diocletian's time, salaries of state officials have been very largely paid in kind; they are somewhat similar—only on a much larger scale—to the emoluments of an agricultural labourer on a contemporary Mecklenburgian estate: a few thousand bushels of grain, so many head of cattle, corresponding quantities of salt, olive oil, etc.; in short, whatever the official needs for his food, clothing, and other sustenance, he draws from the imperial warehouses, in addition to relatively modest pocket money in cash. But in spite of this unmistakable preference for direct satisfaction of material needs, the maintenance of a numerous bureaucracy made considerable money expenses unavoidable. This was true, to a still higher degree, of the military requirements of the Empire.

A continental state with neighbours threatening its frontiers cannot be without a standing army. Already at the end of the Republic, the old citizen militia, based on conscription and self-equipment of all landowners, had been replaced by an army recruited from the ranks of the proletariat and equipped by the state—the main pillar of the power of the Caesars. The emperors created what was, not only in fact but legally, a standing *professional* army. To maintain such an army two things are needed: recruits and money. The need for recruits was the reason why the mercantilist rulers during the epoch of 'enlightened despotism' curbed big enterprise in agriculture and prevented enclosures. This was not done for humanitarian reasons and not out of sympathy with the peasants. The individual peasant was not protected—the squire could drive him out without any scruples by putting another peasant in his place. But if, in the words of Frederick William I, 'a surplus of peasant lads' was to be the source of soldiers, such a surplus had to *exist*. Therefore, any reduction in the number of peasants through enclosures was prevented because it would endanger the recruitment of soldiers and depopulate the countryside. For quite similar reasons, the Roman emperors regulated the status of the *coloni* and prohibited, for example, an increase in the duties imposed on them. There is one difference, however. The mercantilist rulers of the eighteenth century strongly fostered the big manufacturers because they increased the population and, secondly, brought money into the country.

Frederick the Great chased with warrants not only his deserting soldiers, but also his deserting workers and—manufacturers. This part of mercantilist policy the Caesars could not adopt since large industries using free labour and producing for the market did not exist and could not develop in the Roman Empire. On the contrary, with the decay of cities and commerce and with the relapse into a 'natural economy', the country became more and more unable to pay the ever increasing taxes in cash. And under the prevailing scarcity of labour, which resulted from the drying up of the slave market, recruitment of the *coloni* for the army threatened the large estates with ruin, a menace from which they tried to escape by all possible means. The draftee flees from the decaying city to the countryside into the safety of serfdom, because the *possessore*— under the pressure of the existing scarcity of labour—is interested in hiding him from the draft. The later Caesars fight against the flight of townsmen to the countryside exactly as the later Hohen- staufen fight against the flight of the serfs into the cities.

The repercussions of this scarcity of recruits are distinctly re- flected in the army of the imperial epoch. Since Vespasian, Italy is no longer subject to the draft; since Hadrian, the units of the army are no longer composed of contingents from different local dis- tricts; in order to save money, one tries to recruit each army, as far as possible, from the district in which it is stationed—the first symptom of the decomposition of the Empire. But the process goes far beyond this: when we study the places of birth of the soldiers as given in their discharge documents through the centuries, we discover that the number of those characterised as 'natives of the camp' (*castrenses*) rises during the imperial epoch from a few per cent of the total to almost one half—in other words, the Roman army increasingly reproduces itself. Just as the peasant with his individual family takes the place of the celibate barracks slave, so— partly at least—the professional and actually hereditary mercenary soldier, who enjoys a kind of substitute marriage, replaces the celi- bate barracks soldier, or rather, camp soldier, of the earlier period. The increasing recruitment of the army from the ranks of barbar- ians was dictated by the same principal purpose: by the desire to preserve the labour force of the country, especially of the large estates. Finally, for the defence of the frontiers, the Romans com- pletely turn away from the principles of money economy: land- grants are made to barbarians, carrying with them the obligation of military service, and this device, the remote forerunner of the fief, is used with increasing frequency. In this way the army, which controls the Empire, is changed into a horde of barbarians, maintaining weaker and weaker ties with the native population. The victorious invasions by the barbarians *from without*, therefore, meant for the inhabitants of the provinces, at first, nothing but a change in the force billeted on them: even the Roman pattern of billeting was preserved. In some parts of Gaul, the barbarians, far from being feared as conquerors, apparently were welcomed as liberators from the pressure of the Roman administration. And this we can well understand.

For not only was it difficult for the ageing Empire to recruit soldiers from the ranks of its own population, but the provinces, relapsing as they were into a 'natural economy', virtually collapsed under the pressure of the money taxes without which a mercenary army cannot possibly be maintained. Raising of money increasingly became the sole aim of political administration; and it became more and more apparent that the *possessores*, now producing almost exclusively for their own needs, were economically unable to pay *money* taxes. It would have been a different story if the emperor had told them: 'Well, gentlemen, make your *coloni* forge arms for yourselves, mount your horses, and protect with me the soil on which you live!' To *this* task they would have been economically equal. But this would have meant the beginning of the Middle Ages and of the feudal army. The feudal organisation of the army was, indeed, like the feudal structure of society, the end towards which the late-Roman development was tending and which—after the short and only local reverse in favour of colonising peasant armies during the Age of Migrations—was already attained, on the whole, in the Carolingian epoch. But although with feudal armies of knights one can conquer foreign crowns and defend a restricted territory, one cannot preserve with them the unity of a world empire nor hold hundreds of miles of frontiers against the attacks of land-hungry invaders. A transition, therefore, to that army pattern which would have conformed to the 'natural economy' basis of society was impossible during the late-Roman epoch. This was the reason why Diocletian had to attempt the reorganisation of public finances on the basis of uniform *money* taxes, and why, to the very end, the *city* officially remained the lowest cell of the state organism. But the *economic* basis of the great majority of Roman cities was withering away: in the interest of a money-hungry state administration they were sitting, like cupping-glasses, on a soil covered with a net of seigneuries. The fall of the Empire was the necessary political result of the gradual disappearance of commerce and the spread of a 'natural economy.' This fall meant essentially the abolition of that state administration and, hence, of the political super-structure with its money economy character which was no longer adapted to its changed economic basis.

When, after half a millenium, the belated executor of Diocletian's will, Charlemagne, revived the political unity of the Occident, this development took place on the basis of a strictly 'natural' economy. Whoever studies the instructions he gave to the administrators of his domains (the *villici*)—the famous *capitulare de villis*, in its practical sense and the tartness of its language reminiscent of the ukases of Frederick William I of Prussia—will find this fact most impressively illustrated. At the side of the king, the queen appears in a dominant position: the king's wife is his minister of finance—and justly so; 'administration of finance' is here principally concerned with the needs of the royal table and household which is identical with the 'state household'. We read there what the bailiffs have to provide for the king's court: grain, meat, textiles, surprisingly large quantities of soap, etc.; in short whatever the king needs for his own use, for that of his companions, and for political functions, like horses and vehicles for warfare. The standing army has disappeared; so has the salaried bureaucracy and, with it, the very concept of taxation. The king feeds his officials at his own table or he endows them with land. The self-equipped army is about to become, for good, an army on horseback and so a military caste of landowning knights. Interlocal exchange of commodities has disappeared as well; the threads of commerce connecting the self-sufficient cells of economic life are broken, trade is reduced to peddling, carried on by foreigners—Greeks and Jews.

Above all, the *city* has disappeared; the Carolingian epoch does not know this term as a specific concept of administrative law. The seigneuries are the vehicles of civilisation; they also form the basis of the monasteries. The seigneurs are the political officials; the king himself is a seigneur, the biggest of all—rural and illiterate. His castles are situated in the countryside; therefore he has no fixed residence: for the sake of his livelihood he travels even more than some modern monarchs do; for he continuously moves from castle to castle and eats up what has been stored for him. Civilisation has become rural indeed.

The cycle of the economic development of antiquity is now completed. The intellectual achievements of the ancients seem to be totally lost. Gone with commercial traffic is the marble splendour of the ancient cities and, with them, all the intellectual values based on them: art and literature, science and the elaborate forms of ancient commercial law. And on the estates of the *possessores* and seigneurs the songs of the troubadours are not yet heard. We can hardly suppress a feeling of sadness when we witness a culture that seems to aim at perfection lose its material foundation and collapse. But what is it actually that we are witnessing in this gigantic process? In the depth of society organic structural changes occur (and had to occur) which, if we look at them as a whole, must be interpreted as an immense process of recovery. Individual family life and private property were restored to the masses of unfree people; they themselves were raised again, from the position of 'speaking inventory' up into the circle of human beings. The rise of Christianity surrounded their family life with firm moral guarantees: already late-Roman laws for the protection of the peasants recognise the unity of the unfree family to a degree not known before. To be sure, at the same time one sector of the free population was sinking down into actual serfdom, and the highly cultivated aristocracy of the ancient world declined into barbarism. As we have seen, the spread of unfree labour and the increasing differentiation of wealth based on slave-ownership had formed the foundation for the evolution of ancient civilisation. But later, when the centre of political gravity had shifted from the coast to the inland regions and when the supply of human cattle had dwindled away, this new system of 'natural economy', as it had become established on the big estates, had forced its own semi-feudal structure upon the exchange economy originally developed in the coastal cities. So the threadbare wrap of ancient civilisation disappeared, and the intellectual life of Western man sank into a long night. But that fall reminds us of that giant in Greek mythology who gained new strength whenever he rested on the bosom of mother earth. If one of the old classical authors had arisen from his manuscript in Carolingian times and had examined the world through the window of the monk's cell in which he found himself, his surroundings would have looked strange to him, indeed: the dung-heap odour of the manor-yard would have hit his nostrils. But those classics were in deep sleep now, as was all civilisation, hidden away under the cover of an economic life which had returned to rural forms. Neither the songs nor the tournaments of feudal society roused it out of this sleep. Only when, on the basis of free division of labour and of commercial exchange, the *city* had arisen again in the Middle Ages, when, later still, the transition to a national economy prepared the ground for civil liberty and broke the fetters imposed by the external and internal authorities of the feudal age, only then the old giant arose and carried with him the intellectual inheritance of antiquity up to the new light of our modern middle-class civilisation.

(D) The emergence of Capitalism in the Western World[1]

THE MEANING AND PRESUPPOSITIONS OF MODERN CAPITALISM

Capitalism is present wherever the industrial provision for the needs of a human group is carried out by the method of enterprise, irrespective of what need is involved. More specifically, a rational capitalistic establishment is one with capital accounting, that is, an establishment which determines its income yielding power by calculation according to the methods of modern bookkeeping and the striking of a balance. The device of the balance was first insisted upon by the Dutch theorist Simon Stevin in the year 1698.

It goes without saying that an individual economy may be conducted along capitalistic lines to the most widely varying extent; parts of the economic provision may be organised capitalistically and other parts on the handicraft or the manorial pattern. Thus at a very early time the city of Genoa had a part of its political needs, namely those for the prosecution of war, provided in capitalistic fashion, through stock companies. In the Roman Empire, the supply of the population of the capital city with grain was carried out

---

[1] Source: *General Economic History*, pp. 207–9; 258–70.
Footnotes to this passage have been omitted.

by officials who, however, for this purpose, besides control over their subalterns, had the right to command the services of transport organisations; thus the leiturgical or forced contribution type of organisation was combined with administration of public resources. Today, in contrast with the greater part of the past, our everyday needs are supplied capitalistically, our political needs, however, through compulsory contributions, that is, by the performance of political duties of citizenship such as the obligation to military service, jury duty, etc. A whole epoch can be designated as typically capitalistic only as the provision for wants is capitalistically organised to such a predominant degree that if we imagine this form of organisation taken away the whole economic system must collapse.

While capitalism of various forms is met with in all periods of history, the provision of the everyday wants by capitalistic methods is characteristic of the Occident alone and even here has been the inevitable method only since the middle of the nineteenth century. Such capitalistic beginnings as are found in earlier centuries were merely anticipatory, and even the somewhat capitalistic establishments of the sixteenth century may be removed in thought from the economic life of the time without introducing any overwhelming change.

The most general presupposition for the existence of this present-day capitalism is that of rational capital accounting as the norm for all large industrial undertakings which are concerned with provision for everyday wants. Such accounting again involves, first, the appropriation of all physical means of production—land, apparatus, machinery, tools, etc. as disposable property of autonomous private industrial enterprises. This is a phenomenon known only to our time, when the army alone forms a universal exception to it. In the second place, it involves freedom of the market, that is, the absence of irrational limitations on trading in the market. Such limitations might be of a class character, if a certain mode of life were prescribed for a certain class or consumption were standardised along class lines, or if class monopoly existed, as, for example, if the townsman were not allowed to own an estate or the knight or peasant to carry on industry; in such cases neither a free labour market nor a commodity market exists. Third, capitalistic accounting presupposes rational technology, that is, one reduced to calculation to the largest possible degree, which implies mechanisation. This applies to both production and commerce, the outlays for preparing as well as moving goods.

The fourth characteristic is that of calculable law. The capitalistic form of industrial organisation, if it is to operate rationally, must be able to depend upon calculable adjudication and administration. Neither in the age of the Greek city-state (*polis*) nor in the patrimonial state of Asia nor in Western countries down to the Stuarts was this condition fulfilled. The royal 'cheap justice' with its remissions by royal grace introduced continual disturbances into the calculations of economic life. The proposition that the Bank of England was suited only to a republic, not to a monarchy, was related in this way to the conditions of the time. The fifth feature is free labour. Persons must be present who are not only legally in the position, but are also economically compelled, to sell their labour on the market without restriction. It is in contradiction to the essence of capitalism, and the development of capitalism is impossible, if such a propertyless stratum is absent, a class compelled to sell its labour services to live; and it is likewise impossible if only unfree labour is at hand. Rational capitalistic calculation is possible only on the basis of free labour; only where in consequence of the existence of workers who in the formal sense voluntarily, but actually under the compulsion of the whip of hunger, offer themselves, may the costs of products be unambiguously determined by agreement in advance. The sixth and final condition is the commercialisation of economic life. By this we mean the general use of commercial instruments to represent share rights in enterprise, and also in property ownership.

To sum up, it must be possible to conduct the provision for needs exclusively on the basis of market opportunities and the calculation of net income. The addition of this commercialisation to the other characteristics of capitalism involves intensification of the significance of another factor not yet mentioned, namely speculation. Speculation reaches its full significance only from the moment when property takes on the form of negotiable paper.

THE EVOLUTION OF THE CAPITALISTIC SPIRIT

It is a widespread error that the increase of population is to be included as a really crucial agent in the evolution of Western capitalism. In opposition to this view, Karl Marx made the assertion that every economic epoch has its own law of population, and although this proposition is untenable in so general a form, it is justified in the present case. The growth of population in the West made most rapid progress from the beginning of the eighteenth century to the end of the nineteenth. In the same period China experienced a population growth of at least equal extent—from 60 or 70 to 400 millions, allowing for the inevitable exaggerations; this corresponds approximately with the increase in the West. In spite of this fact, capitalism went backward in China and not forward. The increase in the population took place there in different strata than with us. It made China the seat of a swarming mass of small peasants; the increase of a class corresponding to our proletariat was involved only to the extent that a foreign market made possible the employment of coolies ('coolie' is originally an Indian expression, and signifies neighbour or fellow member of a clan). The growth of population in Europe did indeed favour the development of capitalism, to the extent that in a small population the system would have been unable to secure the necessary labour force, but in itself it never called forth that development.

Nor can the inflow of precious metals be regarded, as Sombart suggests, as the primary cause of the appearance of capitalism. It is certainly true that in a given situation an increase in the supply of precious metals may give rise to price revolutions, such as that which took place after 1530 in Europe, and when other favourable conditions are present, as when a certain form of labour organisation is in process of development, the progress may be stimulated by the fact that large stocks of cash come into the hands of certain groups. But the case of India proves that such an importation of precious metal will not alone bring about capitalism. In India in the period of the Roman power, an enormous mass of precious metal—some 25 million *sestertii* annually—came in in exchange for domestic goods, but this inflow gave rise to commercial capitalism to only a slight extent. The greater part of the precious metal disappeared into the hoards of the rajahs instead of being converted into cash and applied in the establishment of enterprises of a rational capitalistic character. This fact proves that it depends entirely upon the nature of the labour system what tendency will result from an inflow of precious metal. The gold and silver from America, after the discovery, flowed in the first place to Spain; but in that country a recession of capitalistic development took place parallel with the importation. There followed, on the one hand, the suppression of the *communeros* and the destruction of the commercial interests of the Spanish grandees, and, on the other, the employment of the money for military ends. Consequently, the stream of precious metal flowed through Spain, scarcely touching it, and fertilised other countries, which in the fifteenth century were already undergoing a process of transformation in labour relations which was favourable to capitalism.

Hence neither the growth of population nor the importation of precious metal called forth Western capitalism. The external conditions for the development of capitalism are rather, firstly, geographical in character. In China and India the enormous costs of transportation, connected with the decisively inland commerce of the regions, necessarily formed serious obstacles for the classes who were in a position to make profits through trade and to use trading capital in the construction of a capitalistic system; while in the West the position of the Mediterranean as an inland sea, and the abundant interconnections through the rivers, favoured the opposite development of international commerce. But this factor in its turn must not be overestimated. The civilisation of antiquity was distinctively coastal. Here the opportunities for commerce were very favourable (thanks to the character of the Mediterranean Sea), in contrast with the Chinese waters with their typhoons, and yet no capitalistic development was much more intense in Florence than in Genoa or in Venice. Capitalism in the West was born in the industrial cities of the interior, not in the cities which were centres of sea trade.

Military requirements were also favourable, though not as such but because of the special nature of the needs of the Western armies. Favourable also was the luxury demand, though again not in itself. In many cases, rather, it led to the development of irrational forms, such as small workshops in France and compulsory settlements of workers in connection with the courts of many German princes. In the last resort the factors which produced capitalism are the rational permanent enterprise, rational accounting, rational technology and rational law, but again not these alone. Necessary complementary factors were the rational spirit, the rationalisation of the conduct of life in general, and a rationalistic economic ethic.

At the beginning of all ethics and the economic relations which result, is traditionalism, the sanctity of tradition, the exclusive reliance upon such trade and industry as have come down from the fathers. This traditionalism survives far down into the present; only a human lifetime back, it was futile to double the wages of an agricultural labourer in Silesia who mowed a certain tract of land on a contract, in the hope of inducing him to increase his exertions. He would simply have reduced by half the work expended because with this half he would have been able to earn twice as much as before (*sic*). This general incapacity and indisposition to depart from the beaten paths is the reason for the maintenance of tradition.

Primitive traditionalism may, however, undergo essential intensification through two circumstances. In the first place, material interests may be tied up with the maintenance of the tradition. When, for example, in China, the attempt was made to change certain roads or to introduce more rational means or routes of transportation, the perquisites of certain officials were threatened; and the same was the case in the Middle Ages in the West, and in modern times when railroads were introduced. Such special interests of officials, landholders and merchants assisted decisively in restricting a tendency toward rationalisation. Stronger still is the effect of the stereotyping of trade on magical grounds, the deep repugnance to undertaking any change in the established conduct of life because supernatural evils are feared. Generally some injury to economic privilege is concealed in this opposition, but its effectiveness depends on a general belief in the potency of the magical processes which are feared.

Traditional obstructions are not overcome by the economic impulse alone. The notion that our rationalistic and capitalistic age is characterised by a stronger economic interest than other periods is childish; the moving spirits of modern capitalism are not possessed of a stronger economic impulse than, for example, an oriental trader. The unchanging of the economic interest merely as such has produced only irrational results; such men as Cortez and Pizzarro, who were perhaps its strongest embodiment, were far from having an idea of a rationalistic economic life. If the economic impulse in itself is universal, it is an interesting question as to the relations under which it becomes rationalised and rationally tempered in such fashion as to produce rational institutions of the character of capitalistic enterprise.

Originally, two opposite attitudes toward the pursuit of gain exist in combination. Internally, there is attachment to tradition and to the pietistic relations of fellow members of tribe, clan, and house-community, with the exclusion of the unrestricted quest of gain within the circle of those bound together by religious ties; externally, there is absolutely unrestricted play of the gain spirit in economic relations, every foreigner being originally an enemy in relation to whom no ethical restrictions apply; that is, the ethics of internal and external relations are categorically distinct. The course of development involves on the one hand the bringing in of calculation into the traditional brotherhood, displacing the old religious relationship. As soon as accountability is established within the family community, and economic relations are no longer strictly communistic, there is an end of the naïve piety and its repression of the economic impulse. This side of the development is especially characteristic in the West. At the same time there is a tempering of the unrestricted quest of gain with the adoption of the economic principle into the internal economy. The result is a regulated economic life with the economic impulse functioning within bounds.

In detail, the course of development has been varied. In India, the restrictions upon gain-seeking apply only to the two uppermost strata, the Brahmins and the Rajputs. A member of these castes is forbidden to practice certain callings. A Brahmin may conduct an eating house, as he alone has clean hands; but he, like the Rajput, would be unclassed if he were to lend money for interest. The latter, however, is permitted to the mercantile castes, and within it we find a degree of unscrupulousness in trade which is unmatched anywhere in the world. Finally, antiquity had only legal limitations on interest, and the proposition *caveat emptor* characterises Roman economic ethics. Nevertheless no modern capitalism developed there.

The final result is the peculiar fact that the germs of modern capitalism must be sought in a region where officially a theory was dominant which was distinct from that of the East and of classical antiquity and in principle strongly hostile to capitalism. The *ethos* of the classical economic morality is summed up in the old judgement passed on the merchant, which was probably taken from primitive Arianism: *homo mercator vix aut numquam potest Deo placere*; he may conduct himself without sin but cannot be pleasing to God. This proposition was valid down to the fifteenth century, and the first attempt to modify it slowly matured in Florence under pressure of the shift in economic relations.

The typical antipathy of Catholic ethics, and following that the Lutheran, to every capitalistic tendency, rests essentially on the repugnance for the impersonality of relations within a capitalist economy. It is this fact of impersonal relations which places certain human affairs outside the Church and its influence, and prevents the latter from penetrating them and transforming them along ethical lines. The relations between master and slave could be subjected to immediate ethical regulation; but the relations between the mortgage creditor and the property which was pledged for the debt, or between an endorser and the bill of exchange, would at least be exceedingly difficult if not impossible to moralise. The final consequence of the resulting position assumed by the Church was that medieval economic ethics excluded higgling, overpricing and free competition, and were based on the principle of just price and the assurance to everyone of a chance to live.

For the breaking up of this circle of ideas the Jews cannot be made responsible as Sombart does. The position of the Jews during the Middle Ages may be compared sociologically with that of an Indian caste in a world otherwise free from castes; they were an outcast people. However, there is the distinction that according to the promise of the Indian religion the caste system is valid for eternity. The individual may in the course of time reach heaven through a series of reincarnations, the time depending upon his deserts; but this is possible only within the caste system. The caste organisation is eternal, and one who attempted to leave it would be accursed and condemned to pass in hell into the bowels of a dog. The Jewish promise, on the contrary, points toward a reversal of caste relations in the future world as compared with this. In the present world the Jews are stamped as an outcast people, either as punishment for the sins of their fathers, as Deutero-Isaiah holds, or for the salvation of the world, which is the presupposition of the mission of Jesus of Nazareth; from this position they are to be released by a social revolution. In the Middle Ages the Jews were a guest-people standing outside of political society; they could not be received into any town citizenship group because they could not participate in the communion of the Lord's Supper, and hence could not belong to the *coniuratio*.

The Jews were not the only guest-people; the Caursines, for example, occupied a similar position. These were Christian merchants who dealt in money and in consequence were, like the Jews, under the protection of the princes and on consideration of a payment enjoyed the privilege of carrying on monetary dealings. What distinguished the Jews in a striking way from the Christian guest-peoples was the impossibility in their case of entering into *commercium* and *connubium* with the Christians. Originally the Christians did not hesitate to accept Jewish hospitality, in contrast with the Jews themselves who feared that their ritualistic prescriptions as to food would not be observed by their hosts. On the occasion of the first outbreak of medieval anti-semitism the faithful were warned by the synods not to conduct themselves unworthily and hence not to accept entertainment from the Jews, who on their side despised the hospitality of the Christians. Marriage with Christians was strictly impossible, going back to Ezra and Nehemiah.

A further ground for the outcast position of the Jews arose from the fact that Jewish craftsmen existed; in Syria there had even been a Jewish knightly class, though only exceptionally were there Jewish peasants, for the conduct of agriculture was not to be reconciled with the requirements of the ritual. Ritualistic considerations were responsible for the concentration of Jewish economic life in monetary dealings. Jewish piety set a premium on the knowledge of the law and continuous study was very much easier to combine with exchange dealings than with other occupations. In addition, the prohibition against usury on the part of the Church condemned exchange dealings, yet the trade was indispensable and the Jews were not subject to the ecclesiastical law.

Finally, Judaism had maintained the originally universal dualism of internal and external moral attitudes, under which it was permissible to accept interest from foreigners who did not belong to the brotherhood or established association. Out of this dualism followed the sanctioning of other irrational economic affairs, especially tax-farming and political financing of all sorts. In the course of the centuries the Jews acquired a special skill in these matters which made them useful and in demand. But all this was pariah capitalism, not rational capitalism such as originated in the West. In consequence, hardly a Jew is found among the creators of the modern economic situation, the large entrepreneurs; this type was Christian and only conceivable in the field of Christianity. The Jewish manufacturer, on the contrary, is a modern phenomenon. If for no other reason, it was impossible for the Jews to have a part in the establishment of rational capitalism because they were outside the craft organisations. But even alongside the guilds they could hardly maintain themsevles, even where, as in Poland, they had command over a numerous proletariat which they might have organised in the capacity of entrepreneurs in domestic industry or as manufacturers. After all, the genuine Jewish ethic is specifically traditionalism, as the Talmud shows. The horror of the pious Jew in the face of any innovation is quite as great as that of an individual among any primitive people with institutions fixed by the belief in magic.

However, Judaism was none the less of notable significance for modern rational capitalism, in so far as it transmitted to Christianity the latter's hostility to magic. Apart from Judaism and Christianity, and two or three oriental sects (one of which is in Japan), there is no religion with the character of outspoken hostility to magic. Probably this hostility arose through the circumstance that what the Israelites found in Canaan was the magic of the agricultural god Baal, while Jahveh was a god of volcanoes, earthquakes and pestilences. The hostility between the two priesthoods and the victory of the priests of Jahveh discredited the fertility magic of the priests of Baal and stigmatised it with a character of decadence and godlessness. Since Judaism made Christianity possible and gave it the character of a religion essentially free from magic, it rendered an important service from the point of view of economic history. For the dominance of magic outside the sphere in which Christianity has prevailed is one of the most serious obstructions to the rationalisation of economic life. Magic involves a stereotyping of technology and economic relations. When attempts were made in China to inaugurate the building of railroads and factories a conflict with geomancy ensued. The latter demanded that in the location of structures on certain mountains, forests, rivers and cemetery hills, foresight should be exercised in order not to disturb the rest of the spirits.

Similar is the relation to capitalism of the castes in India. Every new technical process which an Indian employs signifies for him first of all that he leaves his caste and falls into another, necessarily lower. Since he believes in the transmigration of souls, the immediate significance of this is that his chance of purification is put off until another re-birth. He will hardly consent to such a change. An additional fact is that every caste makes every other impure. In consequence, workmen who dare not accept a vessel filled with water from each other's hands, cannot be employed together in the same factory room. Not until the present time, after the possession of the country by the British for almost a century, could this obstacle be overcome. Obviously, capitalism could not develop in an economic group thus bound hand and foot by magical beliefs.

In all times there has been but one means of breaking down the power of magic and establishing a rational conduct of life; this means is great rational prophecy. Not every prophecy by any means destroys the power of magic; but it is possible for a prophet who furnishes credentials in the shape of miracles and otherwise, to break down the traditional sacred rules. Prophecies have released the world from magic and in doing so have created the basis for our modern science and technology, and for capitalism. In China such prophecy has been wanting. What prophecy there was has come from the outside as in the case of Lao-Tse and Taoism. India, however, produced a religion of salvation; in contrast with China it has known great prophetic missions. But they were prophecies by example; that is, the typical Hindu prophet, such as Buddha, lives before the world the life which leads to salvation, but does not regard himself as one sent from God to insist upon the obligation to lead it; he takes the position that whoever wishes salvation, as an end freely chosen, should lead the life. However, one may reject salvation, as it is not the destiny of everyone to enter at death into Nirvana, and only philosophers in the strictest sense are prepared by hatred of this world to adopt the stoical resolution and withdraw from life.

The result was that Hindu prophecy was of immediate significance for the intellectual classes. These became forest dwellers and poor monks. For the masses, however, the significance of the founding of a Buddhistic sect was quite different, namely the opportunity of praying to the saints. Holy men arose who were believed to work miracles, who must be well fed so that they would repay this good deed by guaranteeing a better reincarnation or by granting wealth, long life and other benefits, that is, this world's goods. Hence Buddhism in its pure form was restricted to a thin stratum of monks. The laity found no ethical precepts according to which life should be moulded; Buddhism indeed had its decalogue, but in distinction from that of the Jews it gave no binding commands but only recommendations. The most important act of service was and remained the physical maintenance of the monks. Such a religious spirit could never be in a position to displace magic but at best could only put another magic in its place.

In contrast with the ascetic religion of salvation of India and its defective action upon the masses, are Judaism and Christianity, which from the beginning have been plebeian religions and have deliberately remained such. The struggle of the ancient Church against the Gnostics was nothing else than a struggle against the aristocracy of the intellectuals, such as is common to ascetic religions, with the object of preventing their seizing the leadership in the Church. This struggle was crucial for the success of Christianity among the masses, and hence for the fact that magic was suppressed among the general population to the greatest possible extent. True, it has not been possible even down to the present day to overcome it entirely, but it was reduced to the character of something unholy, something diabolic.

The germ of this development as regards magic is found far back in ancient Jewish ethics, which are much concerned with views such as we also meet with in the proverbs and the so-called prophetic texts of the Egyptians. But the most important prescriptions of Egyptian ethics were futile when by laying a scarab on the region of the heart one could prepare the dead man to conceal successfully the sins committed, deceive the judge of the dead, and thus get into paradise. The Jewish ethics know no such sophisticated subterfuges and neither does Christianity. In the Eucharist the latter has indeed sublimated magic into the form of a sacrament, but it gave its adherents no such means for evading the final judgement as were contained in Egyptian religion. If one wishes to study at all the influence of a religion on life one must distinguish between its official teachings and this type of actual procedure upon which, in reality, perhaps against its own will, it places a premium, in this world or the next.

It is also necessary to distinguish between the virtuoso religion of adepts and the religion of the masses. Virtuoso religion is significant for everyday life only as a pattern; its claims are of the highest, but they fail to determine everyday ethics. The relation between the two is different in different religions. In Catholicism, they are brought into harmonious union in so far as the claims of the religious virtuoso are held up alongside the duties of the laymen as *consilia evangelica*. The really complete Christian is the monk; but his mode of life is not required of everyone, although some of his virtues in a qualified form are held up as ideals. The advantage of this combination was that ethics were not split asunder as in Buddhism. After all, the distinction between monk ethics and mass ethics meant that the most worthy individuals in the religious sense withdrew from the world and established a separate community.

Christianity was not alone in this phenomenon, which recurs rather frequently in the history of religions, as is shown by the powerful influence of asceticism, which signifies the carrying out of a definite, methodical conduct of life. Asceticism has always worked in this sense. The enormous achievements possible to such an ascetically determined methodical conduct of life are demonstrated by the example of Tibet. The country seems condemned by nature to be an eternal desert; but a community of celibate ascetics has carried out colossal construction works in Lhassa and saturated the country with the religious doctrines of Buddhism. An analogous phenomenon is present in the Middle Ages in the West. In that epoch the monk is the first human being who lives rationally, who works methodically and by rational means toward a goal, namely the future life. Only for him did the clock strike, only for him were the hours of the day divided—for prayer. The economic life of the monastic communities was also rational. The monks in part furnished the officialdom for the early Middle Ages; the power of the doges of Venice collapsed when the investiture struggle deprived them of the possibility of employing churchmen for overseas enterprises.

But the rational mode of life remained restricted to the monastic circles. The Franciscan movement indeed attempted through the institution of the tertiaries to extend it to the laity, but the institution of the confessional was a barrier to such an extension. The Church domesticated medieval Europe by means of its system of confession and penance, but for the men of the Middle Ages the possibility of unburdening themselves through the channel of the confessional, when they had rendered themselves liable to punishment, meant a release from the consciousness of sin which the teachings of the Church had called into being. The unity and strength of the methodical conduct of life were thus in fact broken up. In its knowledge of human nature the Church did not reckon with the fact that the individual is a closed unitary ethical personality, but steadfastly held to the view that in spite of the warnings of the confessional and of penances, however strong, he would again fall away morally; that is, it shed its grace on the just and the unjust.

The Reformation made a decisive break with this system. The dropping of the *concilia evangelica* by the Lutheran Reformation meant the disappearance of the dualistic ethics, of the distinction between a universally binding morality and a specifically advantageous code for virtuosi. The other-wordly asceticism came to an end. The stern religious characters who had previously gone into monasteries had now to practise their religion in the life of the world. For such an asceticism within the world the ascetic dogmas of Protestantism created adequate ethics. Celibacy was not required, marriage being viewed simply as an institution for the rational bringing up of children. Poverty was not required, but the pursuit of riches must not lead one astray into reckless enjoyment. Thus Sebastian Franck was correct in summing up the spirit of the Reformation in the words, 'you think you have escaped from the monastery, but everyone must now be a monk throughout his life'.

The wide significance of this transformation of the ascetic ideal can be followed down to the present in the classical lands of Protestant ascetic religiosity. It is especially discernible in the import of the religious denominations in America. Although state and church are separated, still, as late as fifteen or twenty years ago no banker or physician took up a residence or established connections without being asked to what religious community he belonged, and his prospects were good or bad according to the character of his answer. Acceptance into a sect was conditioned upon a strict inquiry into one's ethical conduct. Membership in a sect which did not recognise the Jewish distinction between internal and external moral codes guaranteed one's business honour and reliability and this in turn guaranteed success. Hence the principle 'honesty is the best policy' and hence among Quakers, Baptists, and Methodists the ceaseless repetition of the proposition based on experience that God would take care of his own. 'The Godless cannot trust each other across the road; they turn to us when they want to do business; piety is the surest road to wealth.' This is by no means 'cant', but a combination of religiosity with consequences which were originally unknown to it and which were never intended.

It is true that the acquisition of wealth, attributed to piety, led to a dilemma, in all respects similar to that into which the medieval monasteries constantly fell; the religious guild led to wealth,

wealth to a fall from grace, and this again to the necessity of recon-
stitution. Calvinism sought to avoid this difficulty through the idea
that man was only an administrator of what God had given him; it
condemned enjoyment, yet permitted no flight from the world but
rather regarded working together, with its rational discipline, as
the religious task of the individual. Out of this system of thought
came our word 'calling', which is known only to the languages influenced by the Protestant translations of the Bible. It expresses the
value placed upon rational activity carried on according to the
rational capitalistic principle, as the fulfilment of a God-given task.
Here lay also in the last analysis the basis of the contrast between
the Puritans and the Stuarts. The ideas of both were capitalistically
directed; but in a characteristic way the Jew was for the Puritan
the embodiment of everything repugnant because he devoted himself to irrational and illegal occupations such as war loans, tax-
farming, and leasing of offices, in the fashion of the court favourite.

This development of the concept of the calling quickly gave to
the modern entrepreneur a fabulously clear conscience—and also
industrious workers; he gave to his employees as the wages of their
ascetic devotion to the calling and of co-operation in his ruthless
exploitation of them through capitalism the prospect of eternal
salvation, which in an age when ecclesiastical discipline took control of the whole of life to an extent inconceivable to us now, represented a reality quite different from any it has today. The Catholic
and Lutheran churches also recognised and practised ecclesiastical
discipline. But in the Protestant ascetic communities admission to
the Lord's Supper was conditioned upon ethical fitness, which
again was identified with business honour, while into the content of
one's faith no one inquired. Such a powerful, unconsciously refined
organisation for the production of capitalistic individuals has never
existed in any other church or religion, and in comparison with it
what the Renaissance did for capitalism shrinks into insignificance.
Its practitioners occupied themselves with technical problems
and were experimenters of the first rank. From art and mining, experimentation was taken over into science.

The world-view of the Renaissance, however, determined the
policy of rulers in a large measure, though it did not transform the
soul of man as did the innovations of the Reformation. Almost all
the great scientific discoveries of the sixteenth century and even the
beginning of the seventeenth were made against the background of

Catholicism. Copernicus was a Catholic, while Luther and Melanchthon repudiated his discoveries. Scientific progress and Protestantism must not all be unquestioningly identified. The Catholic Church has indeed occasionally obstructed scientific progress; but the ascetic sects of Protestantism have also been disposed to have nothing to do with science, except in a situation where material requirements of everyday life were involved. On the other hand it is its specific contribution to have placed science in the service of technology and economics.

The religious root of modern economic humanity is dead; today the concept of the calling is a *caput mortuum* in the world. Ascetic religiosity has been displaced by a pessimistic though by no means ascetic view of the world, such as that portrayed in Mandeville's Fable of the Bees, which teaches that private vices may under certain conditions be for the good of the public. With the complete disappearance of all the remains of the original enormous religious pathos of the sects, the optimism of the Enlightenment, which believed in the harmony of interests, appeared as the heir of Protestant asceticism in the field of economic ideas; it guided the hands of the princes, statesmen, and writers of the later eighteenth and early nineteenth centuries. Economic ethics arose against the background of the ascetic ideal; now it has been stripped of its religious import. It was possible for the working class to accept its lot as long as the promise of eternal happiness could be held out to it. When this consolation fell away it was inevitable that those strains and stresses should appear in economic society which since then have grown so rapidly. This point had been reached at the end of the early period of capitalism, at the beginning of the age of iron, in the nineteenth century.

Max Weber:
A Select Bibliography[1]

Abel, T. L. *Systematic Sociology in Germany* (Columbia Univ. Press, 1929).
—— 'The Operation Called Verstehen', *A.J.S.*, LIV (1948).
Andreski, S. 'Method and Substantive Theory in Max Weber', *B.J.S.*, Vol. XV, No. 1 (March 1964), pp. 1–18.
Antoni, C. *From History to Sociology* (Merlin Press, 1962).
Aron, R. *German Sociology* (Heinemann, 1957).
—— *Introduction to the Philosophy of History* (Weidenfeld-Nicolson, 1961).
—— *Main Currents in Sociological Thought*, Vol. 2 (Weidenfeld-Nicolson, 1968).
Becker, H. 'Culture Case Study and Ideal-Typical Method, with Special Reference to Max Weber', *Social Forces*, Vol. 12, No. 3 (March 1934), pp. 399–405.
—— 'Interpretive Sociology and Constructive Typology' in George Gurvitch and W. E. Moore (eds) *Twentieth Century Sociology* (New York, 1945), pp. 70–95.
Bendix, R. *Max Weber: An Intellectual Portrait* (Heinemann, 1960).
—— 'Bureaucracy and the Problem of Power', *Public Administration Review*, Vol. 5, No. 3 (Summer, 1945), pp. 194–209.
—— 'Max Weber's Sociology Today' (*Int. Soc. Sc. Jnl.*, Vol. 17 (1965), pp. 10–22).
—— 'Bureaucracy: The Problem and Its Setting', *A.S.R.*, Vol. 12 (Oct. 1947), pp. 493–507.
—— 'Max Weber's Interpretation of Conduct and History', *A.J.S.*, Vol. 51, No. 6 (May 1946), pp. 518–26.
—— 'Max Weber and Jacob Burckhardt', *A.J.R.*, Vol. 30, No. 2 (1965).
Bennion, L. L. *Max Weber's Methodology* (Paris, 1934).
Berger, P. L. 'Charisma and Religious Innovation: The Social Location of Israelite Prophecy', *A.S.R.*, Vol. 28, No. 6 (Dec. 1963), pp. 940–50.

[1] With the exception of Marianne Weber's biography only works available in English are cited.

Berger, P. L. and Luckman, T.   *The Social Construction of Reality* (Allen Lane, 1967).

Bergstraesser, A.   'Wilhelm Dilthey and Max Weber: An Empirical Approach to Historical Synthesis', *Ethics*, Vol. LVIII (Jan. 1947).

Bierstedt, R.   'An Analysis of Social Power', *A.S.R.*, Vol. 15, No. 6 (Dec. 1950), pp. 730–8.

Birnbaum, N.   'Conflicting Interpretations of the Rise of Capitalism: Marx and Weber', *B.J.S.*, Vol. 4 (1953), pp. 125–41.

Blum, F. H.   'Max Weber's Postulate of "Freedom"', *A.J.S.*, Vol. L (1944–5).

———   'Max Weber: The Men of Politics and the Men dedicated to Objectivity and Rationality', *Ethics* (1959).

Burin, F. S.   'Bureaucracy and National Socialism: A Reconsideration of Weberian Theory', in R. W. Merton *et al.* (ed.), *Reader in Bureaucracy* (Free Press, 1952).

Commons, J. R.   *The Legal Foundations of Capitalism* (N.Y. Macmillan, 1924).

Diehl, C.   'The Life and Work of Max Weber', *Quarterly Journal of Economics*, Vol. 38 (1924), pp. 87–107.

Eisenstadt, S. N.   'Bureaucracy, Bureaucratisation, Markets and Power Structure', in *Essays on Comparative Institutions* (Wiley 1965), pp. 177–215.

Falk, W.   'Democracy and Capitalism in Max Weber's Sociology', *Sociological Rev.*, Vol. 27 (1935), pp. 373–93.

Fanfani, A.   *Catholicism, Protestantism, Capitalism* (London 1935).

Fischoff, E.   'The Protestant Ethic and the Spirit of Capitalism', *Social Research*, Vol. II, No. 1 (Feb. 1944), pp. 53–77.

Freund, J.   *The Sociology of Max Weber* (Allen Lane, 1968).

Friedland, W. H.   'For a Sociological Concept of Charisma', *Social Forces*, XLIII, No. 1 (October 1964), pp. 23–4.

Friedrich, C. J.   'Political Leadership and The Problem of Charismatic Power', *Jnl. of Politics* (Feb. 1961).

———   'Some Observations on Weber's Analysis of Bureacracy', in R. K. Merton (ed.), *Reader in Bureaucracy* (Free Press, 1952).

Fromm, E.   *Escape from Freedom* (New York, 1941).

Fullerton, K.   'Calvinism and Capitalism', *Harvard Theological Review*, Vol. 21, pp. 163–95.

Gerth, H. and H. I.   'Bibliography on Max Weber', *Social Research*, Vol. 16, No. 1 (March 1949), pp. 70–89.

Goldhammer, H. and Shils, E.   'Types of Power and Status', *A.J.S.*, Vol. 45, No. 2 (Sept. 1939), pp. 171–82.

Goode, W. J.   'A Note on the Ideal Type', *A.S.R.*, Vol. 12, No. 4 (Aug. 1947), pp. 473–4.

Gouldner, A.   'Metaphysical Pathos and The Theory of Bureaucracy', *A. Pol. Sc. Rev.*, Vol. 49, No. 2 (June 1955), pp. 496–507.

Honigsheim, P.   'Max Weber as a Rural Sociologist', *Rural Sociology*, Vol. II, No. 3 (Sept. 1946), pp. 207–18.

———   *On Max Weber.* (Collier-Macmillan, 1968).

Hughes, H. S. *Consciousness and Society: The Re-orientation of European Social Thought 1890–1930* (MacGibbon and Kee, 1959).

Jaspers, K. *Leonardo, Descartes, Max Weber: Three Essays* (Routledge, 1965).

Jordan, H. P. 'Some Philosophical Implications of Max Weber's Methodology', *Ethics*, Vol. 48 (1938), pp. 221–31.

Kaufmann, F. *Methodology of the Social Sciences* (New York, 1944).

Kluver, H. 'Max Weber's Ideal Type in Psychology', *Jnl. of Philosophy*, Vol. 23 (1926), pp. 29–35.

Kolho, G. 'A Critique of Max Weber's Philosophy of History', *Ethics*, Vol. 70 (1959).

Lazersfeld, P. F. 'Some Remarks on the Typological Procedures in Social Research', *Zeitschrift für Sozialforschung*, Vol. 6, No. 1 (1937).

Lazersfeld, P. F. and Oberschall, A. R. 'Max Weber and Empirical Social Research, *A.J.R.*, Vol. 30, No. 2 (1965).

Mayer, J. P. *Max Weber and German Politics: A Study in Political Sociology* (Faber, 1944).

Merton, R. K. 'Bureaucratic Structure and Personality', *Social Forces*, Vol. 18, No. 4 (May 1940), pp. 560–8.

—— 'Science and Economy in 17th Century England', *Science and Society*, Vol. 3, No. 1 (Winter 1939), pp. 3–27.

—— 'Science and the Social Order', *Philosophy of Science*, Vol. 5, No. 3 (July 1938).

—— 'Science Technology and Society in 17th Century England', *Osiris*, Vol. 4, Part II (Bruges, 1938).

Michels, R. *Political Parties* (Collier Books, 1962).

Mills, C. Wright 'Situated Actions and Vocabularies of Motive', *in Power Politics and People* (Oxford 1963).

Mommsen, W. 'Max Weber's Political Sociology and his Philosophy of World History', *Int. Soc. Sc. Jnl.*, Vol. 17 (1965), pp. 23–45.

Nagel, E. 'On the Method of Verstehen as the Sole Method of Philosophy', *in* M. Natanson (ed.), *Philosophy of the Social Sciences: a Reader* (Random House, 1963).

Neumann, F. *Behemoth* (New York, 1944).

Niebuhr, H. R. *The Social Sources of Denominationalism* (New York, 1929).

Oberschall, A. *Empirical Social Research in Germany 1848–1914* (Mouton, 1965).

Parsons, T. *The Structure of Social Action* (Free Press, 1949).

—— 'Evaluation and Objectivity in Social Science: An Interpretation of Max Weber's Contribution', *Int. Soc. Sc. Jnl.*, Vol. 17 (1965), pp. 46–63.

—— 'Max Weber 1864–1964', *A.S.R.*, Vol. 30, No. 2 (1965).

Rex, J. *Key Problems of Sociological Theory* (Routledge & Kegan Paul, 1961).

Robertson, H. M. *Aspects of the Rise of Economic Individualism: A Criticism of Max Weber and his School* (Cambridge, 1933).

Rossi, P. 'Scientific Objectivity and Value Hypotheses', *Int. Soc. Sc. Jnl.*, Vol. 17 (1965), pp. 64–70.

Roth, G. 'Political Critiques of Max Weber: Some Implications for Political Sociology', *A.S.R.*, Vol. 30, No. 2 (1965).

Runciman, W. G. *Social Science and Political Theory* (Cambridge, 1963).

Salomon, A. 'Max Weber's Methodology', *Social Research*, Vol. 1 (1934), pp. 147–68.

—— 'Max Weber's Political Ideas', *Social Research*, Vol. 2 (1935), pp. 368–84.

—— 'Max Weber's Sociology', *Social Research*, Vol. 2 (1935), pp. 60–73.

Samuelsson, K. *Religion and Economic Action. A Critique of Max Weber* (Harper, 1964).

Schutz, A. *The Phenomenology of the Social World* (Northwestern Univ. Press, 1967).

Shils, E. 'Some Remarks on the Theory of Social and Economic Organisation', *Economica*, Vol. 15, No. 57 (1948), pp. 36–50.

—— 'Charisma, Order and Status', *A.S.R.*, Vol. 30, No. 2 (1965).

Simey, T. S. *Social Science and Social Purpose* (Constable, 1968).

—— 'Weber's Sociological Theory of Value: An Appraisal in Mid Century', *Soc. Review*, Vol. 13 (1965, New Series), pp. 45–64.

Speier, H. 'Max Weber', *Enc. Soc. Sc.*, Vol. 15 (New York, 1935), pp. 386–89.

van der Sprenkel, O. B. 'Chinese Religion', *B.J.S.* (Sept. 1954).

Strauss, L. *Natural Right and History* (Chicago, 1953).

Troeltsch, E. *The Social Teaching of the Christian Churches* (2 vols.), (New York 1931).

Udy, S. H. (Jnr) "'Bureaucracy' and 'Rationality' in Weber's Organisation Theory: An Empirical Study", *A.S.R.*, Vol. XXIV, No. 6 (1959), pp. 791–5.

Weber, Marianne *Max Weber, ein Lebensbild* (Tübingen, 1926).

Weber, Max *The Methodology of the Social Sciences* (translated and edited by E. A. Shils and H. N. Finch, with a Foreword by Shils) (Free Press, 1949).

—— *The Protestant Ethic and the Spirit of Capitalism* (translated by T. Parsons, with a Foreword by R. H. Tawney) (Allen & Unwin, 1948).

—— *Basic Concepts in Sociology* (translated and with an introduction by H. P. Secher) (N.Y. Philosophical Library 1962).

—— *The Theory of Social and Economic Organisation*, Part I of *Wirtschaft und Gesellschaft* (translated by A. R. Henderson and Talcott Parsons: edited by Talcott Parsons) (Hodge, 1947).

—— *On Law in Economy and Society* (edited with an introduction and annotations by Max Rheinstein: translated by Edward A. Shils) (Harvard, 1954).

—— *The Sociology of Religion* (translated by E. Fischoff with an Introduction by Talcott Parsons) (Methuen, 1965).

—— *The City* (translated and edited by D. Martindale and G. Neuwirth) (Free Press, 1958).

Weber, Max *The Religion of India: The Sociology of Hinduism and Buddhism* (translated and edited by H. H. Gerth and D. Martindale) (Free Press, 1958).

—— *From Max Weber: Essays in Sociology* (translated, edited and with an Introduction by H. H. Gerth and C. Wright Mills) (Kegan Paul, 1948).

—— 'The Social Causes of the Decay of Ancient Civilisation', *Journal of General Education*, Vol. V (1950), pp. 75–88.

—— 'The Three Types of Legitimate Rule' (translated by H. H. Gerth) in *Society and Institutions*, Vol. IV, No. 1 (Berkley Publications, 1958).

—— *The Rational and Social Foundations of Music* (translated and edited by D. Martindale and others) (Southern Illinois Univ. Press, 1958).

—— *The Religion of China: Confucianism and Taoism* (translated and edited by H. H. Gerth) (Free Press, 1957).

—— *The Religion of India* (translated by H. H. Gerth and D. Martindale) (Free Press, 1958).

—— *Ancient Judaism* (translated and edited by H. H. Gerth and D. Martindale) (Free Press, 1952).

—— *General Economic History* (translated by Frank H. Knight) (Allen & Unwin, 1923).

—— *Economy and Society* (3 Vol.), (edited by Gunther Roth and Claus Wittich) (Bedminster Press, 1968).

Winch, P. *The Idea of a Social Science* (1958).

Worsley, P. *The Trumpet Shall Sound* (MacGibbon and Kee 1968, 2nd edition).

Index

abstract construction of ideal types, 24–5

'acquisition class', 87, 88; significance, 89–90, 92

action, classification of types, 27; concept of, 26, 73, 76 ff.

aktuelles Verstehen, 93n.

Ancient Judaism, 56

Antoni, C., 43, 44

Antonin of Florence, 186

Aristotle, ideal of urban autarchy, 257

Aron, Raymond, 21, 70; *Introduction to the Philosophy of History*, 31

Avineri, S., 223

Bach, J. S., and P. E., 238

Baxter, 48, 175; *Saints' Everlasting Rest*, 173n.

Beethoven, Ludwig van, 239

Bell, Daniel, 166

Bendix, Rheinhard, 39, 45, 59, 60

Bentham, Jeremy, 183n., 188

Bernstein, Eduard, 174n.

Bolshevik government, 215, 217, 219

Book of Sports, 167

Brentano, 37

Buddhism, 285, 287

Calvin, Calvinism, 40, 45, 46, 168n., 169, 170n., 174n., 289; Calvinist International, 47; 'diaspora Calvinism', 47; doctrine of predestination, 42; idea of God, 44; in Holland, 170n., 175

capitalism, 33–53, 275–90; calculable law, 277; commercialisation of economic life, 277; definition, 33; differentiating characteristics 33–5; evolution of spirit, 277–90; 'expansive energy', 41–2; free labour, 277; geographical conditions for development, 279; hypotheses for emergence, 277–9; importance of the skilled artisan, 50; meaning of modern capitalism, 275–7; rational capital accounting, 276; rational and irrational, 34, 35, 51; relation to capitalism of Indian castes, 284–5; political and industrial, 33, 34, 35, 36; and protestantism, 37–45, 167, 172, 173, 174; secularisation of spirit, 42–4; 'spirit' of modern capitalism, 40, 41; traditional, 279–80; in Western societies, 33

Catholicism, 286, 289–90; antipathy to capitalistic tendency, 282

causal analysis, 9, 11, 14, 16, 37, 94n., 96, 97, 98, 100; concept of 'adequate causation', 21, 22, 23; historical interpretation, 97; 'objective possibility', 20; one-way, 38–9; *ratio cognoscendi*, 20, 23, 24; *ratio essendi*, 20, 23, 24; Weber's approach to, 16, 20–5

Chambonnières, 237

charisma, charismatic authority, 54, 55, 77, 229–35; foreign to economic considerations, 232,